THE SCARECROW AUTHOR BIBLIOGRAPHIES

Yvor Winters:
An Annotated Bibliography 1919-1982

by

Grosvenor Powell

Scarecrow Author Bibliographies
No. 66

The Scarecrow Press, Inc.
Metuchen, N.J., & London
1983

Library of Congress Cataloging in Publication Data

Powell, Grosvenor, 1932-
    Yvor Winters, an annotated bibliography, 1919-1982.

    Includes indexes.
    1. Winters, Yvor, 1900-1968--Bibliography. I. Title.
Z8978.25.P68 1983 [PS3545.I765] 016.811'52 83-14466
ISBN 0-8108-1653-9

CONTENTS

PREFACE

This bibliography is an annotated listing of all primary and secondary material relating to the poet and critic, Yvor Winters; it is also a critical guide. Through the annotations and cross-references, it introduces the reader to the materials available for the study of Winters' achievement in verse and prose, to the varying reactions to that achievement, and to the critical position itself.

In order to accomplish this last objective, I have annotated Winters' principal critical statements in great detail. It has then been possible to refer through cross-references to these key annotations throughout the rest of the book. When, for instance, I report objectively what a hostile or imperceptive critic has written of Winters' theory of literature, I can refer the reader to a summary of Winters' actual position; where Winters presents the same argument in two separate essays or books, I can refer the reader to one full statement of that argument.

I have had to face a unique problem in accomplishing this dual objective. Winters characteristically developed his ideas through series of publications of essentially the same ideas and thus has published much the same material in a number of different forms. Essays that had been published independently usually became chapters in books; and, in the case of his one short story, "The Brink of Darkness," the various publications represent significantly different texts of the story. It has been necessary to take the essay, or in a few instances the reprinted chapter, as the basic item, although an item that then becomes an entirely new work when it appears in the context of a book.

I have, therefore, departed from conventional bibliographical procedure in two ways: I have given separate item numbers to the various appearances of essentially the same material where the reappearance constitutes a significant alteration or reworking of the original material; and I have not used cross-references as indexical devices of the see and see also variety. I have used them as a means of indicating the intricate relationships between the various appearances of versions of the same material and as a means of leading the reader from a particular annotation to other annotations that elucidate or provide information relating to the first.

As a part of the entry for each of Winters' books, the reader will find the chapters listed and cross-references leading to entries

Department of Special Collections, Research Library, UCLA.

v

for the individual essays of which the book is composed.   As a part of each of these essay entries, one will find the publishing history of the essay and another cross-reference leading back to the annotation for the book of which the essay is a part.   Whether beginning with the essay entry or the book entry, the reader will be led back to the annotation of the book.   Cross-references to individual chapters of Winters' books direct the reader to the essay entry.   This mode of organization may seem slightly circular, but it has proved to be the simplest way of making cross-references to individual chapters precise while keeping the annotation of each of Winters' books as a single summary of the argument of the book.   It has allowed me to treat Winters' major critical statements as a series of individual essays, each of which has its own publishing history, and as chapters in books that are themselves sustained arguments.

Since these cross-references are being used in a special way, I have enclosed them in parentheses.   They are so organized that a reader can find easily the publishing history of any poem, essay, or book by Winters and a full account of Winters' theory of literature and the critical reception of that theory.

In composing this book, I have incurred many debts.   I wish to thank the members of the staff of the University of British Columbia Library, especially the following whose expert bibliographical knowledge has saved me many hours of searching: Margaret Friesen, Tania Gorn, Alice McNair, Wila Busza, and Rita Penco, of the Interlibrary Loan Division; Elizabeth Caskey and Charles Forbes of the Humanities Division; and Jocelyn Foster of the Information and Orientation Division.   I would also like to thank Doreen Todhunter, of the University of British Columbia English Department, who introduced me to the mysteries of word processing.

I am grateful to many individuals throughout the United States who responded generously to my queries.   In particular, I would like to acknowledge the assistance of Barbara Begley, Manuscripts Specialist, University Archives, Stanford University Libraries; Robert J. Bertholf, Curator, Poetry/Rare Books Collection, University Libraries, State University of New York at Buffalo; Rosemary L. Cullen, Special Collections Librarian, Brown University Library; Ellen S. Dunlap, Research Librarian, University of Texas; Michael Edmunds, Special Collections, Mugar Memorial Library, Boston University; Robert Greenwood, Talisman Press; Beatrice A. Hight, Reference Department, General Library, University of New Mexico; William Jankos, Rare Books Librarian, University Library, University of Southern California; Carol Jarvis, Bancroft Library, University of California, Berkeley; Kenneth A. Lohf, Librarian for Rare Books and Manuscripts, Butler Library, Columbia University; Grace Morledge and J. Richard Phillips, Department of Special Collections, Stanford University Libraries; Richard H. Schimmelpfeng, Director for Special Collections, University Library, University of Connecticut; Carolyn A. Sheehy, Special Collections, Newberry Library; Joseph P. Strelka, Professor of German and Comparative Literature,

State University of New York at Albany; Ulla Sweedler, Reference Librarian, University of California, San Diego; Elizabeth Stege Teleky, Special Collections, University of Chicago Library; and Everett C. Wilkie, Jr., Head Reference Librarian, Lilly Library, Indiana University.

Janet Winters kindly provided me with her own annotated copy of the Lohf and Sheehy bibliography of Winters and encouraged me throughout this project. Jeffrey Akard, of ABI Books in Santa Barbara, made available to me his listing of the contents of Winters' library and helped me to verify and locate a number of obscure items. I wish to thank Donald E. Stanford, editor of The Southern Review, who provided me with copies of numerous items and read and criticized the entire typescript in one of its versions. I am greatly in the debt of William E. Cain of the Department of English, Wellesley College, who initially suggested this project to me, for providing me with expert editorial guidance. I wish to thank Peter Howard of Serendipity Books, Berkeley, for providing me with a prepublication copy of his recent Catalogue 41, "Yvor Winters, Janet Lewis & their Friends," a valuable source of information for the student of Winters.

My greatest single indebtedness is to Charles Gullans of the Department of English, UCLA, who answered, generously and patiently, my many questions relating to difficult aspects of Winters bibliography, shared with me material that he has collected over many years, and read and criticized one version of the typescript. Professor Gullans' extensive knowledge of Winters' poetry and criticism and of the craft of bibliography have proved invaluable to me.

The portrait of Yvor Winters used as a frontispiece is by courtesy of the News and Publications Service of Stanford University. The portrait on page v is reproduced by special arrangement with Bern Porter Books, Belfast, Maine 04915 from their publication Yvor Winters Folio by Harry Bowden housed in the Special Collections Department, Research Library, University of California at Los Angeles.

This bibliography could not have been written without the assistance of these individuals, but the inevitable errors and omissions that it contains are, needless to say, my own.

GROSVENOR POWELL

INTRODUCTION

Yvor Winters' approach to literature, and particularly to poetry, is the result of a special way of reading. Poetry, for him, is a technique of contemplation. It is for this reason that he was attracted to sixteenth- and seventeenth-century poets who still wrote as Christians meditating. Although Winters was not a Christian, his philosophy was Christian and his moral principles were Christian. But Winters combined with this traditional metaphysics a visionary tendency that is a result of the religious revolution that occurred with romanticism. In romantic vision, subject and object fuse. When Winters read a poem, the poem altered his consciousness. Most of us read poems the way we read prose. We listen to the opinions of the author and we entertain them. Winters, of course, read in this way also; but, when he made the experience of a poem part of his private corpus of literary experience, he merged with the poem. He chose, that is, to identify his own consciousness with the universe created by the poem. He fused with the poem just as a religious mystic fuses with the object of his adoration. For this kind of reader, a poem is either successful or unsuccessful. An unsuccessful poem is unsuccessful because it is fraudulent in the following sense: the being to which the poem lays claim is either non-existent, unintelligible, contradictory, or a state of incomplete being disguised as a state of total being. For Winters, a successful poem can be major or minor. A minor poem, when it is neither second-rate nor decadent, and when it does not pretend to more meaning than it actually presents, can be an artistic triumph. A major poem is one that successfully deals with a large and valuable subject. (See item 5.)

The notion of greater and lesser being was not present in Winters' earliest thinking about poetry. In The Testament of a Stone (item 1), the dominant idea is fusion of the details of the poem in the consciousness of a reader who himself fuses his consciousness with the reality created by the poem. By the time Winters began to write his major criticism, the idea of being and its absence had become the central idea determining his critical principles, and the normal conventions of traditional poetry had become the conventions that allow for the creation of the fullest human consciousness or being. (See, for a discussion of normal and abnormal conventions, item 5.) Winters did not begin with traditional poetry and move forward to modern poetry. He began with modern poetry as it appeared in the little magazines of the teens and twenties. Starting

1

out as an Imagist poet, he experimented in extreme ways, and, by the age of twenty-eight, had exhausted the possibilities of Imagist conventions. He had searched intensely and exhaustively the modes of experience possible within these experimental conventions. Reaching the limits of these modes, he found that earlier kinds of poetry provided a different kind of experience, and, in some cases, a richer and fuller experience. (See items 5, 7, 10, 15.)

Winters believed that all important human activity is a product of the conscious will. The will expresses itself through a consciously acquired technique, a fact that applies not only to poets but to athletes and the breeders of champion dogs. The richest state of consciousness is the state of normal alertness. (See item 125.) Special states of hyperintense vision are unavoidable if one is fully alive; and the poet, because he lives more intensely than most people, is particularly vulnerable. But such states of consciousness are not to be sought; they are to be mastered. To judge by the testimony of Winters' early verse, he was invaded by such experience in a way that brought him dangerously close to insanity. (See items 531, 604, 630.) He regained his balance, however, and saw that visionary states are a temptation that the poet masters through mastering the medium in which he lives his life, the language of his poetry.

These views led Winters to regard poets and scholars as either amateurs or professionals. Most romantic poets and scholars, Winters felt, used the romantic position as an excuse for a passive attitude toward experience and toward literature: if we will only let ourselves go, we can each of us become automatically first-rate; the poem comes automatically and is to be appreciated viscerally. The romantic position, or that part of it which Winters rejected, is the position of the passive mystic and the resolute amateur. The distinction between amateur and professional parallels in Winters' mind the distinction between romantic and classical in attitudes toward writing. Winters came to define a classical attitude as one held by a person who was not the passive slave of his or her own inspiration. A classical attitude is characterized by discipline and the exercise of the will in the face of the contingent and the obscure in experience. The distinction, for Winters, was not one of subject-matter; it was one of the degree of will power and self-determination brought to bear on the shaping of one's work and of one's consciousness.

In his review of In Defense of Reason, A. Alvarez makes a distinction between amateurs and professionals that helps to clarify Winters' attitude. The amateurs "love literature for its own sake," while the professionals "are vowed to the job by an act of faith." (See item 478.) Amateurs may be scholarly and genteel and may occupy prestigious chairs of learning, but they lack that seriousness that makes of literature a rule of living and source of values. "In England," Alvarez informs us, "the foremost professional critic is in this sense F. R. Leavis; in America, he is Yvor Winters." Winters regarded himself as a professional critic in this sense, but he also regarded himself as a professional because he was a poet. And he felt that, ultimately, his poetry would be recognized as more important than his criticism:

> Whatever the virtues of my poetry, past or present, absolutely considered, I think one may reasonably say that the later work surpasses the earlier, and will probably prove, in the long run, of greater value than my criticism. (Item 589.)

The activities of the critic and the teacher were, in his view, subordinate to those of the poet, but they nicely complemented professionalism in poetry. Winters taught in order to support himself while studying the art of poetry, and he wrote criticism as a means of exploring the possibilities of his art. He regarded most contemporary poets as amateurs because they had not systematically studied their craft, and most professors of literature as amateurs because they had never written poetry. He maintained that a man is unlikely to become a great critic unless he is a practicing poet. Winters felt that most romantic poets and scholars are amateurs in the sense defined above. (See items 104, 113, 125.) They are the dilettantes of experience.

As a critic, Winters was primarily concerned with the implications for human consciousness of metaphysical and scientific structures of thought as these can be realized within literary forms. (See items 1, 5, 7, 10, 15.) To put it another way, Winters experienced ideas and regarded poetry as the medium in which the experience of ideas could be most fully realized. This point is one that requires some elucidation since a failure to understand it is responsible for a good bit of the failure to understand Winters' criticism. In showing the relationship between ideas and literary forms, Winters concerned himself with two episodes in the history of ideas and with a complex of Renaissance ideas that cannot easily be identified with a specific phase in our history. The first episode is the development from the Calvinism of the New England Puritans through eighteenth-century Unitarianism to nineteenth-century Transcendentalism (for a description of this history as Winters conceives it, see items 81, 84, 103), and the second episode is that developing from the doctrines of associationism and natural goodness as these are expressed in eighteenth- and nineteenth-century English romanticism. (See items 7, 15.) Winters regarded both of these episodes as productive of essentially anti-intellectual and dangerously amoral attitudes that are responsible for the formal and stylistic--and therefore moral--weaknesses of nineteenth- and twentieth-century American and British poetry. (See item 15.) The complex of ideas that Winters saw as a kind of antidote to the romantic situation derives from his discovery that Thomistic ideas provide the ideational background for the Renaissance poetry that most impressed him as stylistic models. (See items 99, 125.)

On a practical level, Winters' attitudes towards the structures of thought that I have just described led him to reject the deterministic notion that our actions and choices are dictated by the age. Winters attacked this notion throughout his career; he attacked it, indeed, in the final paragraph of his final book:

> Finally, let us beware of saying that the best poets of our time deal with the subjects which are most important to our time. This would be a rash thing to say of the poets of any period, but it is infinitely rash in speaking of the poets of our own. This fallacy will mean in practice that we shall praise the poets who write of those subjects which seem important to us in our ignorance and stupidity: Anglicanism, Whitmanism, Agrarianism, Rosicrucianism, Communism, or something else. It will be easy to be moved by the poet who writes badly of our own emotions; in fact this facility has generated most of the criticism of our time. Five hundred years from now the subjects which will appear to have been most important to our time will be the subjects treated by the surviving poets who have written the most intelligently. The best poets have the best minds; ultimately they are the standard. When that time comes, my distinguished reader, his favorite poets, his favorite subjects, and all of the members of his elite group will have turned to dust. (Item 125.)

This is an attack on the tyranny of fashion and on the view that we cannot help but be the products of our time; and it is an attack on the corollary notion that art not only should but must express the age. (See item 7.) Winters did not, however, hold such views in an unqualified way; he simply objected to the dogmatically deterministic view that an artist is limited by his age--that, since the age is chaotic, art must be so also; that, since psychoanalysis has shown us the alogical processes of the mind, the logical processes are invalidated; that the connotative richness of modern poetry invalidates a poetry of plain statement.

After exploring the possibilities of experimental conventions and of romantic sensibility generally, Winters discovered that earlier English poetry provides modes of experience completely outside those created by romantic and modern poetry: the sensibility, for instance, of Campion, Jonson, and Herrick. A successful poem, major or minor, is a triumph of the human spirit. The range of experience discovered or created by such a poem remains permanently valid and permanently available. Winters felt, therefore, that one should ignore fashion and write with the best models in mind. But this view was qualified in important ways. If one lives in a chaotic world, one should be aware of the fact and come to terms with it, just as one must come to terms with the world created by modern technology. Similarly, one should assimilate the genuinely new inventions of recent writers. Winters' belief is that one should try to profit from the conditions imposed by one's age instead of being limited by them.

But a difficulty remains. These recommendations sound

merely theoretical, if not positively petulant, to readers who do not know what Winters means when he speaks of modes of perception that do not appear within the prevailing conventions of twentieth-century poetry. The main object of Winters' criticism is to bring about a revolution in taste through bringing to light the valuable poems and modes of feeling and perception that have been lost through the limiting influence of modern fashions or have been denied value by modern critical dogma. (See items 10, 15.) He did not want to deny what was valuable in modern poetry and he did not want to return to the past. His approach was essentially innovative and looked to the future. Although Winters' judgments have gained for him a certain notoriety as a critic, the judgments are the result of an approach and a preoccupation that have been largely ignored by the critics of his work. Winters' emphasis is always on the technical analysis of the formal possibilities within stylistic conventions and on the relationship between style and ideas. These concerns led him to write anatomies, and most of his seminal critical studies are instances of this approach. The question persistently asked is that of what can be accomplished within the various literary forms and systems of thought available to the poet.

By the age of nineteen, Winters had begun writing a draft of The Testament of a Stone, the only systematic exploration of the possibilities of the Image to be produced by an Imagist poet. This brief anatomy of the Image, along with the "Notes" published in the Modern Review in 1924 (items 1, 45), are the key critical documents for an understanding of the first phase of Winters' thought, the phase that extended from 1919 to 1927. In 1929, while still in his twenties, he explored systematically the structural modes available in modern poetry in "The Extension and Reintegration of the Human Spirit Through the Poetry Mainly French and American Since Poe and Baudelaire." (Item 60.) These early essays employ an approach and a format from which Winters was to vary little in the major critical statements published later in his career. The 1929 essay served as the basis for Winters' first book of criticism, Primitivism and Decadence (1937). In defining the intention behind Primitivism and Decadence and Maule's Curse, which followed in 1938, Winters is quite explicit as to his concern with the relationship between philosophical and theological ideas and the literary forms that embody ideas:

> The relationship of the history of ideas to the history of literary forms, however, or conversely, the intellectual and moral significance of literary forms, has not been adequately studied; yet this subject is the very core of literary criticism and of the understanding of the history of literature. In my previous book [Primitivism and Decadence], I described and endeavored to evaluate forms, primarily, and used writers merely to illustrate them. In the present volume [Maule's Curse] I have examined individual writers, a procedure which enables me to examine subject matter more fully and to relate subject matter more fully to form. (IDR, p. 155.)

Winters' most frequently attacked books, Maule's Curse and The Anatomy of Nonsense, drew him away temporarily from poetic problems into the study of American fiction and the history of ideas in America. Winters has remarked that he wrote these books because, as a professor of American literature, he had to master this material and found the available scholarship useless. Presumably, in reading through the published scholarship, he did not find the sort of clear-sighted anatomies of formal possibilities that he wanted. Therefore, he wrote them himself: Maule's Curse, principally an anatomization of the relationship between form and meaning in American fiction (see item 6), and The Anatomy of Nonsense, a study of the relationship between meaning and ideas in American literary criticism (see item 7). In speaking of his objective in The Anatomy of Nonsense, he says that he will "complete the discussion of style undertaken in my first book, Primitivism and Decadence, which was mainly a discussion of style, and which had little reference to the ideas generating style" (IDR, p. 556).

The books written previous to The Function of Criticism (1957) explored, almost therapeutically, the compositional methods that have dominated modern literature. Winters discovered that most of the compositional techniques employed in modern literature limit consciousness instead of extending it. (See item 9.) With the first essay in The Function of Criticism, "Problems for Modern Critic of Literature," Winters produced his definitive anatomy: he considers the possibilities inherent in each of the viable genres--the novel, the drama, the long narrative poem, the short poem--and he shows, to his own satisfaction, which genre has the greatest possibilities. He writes, in other words, a kind of evaluative anatomy of literature. (See item 115.)

Forms of Discovery (1967) rounds out Winters' career as a critic. Finally, he could write the definitive history of the short poem in English. (See item 15.) He had completed the laborious sifting and anatomization of possibilities. Looking for the fullest realization of human consciousness on the level of form and meaning, he went through English poetry and described the best that he found. But it is quite clear that he undertook the labor only in part for the benefit of mere readers. He was still the professional in poetry who was interested in the writing of poetry and the future of poetry. By describing the richest line of technical development in English and American poetry, he hoped to influence the poetry written today and the poetry to be written in the future.

Those readers, the vast majority of current readers of criticism, who think of Winters as a man unsympathetic with romanticism, might find it instructive to realize that a great part of Winters' criticism is, in fact, a debate with his own romantic self. As I have already indicated, Winters began as an extreme variety of romantic mystic. When he altered his position, he built his new position on the experience of his earlier years. He was not a man of classical temperament attacking romantic innovation. He was a romantic innovator who had discovered the limits and dangers of

such innovation. In Testament of a Stone, Winters had stated quite
unequivocally that the poet is not responsible to his subject matter,
that his sole concern is with the intensity with which the details of
the poem fuse with one another in the consciousness of the poet and
the intensity of fusion in the mind of the reader. (See item 1.)
And the object of the poem itself is here described as the achievement of a mystical trance: "A poem is a state of perfection at
which a poet has arrived by whatever means. It is a stasis in a
world of flux and indecision, a permanent gateway to waking oblivion,
which is the only infinity and the only rest. It has no responsibil-
ities except to itself and its own perfection." (UER, p. 195.)

    Winters came to see that, applied consistently, the critical
position of the solipsistic romantic mystic deprives human experience of all value beyond mere emotional and sensory intensity and
leads to insanity, if rigorously and seriously pursued. The intellectual rejection occurred in 1928, and the criticism subsequent
to that year is written against this early position. Nevertheless,
Winters' experience of this early position was intense and was, indeed, the formative experience of his early years, both in life and
in poetry. In his mature criticism, he continually tested the romantic position against his newly acquired views. The proving
ground of his ideas was the work of those American poets and fic-
tionists and those English poets to whose study he devoted his mature years. I would like to show briefly how Winters turned his
critical work into a debate between romantic and post-romantic
principles through examining his discussion of one poet whom he
disliked intensely, Edgar Allan Poe, and two whom he very much
admired, Jones Very and Emily Dickinson.

    In the essay on Poe in Maule's Curse (item 82), Winters ob-
jects to Poe's belief "that the poet should not deal with human, that
is, moral experience; that the subject-matter of poetry is of an order supra-human; that the poet has no way of understanding his
subject-matter" (IDR, p. 237). The youthful Imagist who wrote
Testament of a Stone would have rejected Poe as an untalented poet,
but he would not have rejected the principles that are here attributed to Poe. Winters goes on to criticize another position that he
had stated forcefully in Testament: the belief that the only criterion
of excellence is the subjective one of degree of fusion and the further
belief that intensity is largely reducible to technical considerations.
(See item 1.) Winters now attributes such views to Poe and rejects
them. Winters objects further that, for Poe, "artistic unity is described specifically as totality of effect," a view essentially similar
to Winters' early view that "the degree of fusion of the poet with his
material" is the sole evaluative criterion. There is in Testament,
it should be noted, a preoccupation with literary judgment and professionalism in poetry that stands as a kind of harbinger of the later
position:

        So that the poem can be judged, not in relation to any
        time or place, nor to any mode of thought, but to itself
        alone, and as a part of literature; for it is not a means,

> but an end. The mind that can judge a poem accurately
> is very rare--even more rare than the mind that can cre-
> ate a poem. For this act of weighing requires a mind
> infinitely balanced, infinitely sensitive, and infinitely fa-
> miliar with all the technical phases of the medium. Such
> a mind is, with one exception in a thousand, the mind of
> the master poet. (UER, p. 197.)

But the general position expressed is the mystical aesthetic of the
romantic solipsist, and it is this position from which Winters drew
back in his later criticism.

The issue that Winters is debating with himself is that of the
attitude to be taken towards the romantic treatment of mystical experience. For Winters, Poe is the spurious romantic mystic.
Winters contrasts Poe's experience with the Christian mysticism of
Jones Very and with Emily Dickinson's awareness of human isolation. (See items 81, 86.) When we look at the discussion of Jones
Very, a poet whom he admired very much, we discover that Winters
is curiously reticent about acknowledging fully those aspects of Very's
poetry that are close to his own early experience. Very's poem,
"The Lost," for example, appears to Winters "to go close to the
heart of the mystical experience, and in spite of the obscurity resulting is unforgettable."

> The fairest day that ever yet has shown,
> Will be when thou the day within shalt see;
> The fairest rose that ever yet has blown,
> When thou the flower thou lookest on shalt be;
> But thou art far away among Time's toys;
> Thyself the day thou lookest for in them,
> Thyself the flower that now thine eye enjoys,
> But wilted now thou hang'st upon thy stem.
> The bird thou hearest on the budding tree,
> Thou hast made sing with thy forgotten voice;
> But when it swells again to melody,
> The song is thine in which thou wilt rejoice;
> And thou new risen midst these wonders live
> That now to them dost all thy substance give.

Winters describes the subject of the poem as follows:

> The subject of the poem is identity with God, and hence
> with all time and place, of the divine life in the unchang-
> ing present of eternity; or rather, the subject is the com-
> parison of that life with the life of man, 'the lost.' The
> nature of the state of beatitude is of necessity communi-
> cated but very imperfectly; the core of the poem is a
> radiant and concentrated cloud of obscurity. (IDR, p.
> 275.)

In the light of Winters' own poetry, of such poems as "A
Prayer for My Son" or "To the Holy Spirit," it is difficult to be-

lieve that he really thinks that this is the subject of the poem. His paraphrase seems a conventional statement of the poem's meaning in conventional theological language. The poem is a statement of the marvel of consciousness; it is about identity with God in the very special sense that the creation within one's consciousness of seemingly and possibly external objects like the flower intimates the creation of one's own consciousness in God. Undoubtedly, Winters knew this and regarded the poem so highly because it expresses what I have just said that it expresses. But to put it as I have put it would be to speak in too mystical a way. In his mature work, Winters can only approach this sort of experience through the indirection of poems.

Although Winters expresses misgivings about Very's mysticism and paraphrases the statement of Very's experience in a relatively conventional way, he understands Very's situation. Very is a genuine mystic, and Winters respects the man and his situation: "for Very it [his religious experience] was a sublime exaltation, which appears to have endured until his death. Very was beyond question a saintly man, and we hesitate to doubt a saint when he states that he is a mystic" (IDR, pp. 263-64). Emily Dickinson, on the other hand, is most impressive for Winters in those poems that express "the tragic finality, the haunting sense of human isolation in a foreign universe ... of which the explicit theme is a denial of this mystical trance" (IDR, p. 288). Winters disapproves of her efforts to write of mystical experience, not only because of his own growing distrust of mysticism, but because he feels that she has not had the experience: "The poems of this variety, and there are many of them, appear rather to be efforts to dramatize an idea of salvation intensely felt, but as an idea, not as something experienced, and as an idea essentially inexpressible" (IDR, p. 288).

I mention this strain in Winters' criticism, his continuing dialogue with his own early assumptions and experience, only in order to counter the bland assumption to be found frequently in the critical response to Winters' work that he is a dogmatic classicist, rule bound and moralistic. In general, Winters, as even antagonistic critics have observed, is a very shrewd and perceptive reader of poetry. This capacity, indeed, is widely recognized as one of his principal virtues. But he was also a man passionately concerned with the experience of poetry as a technique of contemplation and as the most civilized and effective means that we have of relating to the contingent and the undefinable in our experience. The high place given to the art of poetry and the commitment to its spiritual function is a part of Winters' romantic heritage, and it remained with him throughout his career.

When one tries to place Winters within the general context of twentieth-century literary theory, one discovers that he occupies a unique position. Winters maintains that a poem is a statement of the same kind as a prose statement and only "differs from a work in prose by virtue of its being composed in verse." (See items 99, 112.) The most influential twentieth-century critics believe, on the other hand, that a poem is essentially different in kind from a prose statement. They have tried to establish, with Coleridge, a definition of the poem as an organic structure, "proposing to itself such delight from the whole, as is compatible with a distinct gratification from each component part." Winters believed that organic unity is a characteristic of good writing, but this belief did not alter his view of the nature of meaning. Meaning that is expressed in poems is no different from meaning that is expressed in prose or in language generally. But the verse medium makes possible a higher degree of control of the feeling expressed or conveyed: "the rhythm of verse permits the expression of more powerful feeling than is possible in prose when such feeling is needed, and it permits at all times the expression of finer shades of feeling" (IDR, p. 363). The other elements in Winters' mature position follow from the basic assumption as to the nature of poetic meaning that I have just stated: a poem has a paraphrasable meaning, it deals with human experience, and it refers to objective reality. In addition, it involves a judgment that is usually implicit rather than explicit and that is conveyed through the unparaphrasable feeling content of the poem. The feeling content and the unique judgment are a product of the poet's control of poetic convention. (See item 5.)

Placing Winters is not a matter of identifying him with a school since, in these fundamental matters, he stands alone. Even F. R. Leavis, the critic with whom Winters is most frequently paired, is utterly different from Winters in his initial assumptions and modes of proceeding, and, at crucial points, makes clear his allegiance to the Coleridgean distinctions. Winters is a New Critic only in the historical sense that he was one of that generation of critics who first introduced criticism into the universities as an academic discipline. But he was not opposed to historical scholarship as most of them were, and he differs from them in the fundamental respect that I have just defined.

The critics who understand the implications of Winters' position recognize that, as Marshall Van Deusen has put it, Winters believed "that poetry, and literature too, or language in general, for that matter, should tell the truth: all the formal properties of poetry, its meter and its rhetorical devices--in short, all the resources of language--are only the means the good poet uses to render his statements more subtle, more true." (See item 686.) The final cause of poetry is truth. They are conscious, furthermore, of the accuracy of Howard Kaye's assertion that Winters' "criticism aimed at nothing less than a revolution of taste" (see item 584), and of the preeminence in Winters' scale of values of poetry over criticism. The following may be cited as among those who have not failed to appreciate these central Wintersian tenets: Marshall Van Deusen (item 686), Howard Baker (items 480, 481), Donald E. Stanford (items 658, 659, 660, 661, 662, 666, 667), David Levin (items 591, 592), Howard Kaye (items 585, 586), John Fraser (items 540, 541, 542, 543, 544, 545, 546, 547), Kenneth Fields (items 529, 530,

531), Douglas Peterson (items 627, 628), Dick Davis (items 437, 514, 515), Raymond Oliver (item 619), Terry Comito (item 503), Clive Wilmer (item 700), John Baxter (item 484), and John Finlay (item 533).

Most commentators on Winters' criticism, however, have misunderstood it utterly and have done so as a consequence of three pervasive misapprehensions: 1) a failure to appreciate the literalness and consistency with which Winters applies his definition of poetic meaning, 2) a failure to appreciate what Winters means by moral judgment, and 3) a failure to understand the function of Winters' technical vocabulary as a means to the apprehension of the unique quality of the particular poem. At times, this failure is simply a consequence of careless reading, as when Stanley Hyman claims that Winters "detests two things he calls 'primitivism' and 'decadence'." (See item 579.) The terms, primitivism and decadence, are not, for Winters, terms of abuse; they refer, rather, to ways of describing the shifting relationships between qualities of style and subject matter. They are analytical terms, and they make possible comparative judgments. (See item 89.) At other times, the critic seems genuinely unable to understand an argument that goes counter to the critical truisms of the age. Among the more ambitious critiques of Winters' theory of literature, those written by the following critics exhibit one or more, and usually all three, of the failures in understanding that I have just mentioned: Edward Abood (item 477), Cleanth Brooks (item 493), Charles Donahue (item 522), John Holloway (item 574), Thomas Howells (item 577), R. K. Meiners (item 607), and Theodore Weiss (item 691).

In discussing Winters' notion of moral judgment, such critics as William Barrett (item 483), Harry M. Campbell (item 497), Robert Kimbrough (item 588), Roy Harvey Pearce (item 624), John Crowe Ransom (item 640), Delmore Schwartz (item 649), and René Wellek (item 694) make the mistake of assuming that moral judgment is a wholly unlived and objective act. For Winters, however, it is always a lived experience. It is only moral because it is human; there is always an element of feeling, and, in fact, the moral judgment is expressed through the human feeling motivated by the poem. A judgment from the point of view of some extra-human intelligence would be a different judgment from the one made from a human perspective. A Christian poet does not imagine that God makes the value judgment in the poem. Poetry is so highly valued by Winters because it is the only mode of language that provides a more or less objectifiable technique for the complete and experienced evaluation. The intention of a poem, as a composite expression, is both descriptive and directive. Its descriptive aspect allows objective confirmation of its truth; its directive aspect instructs the reader as to how he is to feel about that truth.

The most ambitious, concerted, and impressively argued objections to Winters' critical position are those of James A. Barish (item 482), John Casey (item 501), Andor Gomme (item 552), John Holloway (item 574), and Paul Ramsey (item 639). In each case, the critic has focussed his objections on Winters' technical terminology and has attempted to define its inadequacies. Regarding the distinction between the paraphrasable and rational element in a poem and the feeling content, Ramsey objects as follows:

> The meaning of ordinary language (and poetry builds from ordinary and extraordinary language, not the scrubbed language of the social sciences) is never pure concept plus emotion. Concept and emotion do not sit apart in the reality of meaning: the analytical separation of them has its use but does not really cut where the joints are. Taken seriously, it falsifies. The rhetorical meanings of 'denotation' and 'connotation' are handy, though much less precise than the logical meanings of the same terms; but Winters uses them as though they had strict meanings --'denotation' for concept, 'connotation' for feeling--and hence ends up with a poem that is three-fourths skeleton and one-fourth ghost. (Item 639, p. 452.)

But Winters does not equate his analytical terminology with the language of poetry, as Ramsey and others believe that he does. He is actually at great pains to distinguish between these two uses of language. Barish states the widely held view that Winters' "schemes, whether or not logical, are marked by a forbidding scholastic rigidity. They depend on hard and fast categories and absolute alternatives." (Item 482, p. 420.) And Casey, who imagines that he is making an irrefutable point, exhibits the same confusion:

> Finally, would all of those unfortunate American obscurantists, from Poe and Henry Adams to James, Pound, Eliot and Hart Crane, really have written better, more enduring, more rational works of literature, if only they had read their Nicomachean Ethics? (Item 501, p. 139.)

In general, these assertions by Ramsey, Barish, and Casey can stand as the principal objections raised by the critics whom I have just listed. These critics do justice to the sophistication of Winters' position, however, only in so far as they move away from the incorrect belief that Winters' terms are rigid and are applied mechanically to the experience of reading and toward the position stated by Andor Gomme, that the terms are derived from the reading experience:

> And while there are many occasions when the weight of theory seems to have been too much for a poem to bear, it should be stressed that his various general defenses of his critical position are really a philosopher's abstracts of conclusions drawn from his own positive judgments. (Gomme's italics; item 552, p. 66.)

In most cases, however, the critic fails to understand that Winters is not really talking about logical distinctions but about qualities of perception and consciousness; the technical vocabulary employed could not be made more precise than it is without distorting the nature of the undertaking.

Winters has himself made clear that an abstract technical vocabulary is a limited tool; greater precision in the use of terms would not issue in a more precise treatment of the subject of poetry and consciousness:

> It should be remembered in connection with this and other definitions that a critical term ordinarily indicates a quality and not an objectively demonstrable entity, yet that every term in criticism is an abstraction, that is, in a sense, is statistical or quantitative in its own nature. This means that no critical term can possibly be more than a very general indication of the nature of a perception.... Much of the Socratic hair-splitting of some of the more recent critics arises from a failure to observe in particular instances that any critical definition is merely an indication of a unique experience which cannot be exactly represented by any formula, though it may be roughly mapped out, and it is frequently of greater importance to discover something of the nature of the experience than to reduce the more or less expert formula to something simpler and still less veracious and then to demolish it. (IDR, pp. 75-76.)

Where the critical discussion of Winters' criticism is unfair or inaccurate, it almost always follows the formula that Winters has described in the final sentence just quoted.

We come back to the fact that Winters was essentially a poet and that he praises just those qualities in poetry that most critics think that he rejects: qualities of consciousness, the unparaphrasable feelings motivated by language and form. He was interested in poetry first, not in morality and metaphysics; but critics, unable to intuit what he prized, assume that he was not interested in poetry but in various other things. I do not see that Winters could have succeeded more fully than he has. The qualities that he prized can be conveyed through poetry but can only be crudely described in critical prose. At the same time, the critics can not really be blamed for missing the one great virtue of Winters' work and for being puzzled by what they find. The metaphysical defense of absolutes can be undermined, although it expresses an intuitive understanding of human consciousness that is very accurate; the critical terminology is at times confusing; the lists of poems do look eccentric; and the tone is frequently objectionable. Nor can they be blamed for not giving the poems that Winters prizes the attention that Winters asks that they be given. Winters can not muster the necessary authority to force them to do so. And even when the critics read the poems, they are likely not to perceive their virtues since they won't have heard them. Hence, Winters' emphasis on theories of meter.

Winters discovered those indefinable and unparaphrasable qualities that make the greatest poetry in English so moving and so valuable. He has been misunderstood, rejected, and vilified because we have grown insensitive to those qualities. Undertaking an impossible task, he succeeded, but more through his influence on other poets than through any influence that he has had on the critics. He has had virtually no influence on recent developments in criticism. For the rest of us, the poems that he has discovered are available to be read, and the critical distinctions are there to lead us to perceive those qualities of diction, rhythm, and feeling that we might not have perceived without them.

AA	An American Anthology. Edited by Tom Boggs. Prairie City, Ill.: James A. Decker, 1942.
ABD	A Baker's Dozen: 13 Modern Essays of Excellence. Compiled by Richard H. Haswell and John W. Ehrstine. Dubuque, Iowa: Kendall/Hunt, 1974.
ACE	American Critical Essays: Twentieth Century. Selected, with an introduction by Harold Beaver. London: Oxford University Press, 1959.
AL	American Literature
ALC	American Literary Criticism, 1900-1950. Edited by Charles Irving Glicksberg. New York: Hendricks House, 1951.
AM	American Writing 1942. The Anthology and Yearbook of the American Non-Commercial Magazine. Edited by Alan Swallow. Prairie City, Ill.: Press of James A. Decker, 1942.
AmS	American Scholar
AN	The Anatomy of Nonsense. Norfolk, Conn.: New Directions, 1943.
APS	A Poetry Sampler. Edited by Donald Hall. New York: Franklin Watts, 1962.
APTC	American Poetry of the Twentieth Century. Edited by Hayden Carruth. New York: Bantam Books, 1970.
AQ	Arizona Quarterly
AR	American Review
AS	Anchor in the Sea: An Anthology of Psychological Fiction. Edited by Alan Swallow. New York: Swallow Press and W. Morrow, 1947.

AT	American Transcendentalism: An Anthology of Criticism. Edited by Brian M. Barbour. Notre Dame, London: University of Notre Dame Press, 1973.
AW	American Writing: 1943. The Anthology and Yearbook of the American Non-Commercial Magazine. Edited by Alan Swallow. Boston: Bruce Humphries, 1944.
BAP	A Book of Animal Poems. Edited by William Cole. Viking Press, 1973.
BC	Bear Crossings: An Anthology of North American Poets. Edited by Anne Newman and Julie Suk. Newport Beach, Calif.: The New South Company, 1978.
BD	Before Disaster. Tyron, N. C.: Tyron Pamphlets, 1934.
BH	The Bare Hills. Boston: Four Seas, 1927.
CAAP	A Comprehensive Anthology of American Poetry. Edited by Conrad Aiken. New York: Modern Library 1944.
Cal	California Poets: An Anthology of 244 Contemporaries. Foreword by Helen Hoyt. New York: Henry Harrison, 1932.
CBMV	The Criterion Book of Modern American Verse. Edited by W. H. Auden. New York: Criterion Books, 1956.
CBV	A College Book of Verse. Edited by C. F. Main. Belmont, Calif.: Wadsworth Publishing Co. , 1970.
CEC	Critiques and Essays in Criticism, 1920-1948. Representing the Achievement of Modern British and American Critics. Edited by Robert Wooster Stallman. With a foreword by Cleanth Brooks. New York: Ronald Press, 1949.
Comm	Commonweal
CP	Collected Poems. Denver: Alan Swallow, 1952.
CP(1960)	Collected Poems. Rev. ed. Denver: Alan Swallow, 1960.
CPYW	The Collected Poems of Yvor Winters. With an introduction by Donald Davie. Manchester: Carcanet New Press, 1978.
CR	Chicago Review

Crit Criticism: The Foundations of Modern Literary Judgment. Edited by Mark Schorer, Josephine Miles, and Gordon McKenzie. New York: Harcourt, Brace, 1948.

CVPC Collected Verse by the Poetry Club of the University of Chicago. With an introduction by Robert Morss Lovett. Chicago: Covici-McGee Co., 1923.

DM A Dial Miscellany. Edited with an introduction by William Wasserstrom. Syracuse: Syracuse University Press, 1963.

DP Discussions of Poetry: Form and Structure. Edited with an introduction by Francis Murphy. Boston: D. C. Heath, 1964.

DQ Denver Quarterly

EAR Edwin Arlington Robinson. Norfolk, Conn.: New Directions, 1946.

EASP English and American Surrealist Poetry. Edited with an introduction by Edward B. Germain. New York: Penguin Books, 1978.

ED Emily Dickinson: A Collection of Critical Essays. Edited by Richard B. Sewell. Englewood Cliffs, N.J.: Prentice-Hall, 1963.

ELU Eight Lines and Under. Edited by William Cole. New York: Macmillan, 1967.

EMLC Essays in Modern Literary Criticism. Edited by Ray Benedict West. New York: Rinehart, 1952.

EP The Early Poems of Yvor Winters 1920-28. Chicago: Swallow Press, 1966.

EPMEC Elizabethan Poetry: Modern Essays in Criticism. Edited by Paul J. Alpers. London, New York: Oxford University Press, 1967.

Exp Exploring Poetry. Edited by M. L. Rosenthal and A. J. M. Smith. New York: Macmillan, 1955.

FC The Function of Criticism: Problems and Exercises. Denver: Alan Swallow, 1957.

FD Forms of Discovery: Critical and Historical Essays on the Forms of the Short Poem in English. Chicago: Alan Swallow, 1967.

FEAP   An Anthology of Famous English and American Poetry. Edited by William Rose Benét and Conrad Aiken. New York: Modern Library, 1945.

FOP   The Form of Poetry. Edited by Thomas R. Arp. New York: Macmillan, 1966.

GOA   The Gift Outright: America to Her Poets. Edited by Helen Plotz. New York: Greenwillow Books, 1977.

GW   The Giant Weapon. The Poets of the Year, [vol. 9]. New York: New Directions, 1943.

Gyr   Gyroscope

H&H   Hound & Horn

Haw   Hawthorne: A Collection of Critical Essays. Edited by A. N. Kaul. Englewood Cliffs, N.J.: Prentice-Hall, 1966.

HDPM   How Does a Poem Mean? Edited by John Ciardi. 2d ed. Boston: Houghton Mifflin, 1975.

HIP   The Heath Introduction to Poetry. Edited by Joseph de Roche. New York: D. C. Heath, 1975.

Hop   Hopkins: A Collection of Critical Essays. Edited by Geoffrey H. Hartman. Englewood Cliffs, N.J.: Prentice-Hall, 1966.

HR   Hudson Review

HRA   The Hudson Review Anthology. Edited by Frederick Morgan. New York: Random House, 1961.

HWT   High Wedlock Then Be Honoured. Edited by Virginia Tufte. New York: Viking Press, 1970.

IDR   In Defense of Reason. New York: Swallow Press and W. Morrow, 1947.

InP   Introduction to the Poem. Edited by Robert W. Boynton and Maynard Mack. Rev. 2d ed. New York: Hayden Book Company, 1973.

IP   An Introduction to Poetry. Edited by X. J. Kennedy. 3rd ed. New York: Little, Brown, 1974.

IW   The Immobile Wind. Evanston, Ill.: Monroe Wheeler, 1921.

J   The Journey and Other Poems. Ithaca, N.Y.: Dragon Press, 1931.

JAS	Journal of American Studies
KR	Kenyon Review
LOA	Literary Opinion in America: Essays Illustrating the Status, Methods and Problems of Criticism in the United States Since the War. Edited with an introduction by Morton Dauwen Zabel. New York: Harper & Brothers, 1937.
LOATH	Literary Opinion in America: Essays Illustrating the Status, Methods and Problems of Criticism in the United States in the Twentieth Century. Edited by Morton Dauwen Zabel. 3rd rev. ed. 2 vols. New York: Harper & Row, 1962.
LR	Little Review
LTMP	A Little Treasury of Modern Poetry, English and American. Edited by Oscar Williams. New York: Charles Scribner's Sons, 1946.
MAP	Modern American Poetry. Edited by Louis Untermeyer. 8th rev. ed. New York: Harcourt Brace, 1962.
MC	Maule's Curse: Seven Studies in the History of American Obscurantism. Norfolk, Conn.: New Directions, 1938.
MLC	Modern Literary Criticism: An Anthology. Edited with an introduction by Irving Howe. New York: Grove Press, 1961.
MLR	Modern Language Review
Mod	Modern American Poetry. Edited by B. Rajan. London: Dennis Dobson, 1950.
MP	Modern Poetry: Essays in Criticism. Edited by John Hollander. London, New York: Oxford University Press, 1968.
MPA	Modern Poetry of Western America. Edited by Clinton F. Larson and William Stafford. Provo, Utah: Brigham Young University Press, 1975.
MQR	Michigan Quarterly Review
MR	Modern Review
MS	The Magpie's Shadow. Chicago: Musterhousebook, 1922.

MVE   Modern Verse in English, 1900-1950. Edited by David Cecil and Allen Tate. New York: Macmillan, 1958.

NAMP   The Norton Anthology of Modern Poetry. Edited by Richard Ellman and Robert O'Clair. New York: W. W. Norton, 1973.

NDR   A New Directions Reader. Edited by Hayden Carruth and J. Laughlin. Norfolk, Conn.: New Directions, 1964.

NLH   New Literary History

NMQ   New Mexico Quarterly

NOBA   The New Oxford Book of American Verse. Edited by Richard Ellmann. New York: Oxford University Press, 1976.

NP   The New Poetry. Edited by Harriet Monroe and Alice Corbin Henderson. New York: Macmillan, 1932.

NR   New Republic

NS   New Statesman

NY   New Yorker

NYRB   New York Review of Books

NYTB   New York Times Book Review

NYTBV   The New York Times Book of Verse. Edited by Thomas Lask. New York: Macmillan, 1970.

OBSV   The Oxford Book of Satirical Verse. Compiled by Geoffrey Grigson. New York: Oxford University Press, 1980.

PA   The Poetry Anthology: 1912-1977. Edited by Daryl Hine and Joseph Parisi. Boston: Houghton Mifflin, 1978.

PAM   The Poet in America: 1650 to the Present. Edited by Albert Gelpi. New York: D. C. Heath, 1973.

PBMV   The Pocket Book of Modern Verse. Rev. ed. Edited by Oscar Williams. New York: Washington Square Press, 1954.

PCA   The Poem: A Critical Anthology. Edited by Josephine Miles. Englewood Cliffs, N.J.: Prentice-Hall, 1959.

PCC   Perspectives in Contemporary Criticism: A Collection of Recent Essays by American, English, and European Literary Critics. Edited by Sheldon Norman Grebstein. New York: Harper & Row, 1968.

PD   Primitivism and Decadence: A Study of American Experimental Poetry. New York: Arrow Editions, 1937.

PE   Poetry in English. Edited by Warren Taylor and Donald Hall. New York: Macmillan, 1963.

Per   Perspectives on Poetry. Edited by James L. Calderwood and Harold E. Tolliver. New York, London, Toronto: Oxford University Press, 1968.

PI   Poetry: An Introduction and Anthology. Edited by Edward Proffitt. Boston: Houghton Mifflin, 1981.

PIC   Poetry and Its Conventions: An Anthology Examining Poetic Forms and Themes. Edited by John T. Shawcross and Frederick R. Lapides. New York: Free Press, 1972.

PNR   PN Review

Poems   Poems. Los Altos, Calif.: Gyroscope Press, 1940.

POL   Poems One Line and Longer. Edited by William Cole. New York: Grossman Publishers, 1973.

PPD   Poetry Pilot (December 1972)

PPO   Poetry Pilot (October 1979)

PR   Partisan Review

PRA   Poems to Read Aloud. Edited by Edward Hodnett. Rev. ed. New York: W. W. Norton, 1967.

Proof   The Proof. New York: Coward-McCann, 1930.

PV   The Personal Voice: A Contemporary Prose Reader. Edited by Albert J. Guerard, Maclin B. Guerard, John Hawkes, and Claire Rosenfeld. Philadelphia and New York: J. B. Lippincott, 1964.

QR   Quest for Reality: An Anthology of Short Poems in English. Edited by Yvor Winters and Kenneth Fields. Chicago: Swallow Press, 1969.

QRL   Quarterly Review of Literature

REAP   The Recognition of Edgar Allan Poe: Selected Criticism Since 1829. Edited by Eric W. Carlson. Ann Arbor: University of Michigan Press, 1966.

Ren   Renascence

RF   Robert Frost: A Collection of Critical Essays. Edited by James Melville Cox. Englewood Cliffs, N. J.: Prentice-Hall, 1962.

RLE   Readings for Liberal Education. Edited by Louis G. Locke, William M. Gibson, and George Arms. New York: Rinehart, 1948.

RMML   Room for Me and a Mountain Lion: Poetry of Open Space. Compiled by Nancy Larrick. New York: M. Evans, 1974.

RMR   Rocky Mountain Review

RRHR   The Roses Race Around Her Name: Poems from Fathers to Daughters. Edited by Jonathon Cott. New York: Stonehouse Publishing Co., 1974.

Seq   Sequoia

SP   Studying Poetry: A Critical Anthology of English and American Poems. Edited by Karl Kroeber and John O. Lyons. New York: Harper & Row, 1965.

SR   Southern Review

SRL   Saturday Review of Literature

SV   The Structure of Verse: Modern Essays on Prosody. Edited with an introduction and commentary by Harvey Gross. Greenwich, Conn.: Fawcett Publications, 1966.

SW   1941 Yearbook of Stanford Writing. Edited by Glenn Holland. [Stanford]: Writer's Club of Stanford University, [1941].

Tal   Talisman

TCAP   Twentieth-Century American Poetry. Edited by Conrad Aiken. Rev. ed. New York: Modern Library, 1963.

TCL   Twentieth Century Literature

ThP   Three Poems. Cummington, Mass.: Cummington Press, 1950.

TLS	Times Literary Supplement
TP	Twelve Poets of the Pacific. Norfolk, Conn.: New Directions, 1937.
TPWD	A Treasury of Poems for Worship and Devotion. Edited by Charles L. Wallis. New York: Harper, 1959.
TQ	This Quarter
Trans	Transition
TS	The Sonnet: A Comprehensive Anthology of British and American from the Renaissance to the Present. Edited by Robert M. Bender and Charles L. Squier. New York: Washington Square Press, 1965.
TSE	T.S. Eliot: A Selected Critique. Edited by Leonard Unger. New York: Rinehart, 1948.
TT	The Turquoise Trail: An Anthology of New Mexico Poetry. Compiled by Alice Corbin Henderson. Boston and New York: Houghton Mifflin, 1928.
UER	Uncollected Essays and Reviews. Edited and introduced by Francis Murphy. Chicago: Swallow Press, 1973.
UP	Understanding Poetry. Edited by Cleanth Brooks and Robert Penn Warren. 3rd ed. New York: Holt, Rinehart and Winston, 1960.
UsP	The Uses of Poetry. Compiled by Agnes Stein. New York: Holt, Rinehart and Winston, 1975.
VGW	The Voice That Is Great Within Us: American Poetry of the Twentieth Century. Edited by Hayden Carruth. Toronto, New York: Bantam Books, 1970.
VQR	Virginia Quarterly Review
WCW	William Carlos Williams: A Collection of Critical Essays. Edited by J. Hillis Miller. Englewood Cliffs, N.J.: Prentice-Hall, 1966.
WP	The War Poets: An Anthology of the War Poets of the 20th Century. Edited by Oscar Williams. New York: John Day, 1945.
WS	Wallace Stevens: A Critical Anthology. Edited by Irvin Ehrenpreis. Harmondsworth: Penguin, 1972.

PART ONE

Primary Sources

I

BOOKS AND COLLECTIONS OF ESSAYS

1. "The Testament of a Stone, Being Notes on the Mechanics of the
   Poetic Image." [Secession, no. 8 (1924)], pp. 1-20. Occupies entire issue. UER. Reprinted in abridged form in
   Form, no. 1 (1966), pp. 26-28, with letter from Winters de-
   claring it "essentially worthless."
   CONTENTS: "Foreword"; "Definition of Observation, Perception, Image, and Anti-Image"; "Types of Perception"; "Types
   of the Image and Anti-Image"; "Upon the Nature of Words
   and Their Use"; "Upon the Construction of the Poem, with
   Relation to the Image."
   Describes these notes as "an effort to incite the beginnings of
   a scientific criticism of poetry." The elementary terms of the
   analysis are observation, perception, image, and anti-image.
   An observation is an instance of the passive reception of experience. A perception is an active awareness of that which dif-
   ferentiates two observations and of that which they have in common. An image results when two observations having one quality in common are so superimposed that the shared quality is
   perceived simultaneously as part of each separate observation
   and yet as one; the point of fusion is the image. The two perceptions are both different and the same, and the mental vibra-
   tion of their coming together within the mind of the perceiving
   poet or reader is the aesthetic emotion. The emotion created
   by the image is experienced directly and without the aid of
   thought. The anti-image, on the other hand, is a product of
   thought and occurs when the poet thinks about the relationships
   not evident to the unaided senses that exist between observations.
   In such a case, the emotion is not transferred through fusion,
   as in the case of the image, but through intercomment.
   To clarify the distinctions made possible by this series
   of definitions, divides types of perception into sound-perceptions
   and meaning-perceptions, and further divides meaning-perceptions
   into sense-perceptions and thought-perceptions. Then places the
   types of image and anti-image within a series of categories il-
   lustrating the different possible types of fusion between perception and a poetic rhythm. Concludes by stating a theory of value
   in poetry based on the relative degree of fusion of the elements
   entering the poem: "that poetry is good which is a perfect fusion of perceptions, and that which is an imperfect fusion of

perceptions or depends mainly upon symbolic or other connotations is, to that extent, weak." (See items 2, 4.)

2. "A Method of Critical Approach to Works of Literature Based Primarily upon a Study of the Lyric in French and English." Master's Thesis, University of Colorado, 1925.
Consists of Notes on the Mechanics of the Poetic Image, which is a slightly expanded version of The Testament of a Stone (see item 1), and which was later to appear as a section of Winters' Ph.D. dissertation (see item 4); and Notes on the Mechanics of the Mood in Lyrical Composition, later to appear as a section of "The Extension and Reintegration of the Human Spirit Through the Poetry Mainly French and American Since Poe and Baudelaire" (see item 60) and then, in somewhat altered form, as "The Experimental School in American Thought" in PD (see item 88). Includes also material that had appeared earlier in "Holiday and Day of Wrath" (see item 46), and "Notes" (see item 45).

3. With Frances Theresa Russell. The Case of David Lamson: A Summary. Foreword by Peter B. Kyne. San Francisco: Lamson Defense Committee, printed by the Knight-Counihan Co., 1934.
Argues for the innocence of David Lamson, convicted and sentenced to be hanged for the murder of his wife. Follows "for the greater part the briefs for appeal" to the California Supreme Court filed by Lamson's second lawyer, Edwin V. MacKenzie, "though some additional material and analyses are introduced." Partly as a result of this pamphlet, a second trial was granted and resulted in a deadlocked jury. A third trial was declared a mistrial and a fourth issued once again in a deadlocked jury. The charges were dismissed and Lamson was released. (See items 78, 351, 353, 354.)

4. "A Study of the Post-Romantic Reaction in Lyrical Verse, and Incidentally in Certain Other Forms." Ph.D. dissertation, Stanford University, 1935.
Consists of a version of the material that was to be published in 1937 as Primitivism and Decadence (see item 5), some of which had already appeared in "The Extension and Reintegration of the Human Spirit Through the Poetry Mainly French and American Since Poe and Baudelaire" (see item 60) and in "Poetry, Morality, and Criticism" (see item 67). Includes also an expanded version of The Testament of a Stone (see item 1) and material from essays that had appeared and were to appear under the following titles: "Traditional Mastery" (see item 71), "T. Sturge Moore" (see item 75), "Poets and Others" (see item 72), "The Oxford Book of Sixteenth Century Verse" (see item 76), and Chapter I of Forms of Discovery (see item 125).

5. Primitivism and Decadence: A Study of American Experimental Poetry. New York: Arrow Editions, 1937.
CONTENTS: "The Morality of Poetry" (see item 67); "The Experimental School in American Thought" (see item 88);

"Poetic Convention"; "Primitivism and Decadence" (see item 89); "The Influence of Meter on Poetic Convention."
Establishes, in "The Morality of Poetry," a direct relationship between poetic technique and moral awareness, "for the creation of a form is nothing more nor less than the act of evaluating and shaping (that is, controlling) a given experience." Poetry is a technique of contemplation in which the poet's technical control is the means to spiritual mastery of his material. Moral judgment resides in the feeling defined and motivated by the poem. The feeling motivated is a product of the poet's control of the form and is inseparable from the form. Verse is preferable to prose because its faster rhythms make possible great economy of statement, and its greater complexity of organization is more precisely expressive of feeling than is prose. The poetic discipline sharpens the faculties of the poet, and the resultant poem provides, for both poet and reader, a means of arriving at new perceptions of the objective universe and of human experience. Poetry is not a substitute for philosophy or religion and is not an escape from life or action. "Poetic morality and poetic feeling are inseparable. Technique has laws which govern poetic (and perhaps more general) morality more widely than is commonly recognized." (See item 67.)

Describes and evaluates, in "The Experimental School in American Poetry," structural methods that appear in recent American poetry. Among the traditional modes of construction are the method of repetition, the logical method and narrative. The method of repetition consists of restatement in successive stanzas of a single theme in different terms or images. It is effective in short poems but not in the longer forms of Whitman and Jeffers. The logical method involves rational progression from detail to detail. Narrative depends on necessary and natural causation within a sequence. Causation can be best exposed through the direct authorial comment of the omniscient narrator rather than through the limited point of view of Henry James and James Joyce.

Discusses recent experimental modes of construction: pseudo-reference, qualitative progression, and the double mood. In pseudo-reference, the poet retains "the syntactical form and much of the vocabulary of rational coherence in its absence or at least in excess of its presence." In qualitative progression, the poet abandons rational coherence and "proceeds from image to image wholly through the coherence of feeling: his sole principle of unity is mood, carefully established and varied." Pseudo-reference and qualitative progression are the dominant structural principles of twentieth century poetry and exhibit a failure to adapt motive to feeling within the poem. The double mood is frequent in Pound, Eliot, and Stevens; it is a strategy for indulging feeling without judging it. The strategy consists of expressing romantic feeling and then ridiculing the feeling ironically. These three strategies represent irresponsible indulgence in imprecise and unjustifiable feeling and are extensions of romanticism rather than a development beyond it. (See item 60.)

Distinguishes, in "Poetic Convention," between the perceptual content of a poem and the quality and intensity of feeling to which the poet lays claim. Identifies the convention of a poem with this norm of feeling: "poetic convention is the initial, or basic, assumption of feeling in any poem, from which all departures acquire their significance." Norms of feeling can be divided into the normal conventions of traditional poetry and the abnormal conventions of experimental poetry. Traditional differs from experimental poetry in that it uses the full resources of the language, exhibits a more balanced relationship between motive and feeling, and is capable of expressing a wider range of feeling. The conventions of experimental poetry are a means of widening, altering, or escaping from the human experience. Such conventions are frequently unsuccessful and exhibit an imperception that results from overemphasis.

Traditional poetry is sometimes confused with the pseudo-traditional or "literary." The literary poet has no contact with a living tradition and employs the idioms of the traditional poet as a mannerism. Literary poetry is often mistaken for traditional poetry by readers of popular and academic taste and is preferred by such readers. Pseudo-experimental poetry results when a poet confuses tradition with convention and abandons convention to escape from tradition. The result is the loss of form and the destruction of poetry.

Asserts, in "Primitivism and Decadence," that experimental poetry can be classified as primitive or decadent and that these types correspond to two distinct methods of creating an abnormal convention. The primitive poet limits both his subject matter and the resources of language employed to realize that subject matter. The limitation of subject and the limited form are appropriate to one another; the resulting poem is a balanced, minor performance: "the primitive poet is the major poet on a smaller scale." The decadent poet applies a highly developed technique to a limited subject matter. In such poetry there is an imbalance and a sense of incompleteness: "the decadent poet is the major, or primitive, poet with some important faculty absent from the texture of all his work."

These classifications make possible comparative judgments. The experimental poet is not primitive or decadent in an absolute sense but in comparison to other poets and as a result of the use he makes of his subject matter and technical resources. Hart Crane's "The Dance" is incomplete and decadent if compared with poems by Ben Jonson or George Herbert but represents an advance over Whitman. Crane's sophisticated technique is inappropriate to the imprecise mysticism of his subject matter. In contrast, technique and subject matter are balanced and appropriate to one another in Jonson. Crane's mysticism derives from Whitman, a second-rate poet whose language is as imprecise as his subject and thus appropriate to his subject. Whitman's imprecise language does not make evident the imprecision of his subject matter; his poetry achieves a second-rate balance. Crane's precise language does make clear the imprecision of the Whitmanian theme and thus makes evident the limitations of the theme. Applies this terminology to discussions of Williams and T. Sturge Moore.

Describes, in "The Influence of Meter on Poetic Convention," the principles of traditional English meter, his own method of scanning free verse, the relationship of experimental to traditional meters, and the principles and history of the heroic couplet. Within accentual-syllabic meter, the principal sources of rhythmical variation are substitution, quantity, varying degrees of accent, and sprung rhythm. Within the accentual-syllabic system, a syllable is accented or unaccented only with reference to other syllables in the same foot. The system does not measure length of syllable or the varying degrees of accent within the language itself, but these unmeasured linguistic elements are part of the rhythmical pattern that is given by the meter.

Scans free verse as accentual verse so written that two degrees of accent are perceptible apart from unaccented syllables in a long foot made up of one primary accent, and an indeterminate number of unaccented syllables. This meter creates the effect of two rhythms counterpointed against one another: a free verse pattern marked by the heavy accents and a fragmentary iambic pattern marked by both primary and secondary accents heard against the unaccented syllables. This structure is not as flexible as that based on a fixed meter. Although not capable of accommodating a wide range of feelings, free verse can express qualities of feeling not possible within traditional meter.

The most flexible and expressive form is that which measures most precisely every syllable and provides the clearest convention from which variations in feeling can be measured. The free verse norm is a norm of heightened intensity and one from which it is difficult to depart without damage to the integrity of the form. In free verse, the metrical form and the norm of feeling are closely identified with one another; a marked change in one causes a breakdown of the other. Traditional meter makes possible the establishment of clearly defined norms from which departures can be precisely measured. The flexibility of the heroic couplet lies in its apparent inflexibility. The fact that the form itself accounts for the definition of every syllable and is, as well, the simplest possible form of stanza allows the poet great freedom in the management of tempo, quantity, degree of accent, and the relationship between phrasing and underlying metrical structure. (See item 112.)

5a.   Primitivism and Decadence: A Study of American Experimental
        Poetry.   1937.   Reprint.   New York: Haskell House, 1969.

5b.   Primitivism and Decadence: A Study of American Experimental
        Poetry.   1937.   Reprint.   New York: Gordon Press, 1973.

6.   Maule's Curse: Seven Studies in the History of American Obscurantism.   Norfolk, Conn.:   New Directions, 1938.
        CONTENTS: "A Foreword"; "Maule's Curse, or Hawthorne

and the Problem of Allegory" (see item 84); "Fenimore Cooper, or the Ruins of Time"; "Herman Melville and the Problems of Moral Navigation"; "Edgar Allan Poe: A Crisis in the History of American Obscurantism" (see item 82); "Jones Very and R. W. Emerson: Aspects of New England Mysticism" (see item 81); "Emily Dickinson and the Limits of Judgment" (see item 86); "Maule's Well, or Henry James and the Relation of Morals to Manners" (see item 85); "A Brief Selection of the Poems of Jones Very."

Maintains, in "Maule's Curse, or Hawthorne and the Problem of Allegory," that Hawthorne was essentially an allegorist and a product of the Puritan view of life. The New England Puritans believed in predestination and the inefficaciousness of good works and, at first, that an inner assurance of election was reasonable evidence that one was of the Elect. This mystical tendency was suppressed quite early and replaced by an act of will: the decision to trust in Christ and obey God's will. Individual behavior became an index of God's probable judgment. The effect was to exaggerate the importance of the will while denying that the will had any existence and to encourage an allegorical frame of mind.

Hawthorne was a product of two historical centers, that of the first generation of New England Puritans and that of the post-Unitarian Transcendentalists among whom he lived. In The Scarlet Letter, Hawthorne dealt with the entire subject of sin through treating sexual sin as representative of all sin. He thereby exhausted the subject in so far as his allegorical method could deal with it. In future work, he could only repeat himself, and this he attempted to do in The House of the Seven Gables and The Marble Faun. When he left allegory for the procedures of the novelist, he was unsuccessful. Hawthorne was cut off by his historical position from the meaning that sustained the allegorical explorations of the Puritans, but he could not escape from the allegorical method that required such meaning. In this situation, he developed "the formula of alternative possibilities." In The Scarlet Letter and The Marble Faun, the allegorical meaning or the supernatural causation of a detail or event is indicated clearly, but the detail or event itself is described ambiguously. In The Blithedale Romance and the four unfinished romances, the formula is reversed: the physical detail is rendered precisely, but the meaning is unclear. Separated from his heritage, Hawthorne searched experience for a meaning that would not reveal itself.

Emphasizes, in "Fenimore Cooper, or The Ruins of Time," Cooper's importance as social critic and prose stylist. Cooper defended democracy but feared the power that it gave to uneducated men and to the uncontrolled rule of the majority, a power that could easily lead to oligarchy as unscrupulous demagogues took advantage of it. He describes these dangers perceptively in such otherwise bad novels as The Redskins, Home as Found, and The Ways of the Hour, and deals particularly with the development and dangers of oligarchy in The Bravo and The Monikins. Cooper believed that democracy could be pro-

tected from these dangers through abstract principle embodied
in law and through the perpetuation and extension of a heredi-
tary landed aristocracy with the leisure for self-improvement
but too cultivated to seek power as an end in itself. The failure
of abstract principle and aristocratic tradition to preserve American democracy from corruption left Cooper disillusioned but
still certain that democracy was the least defective of political
systems.

In the Littlepage novels, Cooper defends the property
rights of the landed proprietors and the social value of an
aristocracy. The novels suffer in depth of character portrayal
from Cooper's division of his characters into the Genteel and
the Vulgar, a distinction made on the level of manners rather
than morals and lacking the spiritual intensity of Hawthorne's
distinction between the Good and the Evil. The novels of the
Leatherstocking Series do not deserve the contempt in which
they are held. The social ideal that Cooper defends was already in decay during his lifetime. His rhetoric was appropriate to his social ideals but was frequently damaged by the romantic sentiment of his period.

Demonstrates, in "Herman Melville and the Problems of
Moral Navigation," that Melville's governing theme and his central moral problem is the relationship of principle to perception. In Moby Dick, the theme is realized in an antithesis of
sea and land where the land represents principle, the known
and mastered in human experience, and the sea represents perception, the contingent and half-known realms of instinct, evil,
and death. Ahab is a tragic hero whose sin is attempting to
destroy the evil of the world symbolized by the White Whale, a
denizen of the sea and a symbol of evil and of death. The novel
contains a powerful argument for the "demonism of the world,"
an argument that is "one of the most appalling specimens of
metaphysical argument in all literature."

In Pierre and The Confidence Man, Melville explores the
relationship of principle to perception but now believes that no
judgment is possible. Pierre is unsatisfactory both as philosophy and in the quality of its prose. The Confidence Man is
written in sharp and occasionally brilliant prose despite the unsatisfactory philosophy and the repetitious narrative. Aside
from Moby Dick, Melville's greatest works are Benito Cereno,
The Encantadas, and Billy Budd. In the last of these, Melville
once more takes up the theme of the relationship between principle and perception, here as that of the conflict between established principle supporting public order and private judgment.

Describes, in "Edgar Allan Poe: A Crisis in the History
of American Obscurantism," Poe's poetic theory as one in which
the poet's subject matter is supra-human, poetic unity one of
mood or effect, and unity of effect created mechanically. For
Poe, beauty is the subject of the poem, but Poe fails to realize
that beauty is not itself a subject but exists in the just treatment
of human experience. In attempting to define a pure poetry,
Poe excludes from poetry both subject matter and intellectual
content.

Poe's view that, in English meter, accented syllables are always long made it impossible for him to recognize the subtle sources of variation that result from the counterpoint between metrical accent and length of syllable. Beyond that, Poe had no sense of the gradations in degree of accent that are possible within the English metrical system. (See item 112.)

We must try to understand Poe's theory and practice because the confusion that he exhibits and the exclusions that he practices express aesthetic ideas that have influenced the work of his American contemporaries, the French Symbolists, and the American Experimentalists of the twentieth century. (See item 88.)

Asserts, in "Jones Very and R. W. Emerson: Aspects of New England Mysticism," that Very, the dogmatic Calvinist, and Emerson, the moral relativist, both recommend the submission of the will. The God who controlled Very's will was the Christian God who conforms the believer's will to traditional Christian moral distinctions. Emerson believed that all of creation was equally divine and all impulses of divine origin. Although Emerson's impulses were the product of a traditional moral training, the doctrine of equivalence in which he believed provided no basis for preferring one impulse to another. The amoral implications of this doctrine were not realized in Emerson's own behavior but can be observed in the tradition beginning with Whitman and including Hart Crane that has developed from the doctrine.

In his poetry, Very expresses his longing for and experience of beatitude. Emerson, whose writings demonstrate that he had not undergone the mystical experience that he recommends, confined himself to the theory rather than the actuality of the experience. We must respect Very's saintliness and sincerity, the purity of feeling in his verse, and the skill with which they are communicated. These qualities of feeling can be contrasted with the whimsical facility of Emerson's prose and verse.

Maintains, in "Emily Dickinson and the Limits of Judgment," that Dickinson "is one of the greatest lyric poets of all time" and, among American writers, is only surpassed by Melville. The critical problem is that even her best work is marred by lack of taste. She differs from all major nineteenth century American writers except Melville in that her Calvinistic heritage did not leave her life in moral chaos, although it made her life a moral drama. She is unlike her contemporaries in that her inability to accept Christian mysticism did not cause her to turn to the pantheistic mysticism of the Transcendentalists. Her attitude toward nature was that it is other than and hostile to human consciousness; it is thus a symbol for death and appears as such in her greatest poems.

Her subject matter can be divided into three categories: natural description, mystical experience, and the definition of the limits of human comprehension. Despite brilliant descriptive moments, she can plunge into obscurity and a rhetoric more portentous than is justified by her subject. Her mystical

poems attempt the definition of posthumous beatitude as though
she had already experienced it; since they must employ the
terms of human life, they are forced and theoretical. They
lack the conviction that informs the mystical poems of Very as
well as the tragic sense of human limitation and isolation defined in her own best poems. Her best poems fall into the
third category; their theme is a rejection of the mystical trance
and an acceptance of the limits of human judgment and of the
essential cleavage between man and nature.

Asserts, in "Maule's Well, or Henry James and the Relation of Morals to Manners," that James is "the greatest novelist in English" and "one of the five or six greatest writers of
any variety to be produced in North America." His achievements lie in the creation of memorable characters, in the art
of plot construction, and in the definition of central moral concerns of his culture. His weaknesses are related to these virtues; they proceed from the effort to separate ethical problems
from the unimportant details of life, to analyze them in a pure
state, and to treat them almost as an allegorist would.

James dealt typically with the American moral sense as
it appeared in Americans encountering the rich context of European manners. In this engagement, the American possesses a
moral sense derived from the theological developments from
Calvinism through Unitarianism to Emersonian Transcendentalism, and the European a richer sensibility and a more highly
developed code of manners. The European code, however, is
decadent and no longer expresses the ethical system on which
it was based. This relationship between the American moral
sense and European manners and cultural tradition resembles
that of character to sensibility: up to a certain point, the relationship is enriching and, beyond that point, disintegrating.

Factors leading to James's obscurity are the New England background that encouraged the search for a nonexistent
allegorical meaning, the isolation of James and his characters
from the details of American life and manners, and the resultant divorce between feeling and motive for feeling. In American literature, this obscurity appears as early as Hawthorne
and anticipates the obscurity of twentieth century Experimental
poetry. Its continuing presence indicates the historical conti-
nuity between earlier and present day American culture. (See
items 5, 7.)

6a. Aspects de la Littérature Américaine: Hawthorne, Cooper,
     Melville, Poe, Emerson, Jones Very, Emily Dickinson,
     Henry James.   Translated by Georges Belmont.   Paris:
     Editions du chêne, 1947.   Translation of Maule's Curse.

7.   The Anatomy of Nonsense.   Norfolk, Conn.: New Directions,
     1943.
     CONTENTS: "Preliminary Problems" (see item 99); "Henry
     Adams, or the Creation of Confusion"; "Wallace Stevens, or,
     the Hedonists's Progress" (see item 100); T. S. Eliot, or
     the Illusion of Reaction" (see item 95); "John Crowe Ransom,

or Thunder Without God" (see item 101); "Post Scripta" (see item 94).

Proposes, in "Preliminary Problems," a series of problems designed to demonstrate the impossibility of meaningful value judgments outside of an absolutistic frame of reference and to define the nature of poetry and the central issues and procedures of literary criticism. A poem is "a statement in words" that has "by intention a controlled content of feeling" written in verse rather than prose because "the rhythm of verse permits the expression of more powerful feeling than is possible in prose when such feeling is needed, and it permits at all times the expression of finer shades of feeling." Words have conceptual content and imprecise associations of feeling that are rendered more precise through the control of context and the details of style. The conceptual cannot be eliminated from words, and the poet's task is that of relating concept to feeling through just motive. The romantic practice is to suppress the conceptual content and to present unmotivated feeling for its own sake. (See discussion of pseudo-reference in item 88.)

One determines whether feeling has been justly motivated through an act of moral judgment. In human life, distinctions between better and worse are distinctions between the degrees to which human beings fulfill the potentialities of their nature. The existence of clearly incomplete and unfulfilled human beings indicates the existence of greater or lesser fulfillment and, therefore, of greatest fulfillment. A poem can be judged in terms of the fullness with which it utilizes the possibilities of its medium and the extent to which feeling is adequately and precisely motivated by concept. The poet tries to use the full potentialities of his mind and his medium; and the critic does likewise, considering the relevant history, biography, and literary theory, as well as the paraphrasable content of the poem, the feeling motivated by the details of style, and the final act of judgment. Right judgment, in the case of both poet and critic, is an act of intuition as well as one of rational understanding; but, for the most complete act of human judgment, rational understanding must be fully present. The final judgment is a unique act.

Traces, in "Henry Adams, or the Creation of Confusion," the background necessary for understanding Adams' mind from the Medieval nominalism of William of Ockham. The denial of the reality of universals and of the validity of natural reason directly supported a fideistic Christianity. Deriving all knowledge from faith and Revelation led logically to the determinism of Calvin's doctrines of predestination and of man's utter depravity and complete reliance on God's grace. (See item 84.) The contradiction in later New England Calvinism between the denial of man's free will and the call to an act of will in the form of repentance led to the abandonment of supernatural theology in Unitarianism. (See item 81.) In the thought of Adams, even this last position was found unacceptable and was rejected, and he was left with no means of giving meaning to his experience.

Adams inherited as well the New England Calvinist's habit of searching experience allegorically for signs of God's intentions, a habit persisting after the disappearance of the theology and the belief that gave meaning to the search. In the Education and in Mont Saint-Michel and Chartres, Adams develops a theory of history in which nothing is assumed but relative degree of order: thirteenth century unity as one pole and twentieth century multiplicity as the other. Adams's scheme is too simple to be useful and is pernicious because Adams derives from it the conclusion that the process of deterioration is inescapable. The pattern of deterioration becomes a cosmology and has the force of revealed truth.

Adams was a great historian and his History of the United States During the Administrations of Thomas Jefferson and James Madison is "the greatest historical work in English, with the probable exception of The Decline and Fall of the Roman Empire." He did not see man as heroic, but he had an interest in character like that of Henry James and was able to analyze with great precision the behavior of the major figures of the period he is recounting. Adams' skill is that of a Jamesian novelist, and his material is more important than that of the novelist.

Describes Eliot's critical position, in "T. S. Eliot, or the Illusion of Reaction," as one in which art is autotelic, the poet himself a passive agent in the creative process, and the poet's object that of finding an "objective correlative" for the emotion that he wishes to express. The first of these views deprives poetry of its function as a moral judgment of human experience. The second deprives the poet himself of free will and leads to the determinism made explicit in Eliot's view that the poet expresses his age even when he is not aware of doing so. The third establishes the poet's function as that of expressing emotions rather than understanding them. Eliot frequently writes as though he were unaware of the implications of his own views. He criticizes Gray and Collins for having lost the values that characterized Elizabethan and Jacobean poets. He speaks of the intensity of the process of artistic creation as though the poet were an active agent in the creative process and not a mere catalyst, and he attacks deterministic views in the writings of others even though his own definition of tradition and the individual artist's relationship to tradition is deterministic.

Eliot maintains that poetry should be dramatic in that it should give us the sense that we are in the immediate present of the action described. Such a view leads to emotionalism and away from balanced judgment. Although Eliot's own poetry is at times dramatic, his practice tends more towards a poetry of revery like Pound's. (For further discussion of the poetry of immediacy and the poetry of revery, see item 655.) The subject matter of The Waste Land is Baudelairean; but, whereas Baudelaire understands and judges the spiritual torpor of the modern world, Eliot merely exhibits it: the poet expresses the fragmentariness of modern experience through writing fragmentary revery.

Defines, in "Wallace Stevens, or the Hedonist's Progress," the central attitude expressed in Stevens' poetry as hedonism or cultivation of the emotions for their own sake. The cultivation of the feelings can proceed as a search for more and more intense feeling or as a search for greater and greater subtlety of feeling. The failure to realize that poetry is a moral experience leads to a contempt for the art. The poet who continues nevertheless to practice his art must explore increasingly perverse and elusive feelings if he is to escape the ennui that must otherwise overtake him in a universe in which only intensity of feeling has value. In "Sunday Morning" and in other early poems such as "The Snow Man," "On the Manner of Addressing Clouds," and "Of Heaven Considered as a Tomb," Stevens is a master of style and one of the greatest poets in English. Stevens's work collapses thereafter into the laborious and the trivial, and this result can be directly attributed to the dangers inherent in the hedonistic outlook.

The background necessary for an understanding of Stevens' attitude begins with eighteenth century Deism. The Deists believed that the universe is good, God benevolent, and the feelings a more trustworthy guide to conduct than the reason. A stereotyping of feeling and diction was the poetic result of these beliefs. To extend the possibilities of poetry beyond these narrow limits, Blake and Wordsworth sought to widen its scope through expressing new emotions, largely of an obscurely prophetic variety. The poetry achieved endeavored to free emotions rather than to provide just motivation for them. In the theories and practice of Coleridge, Poe, and the French Symbolists, the purpose of poetry was to express emotion in a language that suppresses rational motivation. This practice reached its greatest subtlety in the poetry of Mallarmé and Rimbaud, who provide the immediate background for Stevens.

Defends critical position, in "John Crowe Ransom, or Thunder Without God," from Ransom's objections to it. (See item 640.) Ransom confuses the ethical and the didactic. He assumes that when Winters refers to poetry as an act of moral judgment, Winters means that poetry is didactic in that it represents a simple act of classification. In fact, Winters means that the poet, through his control of the conceptual and the evocative aspects of language, adjusts motive to concept, and that this adjustment can be made precise through a control of meter.

Ransom believes that the poet imitates a unique experience out of love for the experience imitated. This view fails to explain how we like a poem when we don't like the object imitated. At times, Ransom justifies the artistic imitation by seeing it as a means of separating knowledge from usefulness, but neither the nature of that knowledge nor its value is clearly indicated. The structure of poetry, for Ransom, consists of a logical core and a texture of irrelevance. Figurative language is a means of introducing irrelevance into the text, and metrical irregularities are a form of irrelevance superimposed on meter. The function of these irrelevancies is to provide nonrational and therefore "pure" patterns of various sorts that we

enjoy for their own sake. Ransom's theories render poetry
contemptible. They provide no principles through which one
poem can be preferred to another and no motive for poetry beyond a hedonistic one.

Draws conclusions, in "Post Scripta," from foregoing
studies of weaknesses in the thought of Adams, Stevens, Eliot,
and Ransom. The failure to understand the basic materials of
American literary history and theory is not confined to these
four writers. It can be found in the work of V. L. Parring-
ton, who believes that one can understand the Puritans without
reference to their theology and literature without reference to
its function as art. Similar instances of limited sensitivity and
oversimplification can be found throughout the academic study
of American literature.

To produce first-rate literary critics, it is necessary
to combine "the talents of the poet with the discipline of scholarship" within the institution of the university. Despite the
poor performance of the university, it is the only institution
comparable to the Catholic Church as a preserver of civiliza-
tion. Maintains that there are a large number of talented poets
teaching in the universities. They constitute a group that combines literary perceptivity with academic discipline, and their
presence may improve the quality of American literature and
criticism.

7a. The Anatomy of Nonsense. Folcroft, Pa.: Folcroft Press,
      1970.

8. Edwin Arlington Robinson. Norfolk, Conn.: New Directions,
      1946.
   Discusses briefly Robinson's life, the New England background
   for his work, literary influences on his style, and, at greater
   length, the shorter poems, the three Arthurian poems, other
   long poems, and poems of medium length. (For a summary of
   the background of ideas from New England Calvinism through
   Emersonian Transcendentalism, see items 81, 84, 85, 104.)

        Regards Robinson as essentially a counter-romantic.
   The best poems are to be found among the shorter poems and
   the poems of medium length and include "Hillcrest," "Eros
   Turannos," "The Wandering Jew," "Many Are Called," "The
   Three Taverns," and "Rembrandt to Rembrandt." In discussing
   the three Arthurian poems and the other long poems, summarizes plots and analyzes Jamesian techniques of exposition with
   emphasis on the obscurantism of the method. Although influenced by Robert Browning, W. M. Praed, and various other
   poets, Robinson writes in a prose tradition despite his use of
   a verse medium: "one may find him related to such a mind
   as that of Henry James, but perhaps more obviously to Edith
   Wharton and Motley and Francis Parkman, and perhaps even
   at times to Henry Adams."

8a. Edwin Arlington Robinson. Rev. ed. New York: New Direc-
      tions, 1971. With quotations as first planned. (See discus-
      sion of first edition in FD, pp. 369-70.)

9. In Defense of Reason. New York: Swallow Press and W. Morrow, 1947.

    CONTENTS: Primitivism and Decadence: A Study of American Experimental Poetry (see item 5); Maule's Curse: Seven Studies in the History of American Obscurantism (see item 6); The Anatomy of Nonsense (see item 7); "The Significance of The Bridge, by Hart Crane, or What Are We to Think of Professor X?" (see item 104).

    States, in the Foreword, that the standard literary theories are didactic, hedonistic, or romantic. The limitations of the didactic theory are that moral instruction might be better accomplished through other means than literature and that the theory encourages the identification of a work and its paraphrase. The limitations of the hedonistic theory are that it treats pleasure as an end rather than as a by-product of our recognition of the truth or justice of a statement, and encourages the pursuit of ever more intense varieties of pleasure. The first limitation trivializes literature and the second encourages a destructive self-indulgence. Of these three theories, the romantic theory accounts most satisfactorily for the power of literature. Literature becomes, in this theory, the expression of emotions and frequently the vehicle for pantheistic mysticism. The romantic doctrine is based on a belief in natural goodness that encourages automatism.

    Proposes a fourth theory called moralistic and defined as absolutist: "I believe that the work of literature, in so far as it is valuable, approximates a real apprehension and communication of a particular kind of objective truth." The poet makes a statement that communicates a rational understanding of a human experience that need not be real but must be possible. He does so in language that motivates the emotion proper to that understanding. This theory accounts for the power of poetry and the seriousness of great poets clearly interested in something more important than giving pleasure or expressing their emotions.

    (For annotations of Primitivism and Decadence, see item 5; Maule's Curse, item 6; and The Anatomy of Nonsense, item 7.)

    Considers, in "The Significance of The Bridge, by Hart Crane, or What Are We to Think of Professor X?" Crane's intentions in The Bridge and the moral that we derive from Crane's success and failure in the poem. The poem is based on the thought of Emerson and Whitman: God, man, and the creation are good; man partakes of this universal goodness through suppressing his rational faculties and acting on impulse. (See item 81.) Whereas Emerson's impulses were largely governed by the Christian morality that he repudiated, Crane's were not. Crane cultivated his impulses on principle and from religious conviction, and the result was personal disaster.

    The Bridge consists of a collection of lyrics held together loosely by their connection with the Brooklyn Bridge as a symbol that functions as a bridge between past, present, and future, life and death, non-being and being. The poem is weakened by

the miscellaneous character of the forms used in the individual
poems and by the difficulty inherent in the Whitmanian theme
of imagining salvation as immolation. Nevertheless, the poem
contains great moments. (See item 66.)

Since Crane was a poet of genius and intelligence, the
failure of the poem and of his life must be partly attributed
to the teachings of Emerson and Whitman. These same teachings are recommended by Professor X, the typical teacher of
American literature and history in our universities. Since
Professor X is not a genius and does not possess great moral
energy, he does not go mad and does not live self-destructive-
ly. He does, however, teach a pernicious philosophy, the evil
of which becomes apparent when it is adopted by a man of
Crane's genius and integrity.

9a. In Defense of Reason. Denver: Alan Swallow, 1947.

9b. In Defense of Reason. Denver: University of Denver Press,
     1950.

9c. In Defense of Reason. Denver: University of Denver Press,
     1959.

9d. In Defense of Reason. Denver: Alan Swallow, 1959.

9e. In Defense of Reason. London: Routledge & Kegan Paul,
     1960.

10. The Function of Criticism: Problems and Exercises. Denver:
     Alan Swallow, 1957.
     CONTENTS: "Problems for the Modern Critic of Litera-
     ture" (see item 115); "The Audible Reading of Poetry" (see
     item 112); "The Poetry of Gerard Manley Hopkins" (see item
     110); "Robert Frost, or the Spiritual Drifter as Poet" (see
     item 106); "English Literature in the Sixteenth Century"
     (see item 113).
     Illustrates, in "Problems for the Modern Critic of Literature,"
     through examining the critical positions of Eliot, Ransom,
     Brooks, Blackmur, Tate, and R. S. Crane, the absence of a
     final cause for literature in twentieth century criticism. Pro-
     poses a theory according to which the final end of any literary
     work is a complete moral judgment, both rational and emo-
     tional, of the experience contemplated. Evaluates the relative
     strengths and weaknesses of the principal literary genres:
     the epic, the allegorical epic, historiography, prose fiction,
     poetic drama, and the short poem.
     The epic is damaged by the fact that its subject matter
     is primitive history of an intellectually unsophisticated sort.
     The form is further marred by the inappropriateness of verse
     to the rendering of narrative detail. Milton encountered these
     difficulties in Paradise Lost when he tried to use the epic form
     as a medium through which to express his own sophisticated
     thought. The allegorical epic (The Divine Comedy, The Fairy

Queen) is marred by the frequent arbitrariness of the relationship between details and the meanings that they represent.

Prose fiction is often damaged by the triviality of the
material treated and by the theory that material should be
presented through the limited point of view of a character
within the action rather than from that of the intelligent omniscient author. Believes that such works of history as Macau-
lay's History of England, Motley's Rise of the Dutch Republic,
and Adams's Jefferson and Madison, escape these limitations
and possess the further advantage of dealing with real and important occurrences.

The weakness of poetic drama is that the poet cannot
speak directly but must imitate the speech of a character of a
definable and therefore limited degree of intelligence. The
poet must damage his language and poetic form in the interests
of imitation. The only genre that makes possible maximum
perfection of language and form is the short poem. Unlike
other genres, the short poem is not the imitation of an action
but the contemplation of experience in an essentially expository
form that gains emotional precision from the use of a verse
medium. The poet is free to use the full resources of intelligence, language, and form, and is not hampered by limitations imposed by imitative and narrative forms and objectives.
The greatest achievements in this form appear in the sixteenth
and seventeenth centuries in England, in Paul Valéry's Le
Cimetière Marin and Ebauche d'un Serpent, and in the post-
Symbolist work produced in America during the nineteenth and
twentieth centuries. (See item 15.)

States, in "The Audible Reading of Poetry," that neither
poetry nor prose can be properly understood by a reader incapable of reading it aloud so as to perceive its rhythmical
structure. In the case of poetry, such reading must be a restrained and formal chant that establishes the impersonal and
definite base necessary for the creation of metrical variations.
Analyzes the structure of iambic verse in which the metrical
base is an arithmetic but theoretic norm created by the distinction between accented and unaccented syllables within the
foot. The norm is abstract and theoretic because the linguistic elements that create variation are inescapably present in
the actual line; therefore, the norm almost never exists in a
pure state. These sources of variation are degree of accent,
length of syllable, and rhetorical stress. Iambic verse measures two degrees of accent (accented and unaccented); but, in
the language itself, degrees of accent are infinitely variable.
In such verse, length of syllable, although not measured by
the meter, affects the rhythm. A relationship exists between
rhythmical stress and metrical stress, but the two are not
identical, and it is a part of the art of writing poetry to manage the relationship so that these two kinds of stress support
rather than conflict with one another.

A failure to read properly, usually a tendency to read
dramatically rather than formally, results in an obscuring of
the metrical base and a conflict between metrical stress and

rhetorical stress. When this failure occurs in a poet, the result can be the production of poems in which metrical and
rhetorical stress are awkwardly and unproductively at vari-
ance. Discusses instances of such failure in poems by Hopkins, Eliot, Keats, and Wordsworth.

Analyzes metrical and rhythmical structure of five poems
to illustrate the wide variety of kinds of rhythmical movement
obtainable within the iambic norm. The poems are Googe's
"Of Money," Shakespeare's "When to the sessions of sweet
silent thought," Dowland's "Fine knacks for ladies," Campion's
"Follow your saint," and Hopkins' "No worst, there is none."

Approaches, in "The Poetry of Gerard Manley Hopkins,"
critical problems raised by Hopkins' poetry through comparing
Hopkins' sonnet, "No worst, there is none," with Donne's
"Thou hast made me" and Bridges' "The southwind strengthens
to a gale." The poems by Donne and Bridges conform to
Winters' view that a poem should present a rational understanding of a situation that is both general and personal at
once, as well as the feeling properly motivated by that understanding. (See item 99, and "The Morality of Poetry," item
67.) Hopkins' poem presents obscurely an undefined personal
situation in language that is violently emotional.

Hopkins' theory of meter contributes to these difficulties. In both Running meter and Sprung Rhythm, he introduces innovations that lead to metrical ambiguity and a
rhythmical violence in conflict with the normal pronunciation
of the language. The ambiguity and the violence represent
extreme forms of variation from the metrical norm and function to intensify emotion that is obscurely or inadequately
motivated within the poem. Hopkins normally appends to the
description of landscape an application that is religious and
personal, but the intensity of feeling motivated by the poem
is not justified by the personal application or moral that follows. Analyzes this difficulty as it appears in a number of
poems and, most extensively, in "The Windhover."

Finds the reasons for Hopkins' kind of poetry in his
personal instability and in the romantic background that justifies the expression of strong and unmotivated feeling for its
own sake. The latter tendency was encouraged by Hopkins'
doctrine that the poet should express the "inscape" or in-
dividuating form of an object. The doctrine, when applied to
himself, justifies the romantic view that poetry is self-
expression.

The Thomistic distinction between art and prudence
encouraged Hopkins' self-expressive tendencies and his tendency to separate art and morality. Feels that his own view
of the function of poetry is more Thomistic than the view that
has been derived from Aquinas's writing and claims that the
apparent difference arises from the fact that St. Thomas did
not concern himself with the arts except as illustration of other matters.

States, in "Robert Frost, or the Spiritual Drifter as
Poet," that Frost deserves careful study because he is both

popular and distinguished. Frost's position is the Emersonian version of romantic pantheism: God and nature are one, both are good, and we participate in this goodness by suppressing reason and following impulse. (See items 81, 104.) Frost differs from Emerson in lacking the latter's religious conviction; he is driven by Emersonian relativism to scepticism, uncertainty, and melancholy, and rarely perceives clearly his rootless position. In poems such as "The Road Not Taken," "The Sound of the Trees," and "The Hill-Wife," Frost deals with the theme of moral choice but can only imagine such choice as whimsical and incomprehensible in nature.

Some of Frost's poems are didactic and affirm Emersonianism as it applies both to the individual and to society. The individual is encouraged not to cooperate with society; human affairs should be left to manage themselves. Frost is, however, talented. In poems such as "On Going Unnoticed," "The Last Mowing," and "Spring Pools," he expresses sensitively the romantic love for the dream-like, the fragile, and the tentative as well as a sense of irrational fear. In "Acquainted with the Night" and "The Most of It," he shows an awareness of the true horror of his relativism: the perception that there is no meaning in the universe of the Emersonian individualist.

In "English Literature in the Sixteenth Century," reviews English Literature in the Sixteenth Century, by C. S. Lewis, Sixteenth Century English Poetry, edited by Norman E. McClure, and Sixteenth Century English Prose, edited by Karl J. Holzknecht. Asserts that Elizabethan drama and prose have been overrated; music and poetry are the arts brought to the highest degree of perfection during the period. Considers shortcomings of C. S. Lewis's treatment of the poetry of the period, and states that these shortcomings are apparent in the anthologies under review as well. Lewis concentrates on the identifying eccentricities of the various schools and poets of the century. In his preference for the Golden (the Petrarchan) school to the Drab (the plain), he exhibits the romantic prejudice to which he objects in other scholars. Despite his literary, linguistic, and historical learning, Lewis is not properly qualified to write a history of poetry because he is incapable of identifying the best poems, and the best poems are the essential historical facts upon which such a study must be based.

10a. The Function of Criticism: Problems and Exercises. London: Routledge & Kegan Paul, 1962.

10b. The Function of Criticism: Problems and Exercises. Denver: Alan Swallow, 1966.

11. On Modern Poets. With an Introduction by Keith McKeon. New York: Meridian Books, 1959.
CONTENTS: "Introduction" (see item 598); "Wallace Stevens, or the Hedonist's Progress" (see item 100); "T. S. Eliot, or the Illusion of Reaction" (see item 95); "John

Crowe Ransom, or Thunder Without God" (see item 101);
"The Significance of The Bridge, by Hart Crane, or What
Are We to Think of Professor X" (see item 104); "The
Poetry of Gerard Manley Hopkins" (see item 110); "Robert
Frost, or the Spiritual Drifter as Poet" (see item 106.)

11a. On Modern Poets. London: Routledge & Kegan Paul, 1962.

12. The Poetry of W. B. Yeats. The Swallow Pamphlets Number
10. Denver: Alan Swallow, 1960.
(For annotation, see item 15.)

13. The Poetry of J. V. Cunningham. The Swallow Pamphlets
Number 11. Denver: Alan Swallow, 1961.
(For annotation, see item 15.)

14. The Brink of Darkness. The Swallow Pamphlets Number 15.
Denver: Alan Swallow, n. d.
Author's note reads: "Winters says that this story is a study
of the hypothetical possibility of a hostile supernatural world,
and of the effect on the perceptions of a consideration of this
possibility." PV, ABD, CPYW. (See items 73, 105.)

15. Forms of Discovery: Critical and Historical Essays on the
Forms of the Short Poem in English. Chicago: Alan Swallow, 1967.
CONTENTS: "Introduction" (see item 125); "Aspects of the
Short Poem in the English Renaissance" (see items 76, 92,
113, 116); "The Poetry of Charles Churchill" (see item
119); "The Sentimental-Romantic Decadence of the 18th and
19th Centuries"; "The Turn of the Century" (see items 117,
123); "The Post-Symbolist Methods" (see items 116, 121);
"The Plain Style Reborn" (see item 118); "Conclusions."
Asserts, in the "Introduction," that the book will be concerned
with poetry as an art, with specific reference to poetry in
English of the last five hundred years. Defines art as method
and maintains that "the end, the purpose, of poetry is the understanding of the human condition, the understanding both rational and emotional," and that "this is the most important
activity of the human mind." The language in which the Western mind has realized itself is the product of a long and
unique tradition that began with the Platonic and Aristotelian
exploration of language as a medium of precise thought and was
enriched by the scholastic continuation of this effort. This
linguistic and philosophical heritage becomes in poetry, through
the developing conventions of meter, a vehicle for precise
thought and for the discovery and exploration of precise feeling. The linguistic and poetic modes thus evolved are a method of expressing what we already know, and they are "modes
of being," both the creation and the discovery of reality. The
poet is not hampered by the complexity of his medium; like the
great athlete, he lives most fully in the forms that he has
mastered and has become. The forms create for him a fuller

reality than he would otherwise possess.

Maintains, in "Aspects of the Short Poem in the English Renaissance," that the native plain school is as clearly defined as the Petrarchist, Metaphysical, and Cavalier schools and produced major poetry. A poet of this school expresses a proverbial theme in economical and aphoristic language that conveys feeling restrained to the minimum required by the subject. Rhetoric is here a means of stating and evaluating the subject efficiently. The defect of such verse is a brusque manner resulting partly from technical limitations that were gradually overcome: a heavily stopped line with heavy caesura, heavily accented syllables in accented positions, and excessive use of alliteration. The principal practitioners of the early plain style were Thomas Wyatt, Barnaby Googe, George Gascoigne, and Sir Walter Raleigh.

The major Petrarchists were Sir Philip Sidney, Edmund Spenser, Samuel Daniel, Michael Drayton, the early Fulke Greville, and William Shakespeare. Sidney perfected the relationship between elaborate syntax and stanzaic and linear structures, and created a sensitive rhythmical movement for the iambic line through subtle variations in degree and placement of accent. Like other Petrarchists, he elaborated a technique in excess of that required by his small subjects. The poetry of the songbooks also contributed to the refinement of English style and is important to an appreciation of Jonson, Herrick, and Crashaw. Later poets benefiting from the virtues of the plain style and the technical innovations of the Petrarchists include Fulke Greville, William Shakespeare, Ben Jonson, John Donne, Lord Herbert of Cherbury, George Herbert, Richard Crashaw, Henry Vaughan, Andrew Marvell, and Robert Herrick. The conjunction of these two influences resulted in some of the greatest poems of the English Renaissance.

Among other poets discussed are Andrew Marvell, Thomas Traherne, and John Milton. Milton is criticized for expanding his subjects in the interest of rhetorical decoration, for unnecessarily complex syntax, and for excessive dependence on poetic stereotypes.

Describes, in "The Poetry of Charles Churchill," the development of the short poem as background for a discussion of Churchill. The rational and frequently logical structure of sixteenth and seventeenth century poetry developed along two separate lines, that of the ornate or Petrarchan style and that of the plain style. The rational frame in the ornate style was often used for irrational ends; but, in the continuation of the plain style, it made possible the greatest poems of Greville, Jonson, and George Herbert. In Milton, the rational structure present in the ornate style decays into an associative structure, as in Lycidas. This associationism was justified by Locke's view that ideas arise from sense perceptions. Concrete detail and associative development came to be thought of as the proper components of poetry.

Among eighteenth century masters of the heroic couplet,

Churchill is unique in that he uses abstract language and associationism within an implicitly rational structure. He differs from Dryden and Pope in that he is not a poet whose irony results from parodying the genre that he employs. Such a procedure is dangerous because it is the clichés and weaknesses of the genre that are exploited. Churchill is inferior to Dryden and Pope when writing in their modes; but, at his best, he is the greatest master of the heroic couplet.

In The Dedication, his finest performance, Churchill's irony does not develop at the expense of the genre but at the expense of the subject of the poem. The poet utilizes the strengths and avoids the weaknesses of the earlier tradition. Churchill's couplets are written as long, supple sentences that gain precision from the underlying form of the couplet rather than as epigrammatic fragments; the associative structure is rationally controlled and the language is largely that of abstract analysis.

Maintains, in "The Sentimental-Romantic Decadence of the 18th and 19th Centuries," that the eighteenth and nineteenth centuries were periods of deterioration in the history of English poetry. Attributes the decline to the influence of Shaftesburian sentimentalism and the doctrine of the association of ideas. According to Shaftesbury, our impulses are naturally good and lead to virtue, whereas human reason is evil and leads to error. According to the associationists, ideas arise from sensory experience, can best be expressed through the description of sensory detail, and are related to one another in the mind by way of subjective suggestion and resemblances.

Discusses the decay of structure and of style resulting from these antirational doctrines as they appear in Dyer, Collins, Gray, Smart, Blake, Wordsworth, Coleridge, Shelley, Keats, Tennyson, Browning, Arnold, and Swinburne. Asserts that the recovery from this decline manifests itself in American poetry from Jones Very to the present and in Robert Bridges, Thomas Hardy, and T. Sturge Moore.

Discusses, in "The Turn of the Century," Thomas Hardy, Robert Bridges, W. B. Yeats, and T. Sturge Moore, who, along with Gerard Manley Hopkins, are the principal British poets of the late nineteenth and early twentieth centuries. Hardy is a primitive who belongs to no major tradition. His genius manifests itself in his eye for natural detail and for precise description. Although much of Bridges' work is damaged by the influence of romantic diction, his poetry is at times passionately intellectual in a way comparable to the best of Greville, Jonson, and Herbert. In his experiments with new metrical conventions, classical and syllabic, Bridges has opened up new ranges of feeling and new kinds of poetry.

Yeats is overrated; his work is damaged by self-dramatization and a naive system of occult ideas. Although Yeats has been defended as a Symbolist whose work is not paraphrasable, he is, in fact, a poet who is trying to speak clearly but lacks the necessary skill. T. Sturge Moore understood the late romantic and Symbolist background for modern poetry, and he understood the surrender to pure sensation and oblivion that is central to romantic experience. His best work expresses a recovery from the experience rather than an indulgence in it. He is a poet whom we must understand if we are to understand the poetry of our own time. (For earlier treatment of Moore, see item 75.)

Employs, in "The Post-Symbolist Methods," the term, post-Symbolist, to describe a kind of imagery in which physical detail and abstract significance fuse. (For Winters' earlier treatment of fusion, see item 1.) The intense realization of the physical in such imagery results from the romantic and Symbolist emphasis on sensory perception as opposed to conceptual understanding. In post-Symbolist imagery, the conceptual understanding is not stated abstractly; it is implicit in the sensory detail. Discusses post-Symbolist imagery in F. G. Tuckerman, Emily Dickinson, Wallace Stevens, Edgar Bowers, Louise Bogan, and N. Scott Momaday. One would expect to find a Symbolist influence in these poets. Tuckerman and Dickinson, however, could not have been so influenced. Stevens and Bowers probably were influenced by the Symbolists; Bogan and Momaday probably were not.

In Tuckerman's The Cricket, the imagery permeates a theme that is clearly established on the conceptual level, and the result is the greatest poem in English of the nineteenth century. Dickinson's style shows no literary influences that can be traced but frequently exhibits the post-Symbolist fusion of sense-perception and concept in language that is that of a master. (For another discussion of Dickinson, see item 86.) Stevens' best poems deal with the experience of the isolated man in a meaningless universe and contain descriptive details charged with philosophical significance. (For another discussion of Stevens, see item 100.) Discusses, as further examples of the post-Symbolist procedure, poems by Bogan and Momaday.

Regards J. V. Cunningham as "the most consistently distinguished poet writing in English today, and one of the finest in the language." Objects to Cunningham's belief that any particular act of choice is necessarily a realization of being that excludes other possible realizations and becomes a deprivation of being. Contends also that, in Cunningham's weaker poems, concrete detail is not fully realized and does not fuse with the abstract meaning that it supports. Cunningham's best poems are written in a plain style that is sophisticated, complex, and precise. Although the style resembles Ben Jonson's, the subject matter would not have been possible in the Renaissance. Jonson wrote as a Christian, whereas Cunningham writes from a modern perspective. The style is free of local mannerisms; it is perennially useful and will never appear dated as will the mannered styles of Yeats and Crane or of Pound and his disciples. Discusses, as another instance of the contemporary plain style, the poetry of Catherine Davis.

Discusses briefly, in "Conclusions," a number of twen-

tieth century poets not considered elsewhere in the book.
These include "the great eccentrics of the modern period,"
Robert Frost, Hart Crane, Ezra Pound, William Carlos Williams, Marianne Moore, T. S. Eliot, and Allen Tate, who
are described as, without exception, "nominalists, relativists,
associationists, sentimentalists, and denigrators of the rational
mind." Mentions, as minor poets worth preserving, Adelaide
Crapsey, Janet Lewis, Walter Conrad Arensberg, Donald
Evans, Agnes Lee, John Crowe Ransom, S. Foster Damon,
and Stanley Kunitz. Among the poets with whom he has been
personally associated, discusses Elizabeth Madox Roberts,
Glenway Wescott, Howard Baker, Don Stanford, Ann Stanford,
Alan Stephens, Helen Pinkerton, Wesley Trimpi, Charles Gullans, Thom Gunn, and Ellen Kay. Asserts that the major
poet-translators of our time are Ezra Pound and such transla-
tors of American Indian poetry as Washington Matthews and
Frances Densmore. Concludes that the best poets are simply
those who write the best poems: "Five hundred years from
now the subjects which will appear to have been most important
to our time will be the subjects treated by the surviving poets
who have written the most intelligently. The best poets have
the best minds; ultimately they are the standard."

16. Uncollected Essays and Reviews. Edited and introduced by
Frances Murphy. Chicago: Swallow Press, 1973.
CONTENTS: "Introduction" (see item 615); I. REVIEWS:
"A Cool Master" (see item 39); "A Woman with a Hammer"
(see item 41); "Carlos Williams' New Book" (see item 42);
"Under the Tree" (see item 43); "A Prejudiced Opinion"
(see item 44); "Holiday and Day of Wrath" (see item 46);
"Mina Loy" (see item 47); "Open Letter to the Editors of
This Quarter" (see item 49); "The Indian in English" (see
item 51); "Streets in the Moon" (see item 48); "Hart
Crane's Poems" (see item 50); "Fugitives" (see item 52);
"The Poetry of Louise Bogan" (see item 54); "The Poetry
of Malcolm Cowley" (see item 55); "Robinson Jeffers" (see
item 62); "Foster Damon's Second Book" (see item 63);
"The Progress of Hart Crane" (see item 66); "Edmund
Wilson as Poet" (see item 61); "Recent Verse" (see item
65); "Major Fiction" (see item 69); "The Symbolist Influ-
ence" (see item 70); "Poets and Others" (see item 72);
"Traditional Mastery" (see item 71); "The Objectivists"
(see item 74); "T. Sturge Moore" (see item 75); "Agnes
Lee" (see item 93); "Poetry of Feeling" (see item 91);
"The Poems of Theodore Roethke" (see item 97); "In Plato's
Garden" (see item 96); "Three Poets" (see item 107); "A
Discovery" (see item 111); "The Poetry of Edgar Bowers"
(see item 114); II. ESSAYS: "Notes" (see item 45); "The
Testament of a Stone, Being Notes on the Mechanics of the
Poetic Image" (see item 1); "Statement of Purpose: Gyro-
scope" (see item 56); "Notes on Contemporary Criticism"
(see item 58); "The Extension and Reintegration of the Hu-
man Spirit Through the Poetry Mainly French and American

Since Poe and Baudelaire" (see item 60); "Robert Bridges and Elizabeth Daryush" (see item 83); "Foreword to New England Earth" (see item 98); "Religious and Social Ideas in the Didactic Work of E. A. Robinson" (see item 103); "The Poet and the University: A Reply" (see item 109); "Introduction to The Early Poems" (see item 124).

16a. Uncollected Essays and Review. Edited and introduced by Francis Murphy. London: Allen Lane, 1974.

II

BOOKS--POETRY

17. The Immobile Wind. Evanston, Ill.: Monroe Wheeler, 1921.
    CONTENTS: "Two Songs of Advent"; "One Ran Before";
    "Hawk's Eyes"; "Ballad'; "The Immobile Wind"; "The
    Priesthood"; "The Morning"; "Where My Sight Goes"; "Song
    for a Small Boy Who Herds Goats"; "Ballad of Men"; "Two
    Dramatic Interludes for Puppets"--I. 'Autumn Roadside';
    II. 'The Pines Are Shadows'; "Death Goes Before Me";
    "The Wizard"; "Alone"; "The Chapel"; "I Paved a Sky."

18. Diadems and Fagots. Translations from the Portuguese of
    Olavo Bilac by John Meem and from the French of Pierre
    de Ronsard by Yvor Winters. Santa Fe, N. Mex.: pri-
    vately printed, [1921].
    CONTENTS: Two Sonnets and Two Fragments by Olavo
    Bilac, translated from the Portuguese by John Meem:
    "Down River"; "One Evening in Autumn"; "Waves"; "The
    Valley"; The Last Sonnets of Pierre de Ronsard: I. "Ill-
    natured winter nights, Serpents of Alecto"; II. "Ah, long
    winter nights, hang-women, give me now"; III. "Oh, why
    sleep, my soul, benumbed, with hidden face?"; IV; "One
    has to leave his orchards and his gardens and his doors."

19. The Magpie's Shadow. Chicago: Musterhousebook, 1922.
    CONTENTS: I. "In Winter"--'Myself'; 'Still Morning';
    'Awakening'; 'Winter Echo'; 'The Hunter'; 'No Being'; II.
    "In Spring"--'Spring'; 'May'; 'Spring Rain'; 'Song'; III.
    "In Summer and Autumn"--'Sunrise'; 'Fields'; 'At Evening';
    'Cool Nights'; 'Sleep'; 'The Aspen's Song'; 'The Walker';
    'Blue Mountain'; 'God of Roads'; 'September'; 'A Lady';
    'Alone'; 'A Deer'; 'Man in Desert'; 'Desert'; 'The End';
    'High Valleys'; 'Awaiting Snow.'

20. The Bare Hills. Boston: Four Seas, 1927.
    CONTENTS: I. "Upper River Country: Rio Grande"--1.
    'Hill Burial'; 2. 'The Precincts of February'; 3. 'The
    Resurrection'; 4. 'Tewa Spring'; 5. 'Dark Spring'; 6.
    'The Crystal Sun'; 7. 'José's Country'; 8. 'The Upper
    Meadows'; 9. 'The Moonlight'; 10. 'October'; 11. 'The

Impalpable Void'; 12. 'The Fragile Season'; II. "The
Bare Hills"--1. 'Genesis'; 2. 'Exodus'; 3. 'The Vigil';
4. 'Moonrise'; 5. 'Alba for Hecate'; 1. 'The Cold';
2. 'Digue dondaine, Digue dondon'; 3. 'Nocturne'; 4.
'Quod Tegit Omnia'; 1. 'March Dusk'; 2. 'The Lamplight'; 3. 'Flesh of Flowers'; 4. 'Under Rain'; 5. 'Midnight Wind'; 1. 'Complaint'; 2. 'The Muezzin'; 3. 'Song';
4. 'April'; 5. 'Song'; 1. 'Full Moon'; 2. 'Love Song';
3. 'Sleep'; 1. 'The Cold Room'; 2. 'The Bare Hills';
3. 'The Dead: Mazda Wake'; 4. 'The Barnyard'; 5.
'The Grosbeaks'; 1. 'The Streets'; 2. 'The Rows of Cold
Trees'; 3. 'Prayer Beside a Lamp'; 4. 'Man Regards
Eternity in Aging'; III. "The Passing Night"--1. 'Eternity'; 2. 'The Passing Night. '

21. The Proof. New York: Coward-McCann, 1930.
CONTENTS: I. "The Red Month"; "The Goatherds";
"Orange Tree"; "See Los Angeles First"; "Song of the
Trees"; "To the Painter Polelonema"; "Bison"; "Remem-
bered Spring"; "Wild Sunflower"; "November"; "The Bitter
Moon"; "The Deep"; "Satyric Complaint"; "The Longe
Nightes When Every Creature"; "Snow-Ghost"; "Sonnet";
"The Vigil"; "Strength Out of Sweetness"; "Simplex Mundi-
tiis"; II. "Sonnet"; "Sonnet"; "The Countryless: Refugees
of Science"; "The Moralists"; "To William Dinsmore
Briggs"; "The Proof"; "To Emily Dickinson"; "The Castle
of Thorns"; "Apollo and Daphne"; "The Fable"; III. "The
Empty Hills"; "Hymn to Dispel Hatred at Midnight"; "The
Fall of Leaves"; "Inscription for a Graveyard"; "The Last
Visit"; "Shadows"; "Moonrise"; "The Still Small Voice";
"Snapshots"; "Communion"; "Epilogue: For Howard Baker."

22. The Journey and Other Poems. Ithaca, N.Y.: Dragon Press,
1931.
CONTENTS: "The Critiad"; "Slow Pacific Swell"; "The
Marriage"; "On a View of Pasadena from the Hills"; "The
Grave"; "The Journey"; "A Vision"; "December Eclogue."

23. Before Disaster. Tyron, N.C.: Tyron Pamphlets, 1934.
CONTENTS: "Foreword" (see item 79); "The Dedication";
"To a Young Writer"; "Anacreontic"; "To My Infant Daugh-
ter: I"; "To My Infant Daughter: II"; "For My Father's
Grave"; "The Ancestors"; "By the Road to the Sunnyvale
Air-Base"; "Elegy on a Young Airedale Bitch Lost Two
Years Since in the Salt-Marsh"; "Midas"; "Sonnet to the
Moon"; "The Werwolf"; "A Petition"; "Before Disaster";
"The Prince"; "The Anniversary"; "Orpheus"; "Phasellus
Ille"; "On the Death of Senator Thomas J. Walsh"; "Dedi-
cation for a Book of Criticism"; "On Teaching the Young";
"A Post-Card to the Social Muse, Who Was Invoked More
Formally by Various Marxians and Others in the Pages of
The New Republic during the Winter of 1932-3"; "Chiron."

24. Poems. Los Altos, Calif.: Gyroscope Press, 1940.
    CONTENTS: "A Song of Advent"; "Song"; "To Be Sung by
    a Small Boy Who Herds Goats"; "Alone"; "The Lie"; "Noon";
    "The Shadow's Song"; "The Aspen's Song"; "God of Roads";
    "Asleep"; "The Fragile Season"; "The Impalpable Void";
    "The Moonlight"; "The Precincts of February"; "Jose's
    Country"; "The Upper Meadows"; "The Goatherds"; "Song
    of the Trees"; "The Cold"; "Quod Tegit Omnia"; "Nocturne";
    "Song"; "April"; "The Cold Room"; "The Dead, by Electric
    Light Unshaded"; "The Barnyard"; "The Rows of Cold
    Trees"; "The Lady's Farewell"; "Song of the Girl Who Tore
    Her Dress at the Spring"; "Poem"; "Death's Warnings";
    "Cantabria"; "Rome"; "Sonnet"; "Reflections"; "The Skeleton
    Laborer"; "Green"; "A Sigh"; "Marine"; "Threnody for
    Stéphane Mallarmé"; "The Moralists"; "The Realization";
    "To a Distinguished Scholar Conducting His Seminar"; "The
    Invaders"; "To Emily Dickinson"; "The Castle of Thorns";
    "Apollo and Daphne"; "The Fable"; "The Empty Hills";
    "Hymn to Dispel Hatred at Midnight"; "Moonrise"; "The
    Fall of Leaves"; "Inscription for a Graveyard"; "The Last
    Visit"; "For Howard Baker"; "The Slow Pacific Swell"; "The
    Marriage"; "On a View of Pasadena from the Hills"; "The
    Journey"; "A Vision"; "The Grave"; "Anacreontic"; "To a
    Young Writer"; "To My Infant Daughter"; "For My Father's
    Grave"; "By the Road to the Air-Base"; "Elegy on a Young
    Airedale Bitch Lost Some Years Since in the Salt-Marsh";
    "Midas"; "Sonnet to the Moon"; "The Anniversary"; "The
    Werwolf"; "A Petition"; "Before Disaster"; "The Prince";
    "Phasellus Ille"; "Orpheus"; "A Post-Card to the Social
    Muse Who Was Invoked More Formally by Various Marxians
    and Others in the Pages of The New Republic During the
    Winter of 1932-3"; "On the Death of Senator Thomas J.
    Walsh"; "Dedication for a Book of Criticism"; "A Leave-
    Taking"; "On Teaching the Young"; "Chiron"; "Heracles";
    "Alcmena"; "Theseus: A Trilogy"; "Socrates"; "To Edwin
    V. McKenzie"; "To a Woman on Her Defense of Her Brother
    Unjustly Convicted of Murder"; "To David Lamson"; "John
    Day, Frontiersman"; "John Sutter"; "The California Oaks";
    "On Rereading a Passage from John Muir"; "The Manza-
    nita"; "Sir Gawaine and the Green Knight"; "An October Noc-
    turne"; "A Spring Serpent"; "Much in Little"; "The Crema-
    tion"; "An Elegy"; "Time and the Garden"; "To a Portrait
    of Melville in my Library"; "A Prayer for My Son"; "In
    Praise of California Wines"; "A Summer Commentary"; "On
    the Portrait of a Scholar of the Italian Renaissance"; "A
    Dedication"; "Notes."

25. The Giant Weapon. The Poets of the Year, [vol. 9]. New
    York: New Directions, 1943.
    CONTENTS: "By the Road to the Air-Base"; "The Crema-
    tion"; "Before Disaster"; "To My Infant Daughter"; "The
    Marriage"; "Dedication for a Book of Criticism"; "Sonnet
    to the Moon"; "To Edwin V. McKenzie"; "To David Lamson";

"Heracles"; "Orpheus"; "The Manzanita"; "Elegy on a Young
Airedale Bitch Lost Some Years Since in the Salt-Marsh";
"A Spring Serpent"; "An October Nocturne"; "A Winter
Evening"; "To a Military Rifle"; "For the Opening of the
William Dinsmore Briggs Room"; "John Day, Frontiersman";
"A Summer Commentary"; "John Sutter"; "On Teaching the
Young"; "Sir Gawaine and the Green Knight"; "Chiron";
"On Rereading a Passage from John Muir"; "An Elegy";
"Time and the Garden"; "Much in Little"; "A Prayer for
My Son"; "Midas"; "On the Portrait of a Scholar of the
Italian Renaissance"; "Summer Noon: 1941"; "A Testa-
ment."

26. To the Holy Spirit: A Poem by Yvor Winters. Illustration by
   Nick Carter. The California Poetry Folios, no. 11. San
   Francisco: Book Club of California, 1947.

27. Three Poems. Cummington, Mass.: Cummington Press,
   1950.
   CONTENTS: "To the Holy Spirit from a Deserted Graveyard in the Salinas Valley"; "A Song in Passing"; "A
   Fragment."

28. Collected Poems. Denver: Alan Swallow, 1952.
   CONTENTS: "A Song of Advent"; "Song"; "To Be Sung by
   a Small Boy Who Herds Goats"; "Alone"; "The Lie";
   "Noon"; "The Shadow's Song"; "The Aspen's Song"; "God
   of Roads"; "Sleep"; "The Precincts of February"; "Jose's
   Country"; "The Upper Meadows"; "The Goatherds"; "Song
   of the Trees"; "The Cold"; "Quod Tegit Omnia"; "Noc-
   turne"; "Song"; "April"; "The Cold Room"; "The Barnyard";
   "The Rows of Cold Trees"; "The Lady's Farewell"; "Cos-
   sante"; "Poem"; "Death's Warnings"; "Cantabria"; "Rome";
   "Reflections"; "The Skeleton Laborer"; "Green"; "A Sigh";
   "Marine"; "The Moralists"; "The Realization"; "To William
   Dinsmore Briggs Conducting His Seminar"; "The Invaders";
   "To Emily Dickinson"; "The Castle of Thorns"; "Apollo and
   Daphne"; "The Fable"; "The Empty Hills"; "Hymn to Dispel
   Hatred at Midnight"; "Moonrise"; "The Fall of Leaves";
   "Inscription for a Graveyard"; "The Last Visit"; "For
   Howard Baker"; "The Slow Pacific Swell"; "The Marriage";
   "On a View of Pasadena from the Hills"; "The Journey";
   "A Vision"; "The Grave"; "Anacreontic"; "To a Young Writ-
   er"; "To My Infant Daughter"; "For My Father's Grave";
   "By the Road to the Air-Base"; "Elegy on a Young Airedale
   Bitch Lost Some Years Since in the Salt-Marsh"; "Midas";
   "Sonnet to the Moon"; "The Anniversary"; "Before Disaster";
   "The Prince"; "Phasellus Ille"; "Orpheus"; "A Post-Card
   to the Social Muse Who Was Invoked More Formally by
   Various Marxians and Others in the Pages of The New Re-
   public During the Winter of 1932-3"; "On the Death of Senator Thomas J. Walsh"; "Dedication for a Book of Criti-
   cism"; "A Leave-Taking"; "On Teaching the Young"; "Chiron";

"Heracles"; "Alcmena"; "Theseus: A Trilogy"; "Socrates"; "To Edwin V. McKenzie"; "To a Woman on Her Defense of Her Brother Unjustly Convicted of Murder"; "To David Lamson"; "John Day, Frontiersman"; "John Sutter"; "The California Oaks"; "On Rereading a Passage from John Muir"; "The Manzanita"; "Sir Gawaine and the Green Knight"; "An October Nocturne"; "A Spring Serpent"; "Much in Little"; "The Cremation"; "An Elegy"; "Time and the Garden"; "To a Portrait of Melville in My Library"; "A Prayer for My Son"; "In Praise of California Wines"; "A Summer Commentary"; "On the Portrait of a Scholar of the Italian Renaissance"; "A Dedication in Postscript"; "A Winter Evening"; "Summer Noon: 1941"; "A Testament"; "To a Military Rifle 1942"; "For the Opening of the William Dinsmore Briggs Room"; "Moonlight Alert"; "Defense of Empire"; "Night of Battle"; "An Ode on the Despoilers of Learning in an American University 1947"; "To Herman Melville in 1951"; "To the Holy Spirit"; "A Fragment"; "A Song in Passing"; "To the Moon"; "Note."

28a. Collected Poems. Rev. ed. Denver: Alan Swallow, 1960. CONTENTS, the following poems added: "At the San Francisco Airport"; "Two Old-Fashioned Songs": I. 'Danse Macabre'; II. 'A Dream Vision.'

28b. Collected Poems. Rev. ed. London: Routledge & Kegan Paul, 1962.

29. The Early Poems of Yvor Winters 1920-28. Chicago: Swallow Press, 1966. CONTENTS: The Immobile Wind (see item 17); The Magpie's Shadow (see item 19); The Bare Hills (see item 20); Four Poems Previously Uncollected from Magazines: "The Mule Corral"; "The Schoolmaster at Spring"; "The Solitude of Glass"; "Primavera"; "Fire Sequence"--1. 'Coal: Beginning and End'; 2. 'Liberation'; 3. 'Return of Spring'; 4. 'Bill'; 5. 'The Vanquished'; 6. 'The Victor'; 7. 'A Miner'; 8. 'Vacant Lot'; 9. 'Tragic Love'; 10. 'To the Crucified'; 11. 'O Sun!'; 12. 'November'; 13. 'Genesis'; 14. 'The Bitter Moon'; 15. 'The Deep: A Service for All the Dead'; Poems from The Proof: "The Red Month"; "Incandescent Earth"; "Orange Tree"; "See Los Angeles First"; "Song of the Trees"; "The Goatherds"; "To the Painter Polelonema"; "Bison"; "Remembered Spring"; "Wild Sunflower"; "Satyric Complaint"; "The Longe Nightes When Every Creature"; "Snow-Ghost"; "Sonnet"; "The Vigil"; "Strength Out of Sweetness"; "Simplex Munditiis."

30. The Collected Poems of Yvor Winters. With an introduction by Donald Davie. Manchester: Carcanet New Press, 1978. CONTENTS: Early Poems (see item 29); Collected Poems (1960) (see item 28a); Diadems and Fagots (see item 18); Other Translations: "Old Ballad"; "Sonnet"; "Rondeau of

Antique Love"; "Song"; "The Nemean Lion"; "Forgetfulness"; "Poem in Autumn"; "The Lost Secret"; "The Toad"; "Threnody for Stéphane Mallarmé"; Uncollected Poems: "Lament, Beside an Acéquia, for the Wife of Awa-tsireh"; "Sonnet"; "The Proof"; "Shadows"; "The Still Small Voice"; "Snapshots"; "Communion"; "The Dedication"; "The Ancestors"; "The Werwolf"; "A Petition"; "To Herbert Dean Merritt"; The Brink of Darkness (see item 14).

30a. The Collected Poems of Yvor Winters. With an introduction by Donald Davie. Athens, Ohio: Swallow Press, University of Ohio Press, 1980.

BOOKS EDITED

31. Ed. <u>Twelve Poets of the Pacific</u>. Norfolk, Conn.: New Directions, 1937.
     CONTENTS: Poems by Janet Lewis, Yvor Winters, Don
     Stanford, Howard Baker, J. V. Cunningham, Clayton Stafford, Richard Finnegan, James Atkinson, Ann Stanford,
     Henry Ramsey, Achilles Holt, and Barbara Gibbs. The
     following contributions are by Winters: "Foreword" (see
     item 87); "John Day, Frontiersman"; "John Sutter"; "On
     Rereading a Passage from John Muir"; "Heracles"; "Theseus: A Trilogy"; "Socrates."

32. Ed. <u>Poets of the Pacific, Second Series</u>. Stanford: Stanford: Stanford University Press, 1949.
     CONTENTS: "Introductory Note"; poems by Richard K.
     Arnold, Edgar Bowers, Frances Crawford, Colgate Dorr,
     L. F. Gerlach, Ann Louise Hayes, C. R. Holmes, Melanie
     Hyman, Helen Pinkerton, W. Wesley Trimpi, Pearce Young.

32a. Ed. <u>Poets of the Pacific, Second Series</u>. Granger Index Reprint Series. Freeport, N. Y.: Books for Libraries Press,
     1968.

*   Ed. <u>The Early Poems of Yvor Winters 1920-28</u>. Denver:
     Alan Swallow, 1966. (Cited above as item 29.)

33. Coed. with Janet Lewis and Howard Baker. <u>The Gyroscope</u> 1
     (May 1929-February 1930). Palo Alto, Calif. Publication
     ceased after four issues. (See items 56, 57, 58, 59.)

34. Coed. with Kenneth Fields. <u>Quest for Reality: An Anthology
     of Short Poems in English.</u> Introduction by Kenneth Fields.
     Chicago: Swallow Press, 1969. (See item 530.)

35. Ed. <u>Selected Poems</u>, by Elizabeth Daryush. Foreword by
     Yvor Winters. New York: Swallow Press and William
     Morrow, 1948. (See item 108.)

ESSAYS AND REVIEW-ARTICLES

36. "Concerning Jessie Dismorr." LR 6 (1919): 34-35. (See
    item 647.)
    Objects to Jessie Dismorr's attempt to introduce ideas into
    her poetry and her failure to present emotion directly.
    Agrees implicitly with Pound's objections to ideas and ab-
    stractions in poetry.

37. Foreword to The Keen Edge, by Maureen Smith, Evanston,
    Ill.: Monroe Wheeler, [1920], n. p.
    Notes Maureen Smith's association with the Poetry Club of the
    University of Chicago of which he was a member, her death,
    and his memory of her person and her poetry.

38. "An Orthodox Preacher." Poetry 19 (1920): 49-51. Review
    of The Solitary, by James Oppenheim.
    Objects to Oppenheim as an imitator of Whitman and Sandburg
    and as more preacher than poet.

39. "A Cool Master." Poetry 19 (1922): 278-88. UER. Review
    of Collected Poems, by Edwin Arlington Robinson.
    Associates Robinson with a "tradition of New England hard-
    ness" that includes Emerson, Emily Dickinson, and Robert
    Frost. Robinson has established standards of craftsmanship
    that have been maintained by Stevens, Eliot, and Pound.
    These writers represent "a tradition of culture and clean
    workmanship."

40. "A Distinguished Young Man." Poetry 19 (1922): 337-39.
    Review of The Living Frieze, by Mark Turbyfill.
    States that "his five or six finest poems are perfectly exe-
    cuted, and entirely achieve that which they apparently set out
    to achieve."

41. "A Woman with a Hammer." Poetry 20 (1922): 93-95. UER.
    Review of The Contemplative Quarry and the Man with a
    Hammer, by Anna Wickham.
    Objects to Wickham on the grounds that she writes in plati-
    tudes and is derivative.

42. "Carlos Williams' New Book." Poetry 20 (1922): 216-20.
    Review of Sour Grapes, by William Carlos Williams.
    Asserts that Williams' poems at their best are "as perfect
    and final as Herrick."

43. "Under the Tree." Poetry 22 (1923): 45-48. UER. Review
    of Under the Tree, by Elizabeth Madox Roberts.
    Describes Roberts' art as the juxtaposition of physical details
    of landscape or situation as perceived by a young child. The
    book, popular with children, "is too fine a piece of work to
    be ignored by the sophisticated adult."

44. "A Prejudiced Opinion." Poetry 23 (1924): 218-20. UER.
    Review of Fringe, by Pearl Andelson.
    Maintains that Andelson's book "at its lowest ebb is clean-cut
    and intelligent, and at its highest is extraordinarily fine po-
    etry."

45. "Notes." MR 2 (1924): 86-88.
    States general principles relating to poetry and the other arts,
    to American poetry, and to the purposes served by literary
    criticism. A painting can express the various relationships be-
    tween form and color, and music can express relationships
    between sounds. In poetry, the relationships expressed in-
    clude those existing between form, color, and sound, and
    those made possible by ideas as well. Musical sound is not
    like verbal sound. Such an assumption leads to an emphasis
    on sound alone and to the subordination of meaning to sound.
    The use of language with its possibilities for the expression of
    conceptual and symbolic meaning, its fluidity of expression, and
    its image making properties, make poetry a richer medium
    than painting.
    Although America is large, loosely organized, and
    chaotic, American poetry should not also be chaotic and loose-
    ly organized. The imitation of the form of the subject matter
    leads to a breakdown of the form of expression. The result-
    ing poetry is weak and cannot express any subject matter ef-
    fectively. (See item 79.) The task of criticism is to define
    and evaluate work that has already been done. It can define
    traditions, but it cannot determine the future.

46. "Holiday and Day of Wrath." Poetry 26 (1925): 39-44. UER.
    Review of Observations, by Marianne Moore.
    Praises Marianne Moore as "a poet whose style at once in-
    tensely cultivated and painstakingly honest, never fails to
    charm me, and whose mastery of phrase and cadence over-
    whelms me."

47. "Mina Loy." Dial 80 (1926): 496-99. UER.
    Describes Loy as a writer who has overcome a natural clumsi-
    ness of style to write impressive poems. Maintains that she
    and W. C. Williams are the two living poets who have the
    most to offer to younger poets.

48. "Streets in the Moon." Poetry 29 (1927): 278-81. UER.
    Review of Streets in the Moon, by Archibald MacLeish.
    Maintains that MacLeish, "alone of all the set that have ap-
    peared since the Others-Imagist-Vorticist upheaval of twelve
    or fourteen years ago, can rightly take a place beside the
    most distinguished poets of the preceding generation."

49. "Open Letter to the Editors of This Quarter." TQ 1 (1927):
    286-88. UER.
    Objects to the tawdriness and falseness of certain perform-
    ances of American Indian material at the Sante Fe festival
    that had been praised in a review appearing in This Quarter.

50. "Hart Crane's Poems." Poetry 30 (1927): 47-51. UER.
    Review of White Buildings, by Hart Crane.
    Describes Crane as "one of the small group of contemporary
    masters" and as a poet who "deserves the careful attention
    which a comprehension of his work requires." (See items 66,
    104.)

51. "The Indian in English." Transition, no. 11 (1928), pp. 117-
    25. UER. Review of The Path on the Rainbow: An An-
    thology of Songs and Chants from the Indians of North Amer-
    ica, edited by George W. Cronyn, and American Indian
    Love Lyrics and Other Verse, selected by Nellie Barnes.
    Describes the significant contribution made by such translators
    of American Indian poetry as Frances Densmore, James
    Mooney, Frank Russell, Jeremiah Curtin, and Washington
    Matthews to our understanding of American Indian culture.
    Comments also on the high literary merit of these translations
    as poems in English.

52. "Fugitives." Poetry 32 (1928): 102-107. UER. Review of
    Fugitives: An Anthology of Verse.
    Sees the weaknesses in this body of poetry as a result of the
    negative spiritual and formal influence of T. S. Eliot. The
    most impressive poet in the group is Allen Tate.

53. "In Vindication of Poetry." NR, 17 October 1928, pp. 255-56.
    Review of Mr. Pope and Other Poems, by Allen Tate.
    Compares Tate and Hart Crane as the two poets under thirty-
    five most likely to prove of major importance: "Crane's
    quantitative achievement is much greater, and in all likelihood
    Tate has not as yet quite equaled the quality of Crane's best
    work; but on the other hand Tate's field of awareness, his
    general intelligence, is broader and better disciplined."

54. "The Poetry of Louise Bogan." NR, 16 October 1929, pp.
    247-48. UER. Review of Dark Summer, by Louise Bogan.
    Praises Bogan as a stylist whose best poems can bear com-
    parison with Campion, Jonson, and Dryden. The weaknesses
    of her work are an inability to write free verse and to manage
    effectively the long line and the long poem. In addition, the

absence of a firmly defined intellectual element in her poems keeps her from being a major poet, although she possesses the potentiality of becoming one.

55. "The Poetry of Malcolm Cowley." H&H 3 (1929): 111-13.
    UER. Review of Blue Juniata, by Malcolm Cowley.
    States that Cowley's weaker poems are imitations of the various styles that had been in fashion during the period of their composition. In a few of the later poems, where he is "endeavoring to study and master himself," he is "one of the eight or ten most distinguished poets of his generation."

56. "The Gyroscope." Gyr, [no. 1] (1929), pp. 18-19. UER.
    Announces the editorial policy of The Gyroscope as one that will oppose contemporary forms of spiritual extroversion and will assert that emotion, whether in literature or in life, should be adequately motivated; that art provides the most satisfactory means of evaluating life and of communicating that evaluation; and that precision and strength of spirit are manifested through precision and strength of style.

57. "Further Explanation." Gyr, [no. 2] (1929), pp. 21-23.
    Continues definitions of editorial position of The Gyroscope through reference to works by Irving Babbitt, Ramon Fernandez, René LaLou, Albert Thibaudet, Allen Tate, I. A. Richards, and T. S. Eliot. (See item 56.) Argues that a number of cheaply produced, mimeographed, literary magazines might provide a context in which good creative work, as opposed to criticism, might be published and "would do more to straighten out the confusion into which we have fallen than a score of yearbooks in the hands of professional journalists."

58. "Notes on Contemporary Criticism." Gyr, [no. 3] (1929), pp. 26-29. UER.
    Assumes a dualistic as opposed to a monistic universe, and asserts that such an assumption need not necessarily depend on divine revelation. Attempts to establish the minimum absolute basis on which a system of ethics can rationally be based, and finds such a basis in a distinction between good and evil in which evil results from emotion and good from the capacity for rational choice. There is an "irreducible minimum" of emotion in any human situation, and this irreducible minimum must be defined and integrated into one's rational understanding if it is not to be a source of evil. Since this minimum is unique in each of its occurrences, it cannot be dealt with discursively. The irreducible and unique emotion is defined and controlled through the techniques of art and is expressed in the unique work of art. It is "the poetic content" in a poem and "inheres in the feeling, the style, the untranslatable, and can be reduced to no formula save itself." (See items 60, 67.)

59. "Comment." Gyr, [no. 4] (1930), p. 30.

Announces that The Gyroscope will discontinue publication.
Recommends to subscribers various other literary and critical journals.

60. "The Extension and Reintegration of the Human Spirit Through
    the Poetry Mainly French and American Since Poe and
    Baudelaire." American Caravan 3 (1929): 361-404.   UER.
    Establishes a direct relationship between poetic form and tech-
    nique and the moral apprehension of life.   Regards form as
    the means of discovering and of creating experience and of
    evaluating it.   Poetry is a technique for extending human con-
    sciousness and is the most complete and intense mode of con-
    sciousness.   The function of the artist is to experience fully
    "the metaphysical horror of modern thought" and to produce
    from the experience "a dynamic attitude or state of mind, as-
    serting by that very act his own life and the strength and value
    of his own life."   The artist "who can leave that state of mind
    completed behind him for others to enter has performed the
    greatest spiritual service that can be performed."
         Describes and evaluates modes of organization that have
    appeared or that have been revived in recent years.   These
    include the scattered method, in which details have no intel-
    lectual relationship to one another except their convergence on
    a common theme; the logical method, in which details follow
    rationally or pseudo-rationally from one another and of which
    the logical structure of the metaphysical school is one exam-
    ple; the narrative method, which is a subcategory of the logi-
    cal method in that each detail develops from that which pre-
    cedes it in time; the psychological or dream method, in which
    the connections between details are lowered to or below the
    threshold of consciousness; and the alternation of method, in
    which a single mood is developed through two different methods
    or in which two different moods are developed as ironical com-
    mentaries on one another.   All of these methods, if supported
    by an intellectual substructure, can be valid procedures, al-
    though the last two result in obscurantism and self-deception
    if used habitually and automatically.   (See item 88.)

61. "Edmund Wilson as Poet."   H&H 3 (1930): 291-93.   UER.
    Review of Poets, Farewell, by Edmund Wilson.
    Contends that Wilson, although he achieves a few fine mo-
    ments, is usually journalistic and derivative as a poet.

62. "Robinson Jeffers."   Poetry 35 (1930): 279-86.   LOA, LOATH,
    UER.   Review of Dear Judas, by Robinson Jeffers.
    Asserts that Jeffers is theologically a monist who regards the
    impersonal and amoral nature of the physicist as Deity, and
    who regards humanity as divorced from and unnecessary to
    this nature.   Jeffers believes that the only good lies in the
    extinction of humanity through the extinction of one's individual
    humanity.   Such a view provides no basis for moral distinc-
    tions, for preferring one action to another, or for meaningful
    plot.   Jeffers' plots are mere catalogues repetitiously affirm-

ing the meaninglessness of life. The intricacies of human behavior as expressed in the details of style can find no expression in his work. His plots are repetitious and his style is
numb. (See item 88.)

63.   "Foster Damon's Second Book." Poetry 35 (1930): 340-42.
       UER. Review of Tilted Moons, by S. Foster Damon.
Suggests that the impressiveness of Damon's scholarly work
on Blake leads one to expect too much of his poetry. He has,
as a poet, achieved a few moderate successes.

64.   "Merrill Moore's Poems." Poetry 36 (1930): 104-6. Re-
       printed in Foreword by John Crowe Ransom to THE NOISE
       THAT TIME MAKES: A First Volume of 101 Sonnets by
       Merrill Moore and Some Reviews of This Book. Published
       by the author, 1939, pp. 26-27. Review of The Noise That
       Time Makes, by Merrill Moore.
States that Moore's poems are bad partly because he has not
revised them. If Moore "had spent on two or three of these
poems the time that he frittered away on the book, he might
have accomplished something."

65.   "Recent Verse." H&H 3 (1930): 454-61. UER. Review of
       Selected Poems, by Conrad Aiken; O City, Cities!, by
       R. Ellsworth Larsson; and High Falcon, by Leonie Adams.
Categorizes Aiken's poems as unstructured revery and Aiken
himself as inferior to the best stylists of his generation.
Larsson borrows from T. S. Eliot's manner but treats Eliot's
material as a form of conventional decoration. Leonie Adams,
despite stylistic vices deriving from unnecessarily ambiguous
syntax and the influence of W. B. Yeats, has written a
small number of nearly perfect poems.

66.   "The Progress of Hart Crane." Poetry 36 (1930): 153-65.
       UER. Review of The Bridge, by Hart Crane.
Asserts that The Bridge is structurally a loosely connected
succession of lyrics on Whitmanian themes and that Crane's
epic intentions could not be realized within such a fragmentary
form. Aeneas's acts are given precise significance within The
Aeneid as the effort to achieve a specific destiny; but action,
in the tradition of Whitman, can be no more than the enthusi-
astic affirmation of everything, and destiny itself remains undefined except as energetic movement into the future. Crane's
genius is so great that he produces fragments of major poetry
within poems that are otherwise failures. The concluding section of The River and individual lines and brief passages elsewhere are great poetry. Nevertheless, the failure of The
Bridge as a unified poem illustrates the impossibility of successful poetry within a Whitmanian frame of reference. (See
items 50, 104.)

67.   "Poetry, Morality, and Criticism." The Critique of Humanism:
       A Symposium. Edited by Clinton Hartley Grattan. New

York: Brewer & Warren, 1930, pp. 301-33.
Presents the earliest published version of material that was to appear in his Ph. D. dissertation (see item 4) and as "The Morality of Poetry" in Primitivism and Decadence. (See item 5.)

68. Foreword to Hidden Flame, by Bunichi Kagawa. Stanford, Calif.: Half Moon Press, 1930, pp. 5-8.
Describes Kagawa as a poet whose cultural dilemma is that of the Japanese immigrant to California who cannot return to his own culture and has only partially assimilated a new culture. Despite his use of overly elaborate symbols that, "to the occidental reader at least, now and then seem to lose their anchorage and drift," Kagawa "is creating and endeavoring to master a definite rhetoric." We should not overlook Kagawa's poetry: "its modest, but nevertheless valid and penetrating introspective wisdom, and its elaborately hesitant precision, possess values not duplicated in contemporary poetry."

69. "Major Fiction." H&H 4 (1931): 303-5. UER. Review of Flowering Judas, by Katherine Anne Porter.
States that only W. C. Williams, among living writers, "has written short stories at once so fine in detail, so powerful as units, and so mature and intelligent in outlook."

70. "The Symbolist Influence." H&H 4 (1931): 607-18. UER. Review of L'Influence du Symbolisme Française sur la Poésie Américaine, by René Taupin.
Questions the possibility of defining or determining influence, and points to statements by Taupin asserting influence where it could not exist or in all likelihood did not exist. Questions Taupin's taste in poetry written in English and his knowledge of nineteenth century English and American poetry. Taupin's book is valuable as a compilation of information relating to the French influence on Imagist verse and as a history of the period in American poetry.

71. "Traditional Mastery." H&H 5 (1932): 321-28. LOA. UER. Review of The Shorter Poems of Robert Bridges.
Praises Bridges as the only contemporary rival of Hardy and as the best model of poetic style since Dryden. Bridges possessed greater interest in the possibilities of poetic form than one finds in Pound, Williams, and Marianne Moore. Bridges knew that a change of form results in a change in the aspects of experience perceived and mastered. Instead of developing an identifying mannerism and thereby confining himself to idiosyncrasy and a limited range of experience, he aimed at an impersonally traditional manner that combined restraint and economy of style with generality of import and precision of detail. (See items 15, 83.)

72. "Poets and Others." H&H 5 (1932): 675-86. UER. Review of Poems, 1928-31, by Allen Tate; Poems, by Wilfrid

Owen; The Signature of Pain, by Alan Porter; Thrust at the
Sky, by MacKnight Black; The Dark Land, by Kathleen T.
Young; Thurso's Landing, by Robinson Jeffers; Mortal Triumph, by Selden Rodman; Now That the Hawthorne Blossoms, by Althea Bass; and The Flowering Stone, by George
Dillon.
States that Allen Tate's defects are not defects of overall conception but defects of detail that affect only the passages in
which they appear. Despite many such defects in his work,
Tate remains a major poet. Wilfrid Owen's poetry is damaged by the fact that it was written under the pressures of
military service, but it displays intensity and conviction despite fragmentariness, weak diction, and insensitive rhythms.
The other poets reviewed here are very minor, the best of
them being Porter and Young. As examples of distinguished
poetry not being published or being published obscurely, quotes
poems written by Grant H. Code, Howard Baker, and J. V.
Cunningham.

73. "The Brink of Darkness." H&H 5 (1932): 547-61. (See items
     14, 105.)

74. "The Objectivists." H&H 6 (1932): 158-60. UER. Review
     of An "Objectivists" Anthology. Edited by Louis Zukofsky.
     Maintains that the anthology is "of clinical rather than liter-
     ary interest" and that "the theories that Mr. Zukofsky strug-
     gles hopelessly to express, the methods of composition that
     he and his friends have debauched till they no longer deserve
     even ridicule, seem to be sinking rapidly to lower and lower
     literary levels; they should be in a few years no serious
     cause of consternation." (See items 410, 722.)

75. "T. Sturge Moore." H&H 6 (1933): 534-45. UER. Review
     of The Poems of T. Sturge Moore, vols. 1 and 2.
     Defines Moore's situation as that of the regenerate romantic
     and contrasts his relationship to romanticism with that of W.
     B. Yeats. His major theme is the recovery from the Sym-
     bolist immersion in pure sensation: "his wisdom, which is
     traditional, appears banal to those nourished on the unformu-
     lable; and the precision with which he renders his feelings
     appears mild to those nourished on over-statement." (See
     items 95, 123, 655.)

76. "The Oxford Book of Sixteenth Century Verse." H&H 6
     (1933): 713-20. Review of The Oxford Book of Sixteenth
     Century Verse.
     Criticizes Chambers for concentrating on Petrarchists in his
     selections and for omitting or representing badly such poets
     as Googe, Gascoigne, and Turberville. Objects also to inade-
     quate representation of the poetry of the song-books. (See
     items 15, 92, 113, 116.)

77. "The Younger Writers of the West." The Academy: The

Official Publication of the National Academy of American Literature 1 (1933): 6-7, 11.

States that the poetry of the past two centuries "has suffered from the progressive separation of feeling and understanding." Sees, as exceptions to this tendency, the work of Landor, Bridges, Arnold, Hardy, and T. S. Moore. Attributes the decline in part to the fact that the intellect "has devoted itself to such pursuits as the physical sciences, which have been largely irrelevant to the ethical life, and hence to poetry." This separation has been encouraged by the doctrine of self-expression, "that the poet should express himself rather than correct and civilize himself in the attempt to express the universal," and the doctrine of expressive form, "that the form should 'express' the matter, the meter follow the mood, and so on, instead of ordering and criticizing the matter." (For further discussion of expressive or imitative form, see items 5, 7, 45, 79.)

Quotes and discusses poems by Howard Baker, Clayton Stafford, and J. V. Cunningham, as examples of recent work that counters the historical tendencies that he has outlined.

78. "More Santa Clara Justice." NR, 10 October 1934, pp. 239-41.

Outlines principal reasons for believing in the innocence of David Lamson, convicted and sentenced to be hanged for the murder of his wife, and requests support for the appeal of his conviction: "Lamson is far more pathetic than are most of the victims of the economic struggle and of racial prejudice ... he has no class or group for his partisans. He is merely a gentle and amiable man who appears to be innocent of the crime for which he has been sentenced to death." (See items 3, 351, 353, 354.)

79. "Foreword." Before Disaster. Tyron, N. C.: Tyron Pamphlets, 1934, pp. 3-6.

Describes the subject matter of the poems in the volume as "the stress to which the permanent, or ideal, elements of the human character are subjected by the powers of disintegration, by the temptations of Hell, which, though permanent in their general nature, usually take particular forms from the age." Explains that the most important formal principle operating in the poems is "the rule of minimum variation": "that the source of variation to be most extensively employed is quantity, that (in iambic verse) substitution should be restricted as far as possible to inversion of accent, and that in trisyllabic feet the two light syllables should be as light and as short as possible." Objects to "the fallacy of expressive form" that leads to poetry that imitates the form of its subject instead of imposing a controlled form on the expression of subject matter. "To let the form of the poem succumb to its matter is and will always be the destruction of poetry and may be the destruction of intelligence." (See item 88.)

80. [Don Stanford]. Trial Balances. Edited by Ann Winslow.
New York: Macmillan, 1935, pp. 117-18.
States that Stanford's poetry "shows an extraordinary sweetness and soundness of feeling: the feeling is often sound even
when the idea is awry for a moment." His poems "are not
merely interesting indications of work to come; they are
achievements and will survive."

81. "Jones Very: A New England Mystic." AR 7 (1936): 159-78.
Reprinted as "Jones Very and R. W. Emerson: Aspects of
New England Mysticism" in MC and IDR.
(For annotation, see item 6.)

82. "Edgar Allan Poe: A Crisis in the History of American Obscurantism." AL 8 (1937): 379-401. MC, IDR, REAP.
(For annotation, see item 6.)

83. "Robert Bridges and Elizabeth Daryush." AR 8 (1937): 353-
67. UER.
Claims that Bridges and Hardy are the two most impressive
poets to have appeared since Milton, and that Bridges' daughter, Elizabeth Daryush, along with Yeats, T. Sturge Moore,
and Viola Meynell, are the only significant poets to have been
produced by the British Isles since Bridges and Hardy. Both
Bridges and Daryush are impressive in their ability to treat
complex themes in an unmannered way that conveys rich associations of feeling. The difference between them is that
Bridges is more impersonal than Daryush. Both are master
metrists: Bridges has experimented with accentual, syllabic,
and quantitative verse, and Daryush with purely syllabic meters. Since both are stylists who have transcended the identifying mannerisms of their age, they have been neglected by
readers who identify poetry with mannerism.

84. "Maule's Curse: Hawthorne and the Problem of Allegory."
AR 9 (1937): 339-61. MC, IDR, ACE, MLC, Haw.
(For annotation, see item 6.)

85. "Henry James and the Relation of Morals to Manners." AR
9 (1937): 482-503. MC, IDR. Although a note on p. 503
indicates that the essay is "to be concluded," the American
Review ceased publication with this issue.
(For annotation, see item 6.)

86. "Emily Dickinson and the Limits of Judgment." MC, IDR, ED.
Reprinted in part as "The Defects of Emily Dickinson."
A New Directions Reader. Edited by Hayden Carruth and
J. Laughlin. Norfolk, Conn.: New Directions, 1964, pp.
9-12.
(For annotation, see item 6.)

87. "Foreword." Twelve Poets of the Pacific. Norfolk, Conn.:
New Directions, 1937, pp. 9-10. (See item 31.)

States that the aims of the poets included are the following: "in the matter of conception, clarity, as opposed to contemporary obscurantist tendencies, or, to put it otherwise, the expression of the feelings in terms of the motive; in matter of style, purity and freedom from mannerism, as distinct from the contemporary tendency to substitute mannerism for true originality." (See items 9, 15.)

88. "The Experimental School in American Thought." PD, IDR, Crit, DP.
(For annotation, see item 5.)

89. "Primitivism and Decadence." PD, IDR, EMLC.
(For annotation, see item 5.)

90. Review of Collected Poems, by E. E. Cummings. AL 10 (1939): 520-23.
Asserts that the artistry to be found in the poetry of such members of the Experimental Generation as Stevens, Williams, Marianne Moore, Pound, Eliot, H. D., and Crane is absent from Cummings' work. In the poetry of Cummings, "the romantic notions which in various ways and degrees limit or damage their work have been pushed to their ultimate logical development; namely, to a more or less infantile exhibitionism, at once mildly unpleasant and infinitely tedious."

91. "Poetry of Feeling." KR 1 (1939): 104-7. WCW, UER.
Review of The Complete Collected Poems, by William Carlos Williams.
Maintains that Williams distrusts the intellect and does not understand the function of traditional form. These attitudes impose limitations on his capacity for understanding experience and on the formal possibilities that can be realized in his poems. Since Williams has an excellent ear, he makes of his own free verse a complex and subtle form of accentual meter. When he remains within those areas of experience that he understands, he writes poetry that "though in certain ways limited, is at its best not confused or sentimental." (See discussion of primitivism and decadence in item 5.) Williams is, along with Wallace Stevens, "one of the two best poets of his generation." (See item 122.)

92. "The 16th Century Lyric in England." Poetry 53 (1939): 258-72, 320-35; 54 (1939): 35-51. FD, EPMEC.
(For annotation, see item 15.)

93. "Agnes Lee." Poetry 54 (1939): 335-38. UER.
States that "Agnes Lee's power was a power of personal character united to an extraordinary grasp of certain poetic conventions. When the character, the convention, and the subject were happily met, the result was magnificent; when unhappily, the result was a loss of control almost complete."

94. "On the Possibility of a Co-operative History of American
    Literature." AL 12 (1940): 297-305.
    Points out the dangers of unintelligent academic specialization
    in the study of American culture and states that there are
    specialists in Emerson with no detailed knowledge of his con-
    temporaries or of writers such as Hart Crane, and specialists
    in Poe unfamiliar with the French Symbolists. Refers to V.
    L. Parrington's attempt to understand the Puritans without
    reference to their theology or to the literary qualities of their
    work. Maintains that to ignore the theology is to "neglect
    ninety-nine hundredths of what the Puritans wrote during their
    first century and a half," and to ignore the artistic treatment
    of the ideas in literature is to confuse mere paraphrase with
    total meaning. (Some of this material reappears in "Post
    Scripta," The Anatomy of Nonsense; see item 7.)

95. "T. S. Eliot: The Illusion of Reaction." KR 3 (1941): 7-30,
    221-39. AN, IDR, TSE.
    (For annotation, see item 7.)

96. "In Plato's Garden." NMQ 11 (1941): 110-11. UER. Review
    of In Plato's Garden: Poems 1928-1939, by Lincoln Fitzell.
    States that Fitzell's poetry, although minor, of limited scope,
    and sometimes mannered in style, is capable of great power.
    The best of his poems are of permanent value.

97. "The Poems of Theodore Roethke." KR 3 (1941): 514-16.
    UER. Review of Open House, by Theodore Roethke.
    Asserts that the weak poems in Roethke's collection are the
    result of easy irony, jingling meters, imprecise psychological
    jargon, and fashionable imagery. He is sometimes brilliant
    as a poet of pure description and in his handling of precise
    abstractions. "It requires courage to deal with Platonic ab-
    stractions in a season of nominalists triumphant and untram-
    meled--and, were they not so learned, one would add unedu-
    cated." Praises Roethke for having a subject matter and for
    treating it "in a style that is good in this period and would be
    good in any other."

98. Foreword to New England Earth, by Don Stanford. San Fran-
    cisco: Colt Press, 1941, pp. 5-8. UER.
    Describes Stanford's concern to realize sensual beauty modi-
    fied by the intellect within rhetorical and poetic forms modeled
    on such masters as Donne, Rochester, and Dryden. Stanford's
    poetry combines the qualities of these earlier writers with an
    awareness of the spiritual dangers of the romantic experience
    through which our culture has passed since the time of Dry-
    den. The result is the expression of a sensibility both tradi-
    tional and modern.

99. "Preliminary Problems." AN, IDR, CEC, ALC. Translated
    into German as "Einleitende Problemstellungen." Moderne
    Amerikanische Literaturtheorien. Edited by Joseph Strelka

and Walter Hinderer. Frankfurt am Main: S. Fischer, 1970, pp. 231-43.
(For annotation, see item 7.)

100. "Wallace Stevens, or the Hedonist's Progress." AN, IDR, RLE, WS.
(For annotation, see item 7.)

101. "John Crowe Ransom, or Thunder Without God." AN, IDR, Per. (For annotation, see item 7.)

102. "The Critical Method of T. Weiss." QRL 2 (1945): 133-41. (See item 691.)
Replies to the criticisms of Theodore Weiss, "whose remarks on general principles are so brief and so general that it is possible to discuss them only in the most brief and general terms." Corrects Weiss's mistakes with regard to Thomism, Christianity, and Platonism as these relate to Winters' own position. Quotes a number of Weiss's "bald misstatements of what I say."

103. "Religious and Social Ideas in the Didactic Works of E. A. Robinson." AQ 1 (1945): 70-85. UER.
Summarizes the New England background that influenced Robinson: the contradictions in Calvinism led to the Unitarian distrust of theology, and the absence of a mystical element in Unitarianism created an emotional need that was filled by the rebirth of mysticism in Emerson's affirmation of the value of intuition and impulse. (See items 81, 84.) Robinson was poorly equipped to deal with ideas and generalized thought except as they illuminated a human situation. In those poems in which he tried to express religious ideas in general, he achieves only a vague mysticism. Similarly, those poems expressing social ideas exhibit no more than an imprecise distrust in the common man and a tendency to confuse the vices of mankind with the vices of his own country. The poems expressing Robinson's religious and social ideas are his least satisfactory; his best poetry is of a different sort. If he is to be properly evaluated, he should be admired for the great poems that he did write. His poorer work and intellectual weaknesses should not be admired out of respect for his more successful performances. (See item 8.)

104. "The Significance of The Bridge, by Hart Crane, or What Are We to Think of Professor X?" IDR, MP, AT.
(For annotation, see item 9.)

105. "The Brink of Darkness." Anchor in the Sea: An Anthology of Psychological Fiction. Edited by Alan Swallow. New York: Swallow Press and William Morrow, 1947, pp. 137-53. Revised version. (For earlier version, see item 73.) Reprinted with author's note (see item 14). Trans-

lated into French as "Au Bord de la Nuit." Ecrit aux
U.S.A.: Antologies des Prosateurs Américains du XXe
Siècle. 14th ed. Edited by Albert-J. Guérard. Paris:
Robert Laffont, 1947, pp. 331-43.

106. "Robert Frost: Or, the Spiritual Drifter as Poet." SewR
56 (1948): 564-96. FC, LOATH, RF.
(For annotation, see item 10.)

107. "Three Poets." HR 1 (1948): 402-6. UER. Review of
Losses, by Randall Jarrell; The Dispossessed, by John
Berryman; and The Judge Is Fury, by J. V. Cunningham.
Dismisses Jarrell as a writer with no talent for language
and Berryman as a writer whose work is vitiated by self-
pity and an inability to think clearly. Cunningham's work,
on the other hand, is characterized by the clarity of his
thought and the skill with which he controls language and
form.

108. Foreword to Selected Poems, by Elizabeth Daryush. New
York. Swallow Press and William Morrow, 1948, pp.
9-14.
Discusses technical aspects of Daryush's use of syllabic
meter and some of the advantages of the form: "syllabic
meters within short patterns permit curious arrangements
of stresses, including unbroken series of three of four
stresses, and the rhythms thus achieved are often not only
beautiful in themselves but quite foreign to anything possible
in standard meter." Discusses Daryush's principal themes,
including that of the impermanence of life and the precari-
ousness of personal integrity. States that her best poems
are sufficient to prove her "one of the few distinguished
poets of our century and a poet who can take her place
without apology in the company of Campion and Herrick."

109. "The Poet and the University: A Reply." Poetry 75 (1949):
170-78. UER. (See item 499.)
Defends the academic profession as an appropriate one for
poets against objections to this view stated by Hayden Carruth. The patronage that was once available damages one's
self-respect, and the professions suggested by Carruth re-
move one from the intellectual life and community with mankind. The academic profession allows a poet to concentrate
on matters of primary interest to him and does not cut him
off from engagement with the world.

110. "The Poetry of Gerard Manley Hopkins." HR 1 (1949): 455-
76.; 2 (1949): 61-93. FC, Hop.
(For annotation, see item 10.)

111. "A Discovery." HR 3 (1950): 453-58. UER. Review of
The Cricket, by Frederick Goddard Tuckerman.
Argues that Tuckerman, in some of his sonnets and in The

Cricket, is one of the major American poets of the nineteenth century. In The Cricket, Tuckerman meditates on
death conceived as union with nature, but he rejects the
Emersonian pantheism that informs most American poetry
on the subject. The Cricket is "probably the greatest single
American poem of the nineteenth century; and the British
poems of the same period which can be compared with it are
few indeed." (See item 121.)

112.   "The Audible Reading of Poetry." HR 4 (1951): 433-47.
        FC, SV, PCC.
        (For annotation, see item 10.)

113.   "English Literature in the Sixteenth Century." HR 8 (1955):
        281-87. FC.
        (For annotation, see item 10.)

114.   "The Poetry of Edgar Bowers." SewR 64 (1956): 657-62.
        UER. Review of The Form of Loss.
        Contends that Bowers' style is both traditional and modern.
        At times, Bowers employs the abstract vocabulary and the
        rational structure to be found in such poets as Fulke Gre-
        ville. More frequently, he writes in a modern tradition in
        which sensory details are sharply realized and charged with
        explicit meaning by the total context. Nine or ten of Bowers'
        poems are among the greatest in English. (See discussion
        of post-Symbolist imagery in item 15.)

115.   "Problems for the Modern Critic of Literature." HR 9
        (1956): 325-86. FC.
        (For annotation, see item 10.)

116.   "Poetic Styles, Old and New." Four Poets on Poetry.
        Edited by Don Cameron Allen. Baltimore: Johns Hopkins
        University Press, 1959, pp. 44-75. FD.
        Establishes the historical framework in which post-Symbolist
        imagery can be placed through examining the shifting relation-
        ships between rational meaning and sensory perception in
        poems by Donne, Shakespeare, Jonson, and Wallace Stevens.
        Includes material that had appeared in "The 16th Century
        Lyric in England." (See items 15, 76, 92, 100, 113.)

117.   "The Poetry of W. B. Yeats." TCL 6 (1960): 3-24. Re-
        printed in Dubliner, no. 2 (1962), pp. 7-33. FD. Re-
        printed as pamphlet (see item 12).
        (For annotation, see item 15.)

118.   "The Poetry of J. V. Cunningham." TCL 6 (1961): 159-71. FD.
        Reprinted as pamphlet (see item 13).
        (For annotation, see item 15.)

119.   "The Poetry of Charles Churchill." Poetry 98 (1961): 44-53;
        98 (1961): 104-17. FD.
        (For annotation, see item 15.)

120. "By Way of Clarification." TCL 10 (1964): 130-35.
Argues that Alan Stephens, in his review of the Collected
Poems (see item 671), had misinterpreted many of the poems
through assuming "first, that from the beginning of my career I knew everything that I know at present, but merely
made arbitrary choices with regard to what I would or would
not use," and "second, that the poems are absolutely in
chronological order." Illustrates the consequent misreadings
as these appear in a number of poems. Replies to Stephens's
charge that poems such as "A Spring Serpent" are cultish by
asserting that the complex of ideas alluded to in the poem
are a part of the common knowledge of scholars.

121. "Critical Foreword." The Complete Poems of Frederick
Goddard Tuckerman. Edited with an introduction by N.
Scott Momaday. New York: Oxford University Press,
1965. FD.
(For annotation, see item 15.)

122. "In Postscript." WCW, p. 69. UER.
States that he still holds the view expressed in the 1939 review (see item 91) but would restrict further the number of
Williams' poems to be regarded as successful. Emphasizes
more emphatically the limitations imposed by Williams' anti-
intellectualism.

123. "The Poetry of T. Sturge Moore." SR 2 (1966): 1-16. FD.
(For annotation, see item 15.)

124. "Introduction." The Early Poems of Yvor Winters 1920-
1928. Denver: Alan Swallow, 1966, pp. 7-16. UER,
DQ, CPYW. (See item 29.)
Recounts biographical details relevant to an understanding of
his early poetry. Discusses the shift in method from free
verse to traditional meters that occurred in 1928, asserting
that it took place because he realized that he could not achieve
the level of excellence found in Baudelaire, Valéry, Hardy,
Bridges, and Stevens through his earlier procedures. Insists
that the early and "experimental" work contained in The Early
Poems is good work of its kind but is inferior to his later
work in traditional forms.

125. "Forms of Discovery: A Preliminary Statement." SR 3
(1967): 1-12. FD.
(For annotation, see item 15.)

126. "Alan Swallow: 1915-1966." SR 3 (1967): 796-98.
Recalls his acquaintance with his publisher and friend, Alan
Swallow, a man who, though not a good poet himself, "had
a remarkable sense for style in the work of others."

V.

POEMS

127. "Round Eyes." Others 5 (1919): 21.

128. "Profiles and Afternoons: Prelude." LR 6 (1919): 60.

129. "Monodies." Poetry 14 (1919): 301-5. Collective title for
     six poems: 'Concerning Blake'; 'Little Rabbit'; 'Monte-
     zuma'; 'The Old Weep Gently'; 'On the Mesa'; 'Wild
     Horses.'

130. "Carl Sandburg." Youth 1 (1919): 60.

131. "Slag." Youth 1 (1919): 59.

132. "White Song." Youth 1 (1919): 59-60.

133. "Ballad." Poetry 17 (1920): 143. IW, EP, CPYW.

134. "Ballad of Men." Poetry 17 (1920): 145. IW, EP,
     CPYW.

135. "Death Goes Before Me." Poetry 17 (1920): 147. IW,
     CVPC, TT, NP, EP, CPYW.

136. "The Far Voice." Poetry 17 (1920): 142.

137. "Hawk's Eyes." Poetry 17 (1920): 142. IW, PA.

138. "The Immobile Wind." Poetry 17 (1920): 144. IW, NP, EP,
     CPYW.

139. "The Priesthood." Poetry 17 (1920): 146. IW, NP.

140. "To Be Sung by a Small Boy Who Herds Goats." Poetry 17
     (1920): 144-45 (under title "Song for a Small Boy Who
     Herds Goats"). IW (under earlier title), CVPC (under
     earlier title), TT (under earlier title), Poems, CP,
     CP(1960), EP (under earlier title), CPYW.

141. "Two Songs of Advent." <u>Poetry</u> 17 (1920): 142. <u>IW</u>, <u>TT</u>, <u>NP</u>, <u>EP</u>, <u>CPYW</u>. Translated into French as "<u>Deux</u> <u>Chan</u>sons de l'Avent" in <u>Anthologies de la Nouvelle Poésie Américaine.</u> Edited by Eugène Jolas. Paris: Kra, 1928, p. 254. The Poem is in two parts; part I is reprinted in <u>Poems</u>, <u>CP</u>, <u>CP(1960)</u>, and <u>CPYW</u> under title "A Song of Advent."

142. "The Walker" (A leaf turns--). <u>Poetry</u> 17 (1920): 143. <u>NP</u>.

143. "Where My Sight Goes." <u>Poetry</u> 17 (1920): 146-47. <u>IW</u>, <u>CVPC</u>.

144. "Alone" (I, one who never speaks). <u>IW</u>, <u>Poems</u>, <u>CP</u>, <u>CP(1960)</u>, <u>CPYW</u>.

145. "The Chapel." <u>IW</u>, <u>CPYW</u>.

146. "The Lie." <u>IW</u> (under title "I Paved a Sky"), <u>Poems</u>, <u>CP</u>, <u>CP(1960)</u>, <u>EP</u> (under earlier title), <u>CPYW</u>.

147. "The Morning." <u>IW</u>, <u>EP</u>, <u>CPYW</u>.

148. "My Memory." <u>IW</u>, <u>EP</u>, <u>CPYW</u>.

149. "Song" (I could tell). <u>IW</u> (under title "One Ran Before"), <u>Poems</u>, <u>CP</u>, <u>CP(1960)</u>, <u>EP</u> (under earlier title), <u>CPYW</u>.

150. "Two Dramatic Interludes for Puppets" (I. 'Autumn Roadside'; II. 'The Pines Are Shadows'). <u>IW</u>, <u>EP</u>, <u>CPYW</u>.

151. "The Wizard." <u>IW</u>, <u>EP</u>, <u>CPYW</u>.

152. "Chicago Spring: Before Returning to Santa Fe." <u>Poetry</u> 20 (1922): 319.

153. "Lament, Beside an Acéquia, for the Wife of Awa-tsireh." <u>Poetry</u> 20 (1922): 321. <u>CPYW</u>.

154. "Late Winter." <u>Poetry</u> 20 (1922): 318.

155. "The Little Deity Alone in the Desert." <u>Poetry</u> 20 (1922): 318. <u>TT</u>.

156. "Old Spring." <u>Poetry</u> 20 (1922): 320.

157. "A Requiem for the Memory of Bees." <u>Poetry</u> 20 (1922): 318-19.

158. "The Silent Days." <u>Poetry</u> 20 (1922): 320-21. <u>TT</u>.

159. "The Fragile Season." <u>Poetry</u> 20 (1922): 322. <u>BH</u>, <u>Poems</u>, <u>EP</u>, <u>CPYW</u>.

160. "Hill Burial." Milwaukee Arts Monthly, 21 October 1922, pp. 21. BH, EP, CPYW.

161. "The Mule Corral." Milwaukee Arts Monthly, 21 October 1922, pp. 21. EP, CPYW.

162. "The Stone Mountain." Milwaukee Arts Monthly, 21 October 1922, pp. 22.

163. "Apocalyptic Harvest." Broom 3 (1922): 29.

164. "Drifting Deer." Broom 3 (1922): 30.

165. "Of a Day." Broom 3 (1922): 29.

166. "Alone" (I saw day's shadow strike). MS, EP, CPYW.

167. "The Aspen's Song." MS, Poems, CP, CP(1960), EP, POL, CPYW.

168. "At Evening." MS, EP, CPYW.

169. "Awaiting Snow." MS, EP, CPYW.

170. "Awakening." MS, EP, CPYW.

171. "Blue Mountain." MS, EP, CPYW.

172. "Cool Nights." MS, EP, CPYW.

173. "A Deer." MS, EP, CPYW.

174. "Desert." MS, EP, CPYW.

175. "The End." MS, EP, CPYW.

176. "Fields." MS, EP, CPYW.

177. "God of Roads." MS, Poems, CP, CP(1960), CPYW.

178. "High Valleys." MS, EP, CPYW.

179. "The Hunter." MS, EP, CPYW.

180. "A Lady." MS, EP, CPYW.

181. "Man in Desert." MS, EP, CPYW.

182. "May." MS, EP, CPYW.

183. "Myself." MS, EP, CPYW.

184. "No Being." MS, EP, CPYW.

185. "September." MS, EP, CPYW.

186. "Sleep" (Like winds my eyelids close). MS, EP, CPYW.

187. "Song" (Why should I stop). MS, EP, CPYW.

188. "Spring." MS, EP, CPYW.

189. "Spring Rain." MS, EP, CPYW.

190. "Still Morning." MS, EP, CPYW.

191. "Sunrise." MS, EP, CPYW.

192. "The Walker" (In dream, my feet are still). MS, EP, CPYW.

193. "Winter Echo." MS, EP, CPYW.

194. "Eternity." Dial 74 (1923): 255. BH, EP, CPYW.

195. "The Dry Year." Poetry 22 (1923): 86.

196. "The Schoolmaster and the Queres of the Mines." Poetry 22 (1923): 84-85.

197. "The Schoolmaster at Spring." Poetry 22 (1923): 84. EP, CPYW.

198. "The Schoolmaster Writes to a Poet." Poetry 22 (1923): 86-87.

199. "Static Autumn." Poetry 22 (1923): 87. PA.

200. "The Precincts of February." Dial 75 (1923): 72. BH, Poems, CP, CP(1960), EP, CPYW. Translated into Japanese as "Ni-gwatsu no shui" in Gendai Sekai Shika Sen. Selection of Poetical Blossoms from the Modern World. Tôkyô: Kinseidô Co., 1931.

201. "The Crystal Sun." Dial 75 (1923): 363-64. BH, EP, CPYW.

202. "The Moonlight." Secession 7 (1924): 15. BH, Poems, EP, CPYW.

203. "The Resurrection." Secession 7 (1924): 20. BH, EP, CPYW.

204. "Tewa Spring." Secession 7 (1924): 15. BH, EP, CPYW. Translated into Japanese as "Tewa no haru" in Gendai Sekai Shika Sen (see item 200).

205. "Jose's Country." MR 2 (1924): 59. BH, Poems, CP, CP(1960), EP, CPYW.

206. "The Return." Forge 1 (1924): 7.

207. "The Schoolmaster Alone." Forge 1 (1924): 7.

208. "Primavera." 1924, no. 3 (1924), p. 75.

209. "The Rows of Cold Trees." 1924, no. 3 (1924), p. 74. BH, CP, CP(1960), EP, NAMP, NOBA, CPYW.

210. "The Streets." 1924, no. 3 (1924), p. 76. BH, EP, CPYW.

211. "July." Forge 2 (1924): 17.

212. "October." Voices (1924): 142 (under title "October Night"). BH, EP, CPYW. Translated into Japanese as "Jû-gwatsu," in Gendai Sekai Shika Sen (see item 200).

213. "The Solitude of Glass." Poetry 25 (1925): 186. TT, EP, CPYW.

214. "The Upper Meadows." Poetry 25 (1925): 187. BH, Poems, CP, CP(1960), EP, PPO, PAM, CPYW.

215. "Dark Spring." TQ 1 (1925): 27. BH, EP, CPYW.

216. "Digue Dondaine, Digue Dondon." TQ 1 (1925): 24. BH, EP, CPYW.

217. "Man Regards Eternity in Aging." TQ 1 (1925): 25 (under title "Man Betrothed to Death, Regards Eternity in Aging"). BH, EP, CPYW.

218. "Quod Tegit Omnia." TQ 1 (1925): 26. BH, Poems, CP, MVE, CP(1960), EP, QR, CPYW.

219. "The Cold." Guardian 2 (1925): 424 (under title "The Cold Air"). BH, Poems, CP, CP(1960), EP, CPYW.

220. "Prayer Beside a Lamp." Dial 80 (1926): 234. Quoted in Bookman 67 (1928): 441. Translated into Japanese as "Rampu no hotori no inori," in Gendai Sekai Shika Sen (see item 200).

221. "The Barnyard." Dial 82 (1927): 31. BH, CP, CP(1960), EP, CPYW.

222. "The Longe Nightes When Every Creature." Trans, no. 4 (1927), p. 142. Proof, EP, CPYW.

223. "Chrysanthemums: for F.G.E. 1905-1926." Trans, no. 7 (1927), p. 118.

224. "Demigod." <u>Trans</u>, no. 7 (1927), p. 117.

225. "Satyric Complaint." <u>Trans</u>, no. 7 (1927), pp. 115-16.
      <u>Proof</u>, <u>EP</u>, <u>CPYW</u>.

226. "Triumph." <u>Trans</u>, no. 7 (1927), p. 119.

227. "Bison." <u>Trans</u>, no. 9 (1927) p. 131. <u>Proof</u>, <u>EP</u>, <u>CPYW</u>.
      French translation in <u>Anthologie de la Nouvelle Poésie
      Américaine</u>. Edited by Eugène Jolas. Paris: Kra, 1928,
      p. 255.

228. "See Los Angeles First." <u>Trans</u>, no. 9 (1927), p. 130.
      <u>Proof</u>, <u>EP</u>, <u>CPYW</u>.

229. "The Bitter Moon." <u>American Caravan</u> 1 (1927): 483-84.
      <u>Proof</u>, <u>EP</u>, <u>CPYW</u>.

230. "The Deep." <u>American Caravan</u> 1 (1927): 484 (under title
      "The Deep: A Service for All the Dead"). <u>Proof</u>, <u>EP</u>,
      <u>CPYW</u>.

231. "Incandescent Earth." <u>American Caravan</u> 1 (1927): 480-81.
      <u>EP</u>, <u>CPYW</u>.

232. "November." <u>American Caravan</u> 1 (1927): 482. <u>Proof</u>, <u>EP</u>,
      <u>CPYW</u>.

233. "Orange Tree." <u>American Caravan</u> 1 (1927): 481. <u>Proof</u>,
      <u>EP</u>, <u>CPYW</u>.

234. "Fire Sequence." <u>American Caravan</u> 1 (1927) 473-84. <u>EP</u>,
      <u>CPYW</u>.
      Collective title for seventeen poems: 'Coal: Beginning and
      End'; 'Liberation'; 'Return of Spring'; 'Bill'; 'The Van-
      quished'; 'The Victor'; 'A Miner'; 'Vacant Lot'; 'Tragic
      Love'; 'To the Crucified'; 'O Sun!'; 'Incandescent Earth';
      'Orange Tree'; 'November'; 'Genesis'; 'The Bitter Moon';
      'The Deep: A Service for All the Dead.'

235. "Alba for Hecate." <u>BH</u>, <u>EP</u>, <u>CPYW</u>.

236. "April." <u>BH</u>, <u>Poems</u>, <u>CP</u>, <u>CP(1960)</u>, <u>EP</u>, <u>ELU</u>, <u>RMML</u>,
      <u>CPYW</u>.

237. "The Bare Hills." <u>BH</u>, <u>EP</u>, <u>CPYW</u>.

238. "The Cold Room." <u>BH</u>, <u>Poems</u>, <u>CP</u>, <u>CP(1960)</u>, <u>EP</u>, <u>CPYW</u>.

239. "Complaint." <u>BH</u>, <u>EP</u>, <u>CPYW</u>.

240. "The Dead: Mazda Wake." <u>BH</u>, <u>Poems</u> (under title "The
      Dead, by Electric Light Unshaded"), <u>EP</u>, <u>CPYW</u>.

241. "Exodus." BH, EP, CPYW.

242. "Flesh of Flowers." BH, EP, CPYW.

243. "Full Moon." BH, EP, CPYW.

244. "Genesis" (The door became a species of mystery). BH, EP, CPYW.

245. "The Grosbeaks." BH, EP, CPYW.

246. "The Impalpable Void." BH, Poems, EP, CPYW.

247. "The Lamplight." BH, EP, CPYW.

248. "Love Song." BH, EP, CPYW.

249. "March Dusk." BH, EP, CPYW.

250. "Midnight Wind." BH, EP, CPYW.

251. "Moonrise" (The branches, jointed, pointing). BH, EP, CPYW.

252. "The Muezzin." BH, EP, CPYW.

253. "Nocturne." Larus 1 (1927): 21. BH, Poems, CP, CP(1960), CPYW.

254. "The Passing Night." BH, EP, CPYW.

255. "Sleep" (O living pine, be still). BH, Poems, CP, CP(1960), EP, POL, CPYW.

256. "Song" (Now the precise, remote, and). BH, EP, CPYW.

257. "Song" (Where I walk out). BH, Poems, CP, CP(1960), EP, BAP, POL, CPYW.

258. "Under Rain." BH, EP, CPYW.

259. "The Vigil" (These were moments saved from sleep). BH, EP, CPYW.

260. "The Precision." Trans, no. 10 (1928), p. 108. EASP.

261. "The Bed." Larus 1 (1928): 39.

262. "Song of the Trees." Dial 84 (1928): 504. Proof, Poems, CP, CP(1960), EP, CPYW.

263. "The Realization" (under title "Sonnet"). American Caravan 2 (1928): 118. Proof (under earlier title), Poems, CP,

PBMV, CP(1960), CPYW. A slightly different version appears in Poems and subsequently.

264. "Sonnet" (The fact that neither cause nor gain). American Caravan 2 (1928): 118. Proof, CPYW.

265. "Simplex Munditiis." Dial 86 (1929): 204. Proof, EP, CPYW.

266. "The Invaders." Gyr, [no. 1] (1929), p. 7 (under title "The Countryless: Refugees of Science"), Proof (under earlier title), Poems, CP, PBMV, CP(1960), PAM, CPYW. A slightly different version appears in CP and subsequently.

267. "The Proof." Gyr, [no. 1] (1929), p. 8. Proof, CPYW.

268. "To Emily Dickinson." Gyr, [no. 1] (1929), p. 8. Proof, Poems, CP, CP(1960), TS, PAM, CPYW. A slightly different version appears in CP and subsequently. Reprinted in Perspectives USA, no. 15 (1956), p. 100. Reprinted with translation into French as "A Emily Dickinson" in Profils, no. 15 (1956), pp. 12-13. Reprinted with translation into German as "An Emily Dickinson" Perspektiven, no. 15 (1956), pp. 106-107. Reprinted with translation into Italian as "A Emily Dickinson" in Prospetti, no. 15 (1956), pp. 124-25.

269. "To William Dinsmore Briggs Conducting His Seminar." Gyr, [no. 1] (1929), p. 7. Proof, Poems (under title "To a Distinguished Scholar Conducting His Seminar"), CP, CP(1960), CPYW. A slightly different version appears in CP and subsequently.

270. "Apollo and Daphne." Gyr, [no. 2], (1929), p. 9. Proof, Poems, CP, CP(1960), TS, PAM, CPYW.

271. "The Castle of Thorns." Gyr, [no. 2] (1929), p. 20. Proof, Poems, CP, CP(1960), NAMP, CPYW. A slightly different version appears in Poems and subsequently.

272. "The Fable." Gyr, [no. 2] (1929), p. 20. Proof, Poems, CP, CP(1960), CPYW. The last three lines of this poem are dropped in Poems and subsequently.

273. "The Moralists." Gyr, [no. 2] (1929), p. 19. Proof, Poems, CP, CP(1960), PAM, CPYW. A slightly different version appears in CP and subsequently.

274. "Sonnet" (This God-envenomed loneliness, the stain). Gyr, [no. 2] (1929), p. 18.

275. "Sonnet" (Treading infinity, alone I go--). Gyr, [no. 2] (1929), p. 18.

276. "The Empty Hills." Gyr, [no. 3] (1929), p. 20. Proof, Poems, CP, CP(1960), CPYW.

277. "To the Painter Polelonema." Pagany 1 (1930): 81. Proof, CPYW.

278. "Wild Sunflower." Pagany 1 (1930): 80. Proof, CPYW.

279. "For Howard Baker." Gyr, [no. 4] (1930), p. 7 (under title "Epilogue: For Howard Baker"). Proof (under earlier title), Poems, CP, CP(1960), CPYW.

280. "Moonrise" (The slow moon draws). Gyr, [no. 4] (1930), p. 7. Proof, Poems, CP, CP(1960), CPYW.

281. "The Still Small Voice." Gyr, [no. 4] (1930), p. 6. Proof, CPYW.

282. "The Last Visit." Miscellany 1 (1930): 10. Proof, Poems, CP, CP(1960), CPYW.

283. "Hymn to Dispel Hatred at Midnight." H&H 3 (1930): 314. Proof, Poems, CP, CP(1960), CPYW, PPO.

284. "The Fall of Leaves." H&H (1930): 315. Proof, Poems, CP, CP(1960), CPYW.

285. "Strength Out of Sweetness." Pagany 1 (1930): 75. Proof, CPYW.

286. "Shadows." Roon 2 (1930): 5. Proof, CPYW.

287. "Snow-Ghost." Pagany 1 (1930): 71. Proof, EP, CPYW.

288. "Communion." Proof, CPYW.

289. "The Goatherds." Proof, Poems, CP, CP(1960), EP, CPYW.

290. "Idaho." Pagany 1 (1930): 80-81.

291. "Inscription for a Graveyard." Proof, Poems, CP, CP(1960), CPYW.

292. "The Red Month." Proof, EP, CPYW.

293. "Remembered Spring." Proof, EP, CPYW.

294. "Snapshots." Proof, CPYW.

295. "Sonnet" (The table softly flames with flowers and candles). Proof, EP, CPYW.

296. "The Vigil" (To grind out bread by facing God).   Proof, EP, CPYW.

297. "Anacreontic."   NR, 1 April 1931, p. 176.   BD, Poems, CP, CP(1960), CPYW.

298. "The Ancestors."   NR, 6 May 1931, p. 327.   BD, CPYW.

299. "The Marriage."   Smoke 1 (1931): n. p.   J, Poems, GW, MVE, CP, CP(1960), QR, HWT, CPYW.

300. "On a View of Pasadena from the Hills."   H&H 4 (1931): 498-500.   J, Cal, Poems, CP, CP(1960), QR, CPYW.

301. "The Slow Pacific Swell."   Procession 1 (1931): 13-14.   J, Poems, CP, CP(1960), FOP, QR, CBV, NAMP, PAM, HIP, NOBA, CPYW.

302. "The Critiad: A Poetical Survey of Recent Criticism."   TQ 3 (1931): 738-43.   J.

303. "The Journey."   Pagany 2 (1931): 49-50.   J, Poems, CP, MVE, CP(1960), CPYW.

304. "The Grave."   J, Poems, CP, MVE, CP(1960), NAMP, CPYW.

305. "A Vision."   J, Poems, CP, MVE, CP(1960), CPYW.

306. "December Eclogue."   Procession 1 (1932): 31.   J.

307. "Chiron."   Contact n. s. 1 (1932): 49.   BD, Poems, CP, CP(1960), CPYW.

308. "Midas."   NR, 19 October 1932, p. 254.   BD, Poems, GW, CP, CP(1960), CPYW.

309. "Sonnet to the Moon."   Contact n. s. 1 (1932): 48.   BD, GW, Poems, CP, CP(1960), TCAP, CPYW.

310. "To My Infant Daughter."   NR, 12 October 1932, p. 224. In two parts; only part II appears in The New Republic. BD, Poems, GW, CP, CP(1960), VGW (part II only), CPYW.

311. "A Post-Card to the Social Muse Who Was Invoked More Formally by Various Marxians and Others in the Pages of The New Republic During the Winter of 1932-3."   NR, 8 February 1933, pp. 348 (under title "A Post-Card to the Social Muse").   BD, Poems, CP, CP(1960), CPYW.

312. "On the Death of Senator Thomas J. Walsh."   NR, 29 March 1933, p. 185.   BD, Poems, CP, CP(1960), CPYW.

313. "Theseus: A Trilogy" (in three parts: 'The Wrath of Ar-
temis'; 'Theseus and Ariadne'; 'The Old Age of Theseus').
H&H 6 (1933): 635-39. TP, Poems, CP, CP(1960),
NOBA, CPYW.

314. "Before Disaster." NR, 20 September 1933, p. 155. BD,
Poems, AA, GW, CP, HDPM, CP(1960), QR, CPYW.
Reprinted in Ginn Elements of English 7, by Charles R.
Neuschafer. Boston: Ginn & Co., 1971, p. 135.

315. "The Prince." Magazine 1 (1933): 17. BD, Poems, AA,
CP, CP(1960), CPYW.

316. "To a Young Writer." Magazine 1 (1934): 76. BD, Poems,
CP, CP(1960), CPYW.

317. "On Teaching the Young." Magazine 1 (1934): 76. BD,
GW, CP, CP(1960), Seq, NAMP, NOBA, CPYW. Reprinted in Perspectives USA, no. 15 (1956), p. 101. Reprinted with translation into French as "Sur l'Instruction
des Jeunes" in Profils, no. 15 (1956), pp. 12-15. Reprinted with translation into Italian as "Insegnare ai Gio-
vani" in Prospetti, no. 15 (1956), pp. 124-27.

318. "Heracles." Lion and the Unicorn 1 (1934): 26-27; Rocking
Horse 2 (1935): 1-3. Author's note in Rocking Horse
reads in part: "Heracles was printed some months ago in
another magazine, but mangled beyond recognition. This
is the correct version." TP, Poems, GW, CP, CP(1960),
TCAP, QR, CPYW.

319. "John Day, Frontiersman." NR, 7 November 1934, p. 360.
TP, Poems, GW, CP, CP(1960), APS, CPYW.

320. "The Anniversary." BD, Poems, CP, CP(1960), CPYW.

321. "By the Road to the Air-Base." BD (under title "By the
Road to the Sunnyvale Air-Base"), Poems, CP, CBMV,
PCA, CP(1960), PPD, CPYW.

322. "The Dedication." BD, CPYW.

323. "Dedication for a Book of Criticism." BD, Poems, SW, GW,
CP, CP(1960), CPYW.

324. "Elegy on a Young Airedale Bitch Lost Some Years Since in
the Salt-Marsh." BD, Poems, GW, CP, CP(1960), PPD,
CPYW.

325. "For My Father's Grave." BD, Poems, CP, CP(1960),
CPYW.

326. "Orpheus." BD, Poems, GW, CP, MVE, CP(1960), VGW,
PAM, NOBA, CPYW.

327. "A Petition." BD, Poems, CPYW.

328. "Phasellus Ille." BD, Poems, CP, CP(1960), CPYW.

329. "The Werwolf." BD, Poems, CPYW.

330. "Alcmena." Rocking Horse 2 (1935): 1-3. Poems, CP, CP(1960), CPYW.

331. "John Sutter." NR, 28 August 1935, p. 67. TP, Poems, GW, CP, CP(1960), NAMP, NOBA, CPYW.

332. "Socrates." Avenue 1 (1935): 162. Author's note in Rocking Horse 2 (1935) 1 reads in part: "From the first line of the last stanza of Socrates as misprinted in Avenue, the word us should be stricken." TP, Poems, CP, CP(1960), CPYW.

333. "The California Oaks." SR 1 (1936): 846-47. Poems, CP, CP(1960), CPYW, PPO. A slightly different version appears in CP(1960) and subsequently. Reprinted in Perspectives USA, no. 15 (1956), pp. 99-100. Reprinted with translation into French as "Les Chênes de Californie" in Profils, no. 15 (1956), pp. 14-17. Reprinted with translation into German as "Die Kalifornischen Eichen" in Perspektiven, no. 15 (1956), pp. 110-13. Reprinted with translation into Italian as "Querce della California" in Prospetti, 15 (1956), pp. 122-25.

334. "A Spring Serpent." NR, 12 August 1936, p. 20. Poems, GW, CP, Exp, CP(1960), CBV, CPYW.

335. "On Rereading a Passage from John Muir." TP, Poems, GW, CP, CP(1960), CPYW.

336. "Sir Gawaine and the Green Knight." NR, 2 June 1937, p. 98. Poems, GW, CAAP, FEAP, Mod, CP, MVE, CP(1960), Seq, PE, TCAP, PRA, QR, VGW, PIC, NAMP, CPYW. (See item 407.)

337. "In Praise of California Wines." Poetry 51 (1938): 321-22. Poems, CP, CP(1960), CPYW.

338. "The Manzanita." New York Times, 3 June 1938, p. 20. Poems, GW, CP, CP(1960), NYTBV, VGW, CPYW.

339. "An October Nocturne." Poetry 51 (1938): 320 (under title "A Nocturne for October 31st"). Poems, GW, CP, CP(1960), CBV, PA (under earlier title), CPYW.

340. "A Summer Commentary." Poetry 51 (1938): 320-21. Poems, GW, LTMP, CP, CP(1960), UP, QR, PPD, CPYW, PPO.

341. "The Cremation." Twentieth Century Verse 12-13 (1938):
      98. Poems, GW, CP, CP(1960), CPYW.

342. "Much in Little." Twentieth Century Verse 12-13 (1938):
      98. Poems, GW, CP, CP(1960), PPD, CPYW.

343. "On the Portrait of a Scholar of the Italian Renaissance."
      Poetry 51 (1938): 323. Poems, GW, CP, CP(1960),
      CPYW. Reprinted in Perspectives USA, no. 15 (1956),
      p. 98. Reprinted with translation into French as "Sur
      le Portrait d'un Savant de la Renaissance Italienne" in
      Profils, no. 15 (1956), pp. 16-17. Reprinted with trans-
      lation into German as "Zum Bildnis eines Gelehrten der
      Italienischen Renaissance" in Perspektiven, no. 15 (1956),
      pp. 108-9. Reprinted with translation into Italian as "A
      Proposito del Ritratto di un Dotto del Rinascimento Italia-
      no" in Prospetti 15 (1956), pp. 120-21.

344. "A Dedication in Postscript." Poems, CP, CP(1960), CPYW.

345. "A Leave-Taking." Poems, CP, CP(1960), CPYW.

346. "Noon." Poems, CP, CP(1960), CPYW.

347. "A Prayer for My Son." Poems, GW, CP, CBMV, TPWD,
      CP(1960), CPYW, PPO.

348. "The Shadow's Song." Poems, CP, CP(1960), POL, CPYW.

349. "Time and the Garden." Poems, GW, CP, CP(1960), MAP,
      NDR, QR, VGW, NAMP, CPYW.

350. "To a Portrait of Melville in My Library." Poems, CP,
      CP(1960), CPYW.

351. "To a Woman on Her Defense of Her Brother Unjustly Con-
      victed of Murder." Poems, CP, CP(1960), CPYW.

352. "An Elegy: For the U. S. N. Dirigible Macon." Modern
      Verse 1 (1941): 3-4. Poems, AM, GW, CP, CP(1960),
      APTC, VGW, CPYW.

353. "To David Lamson." Modern Verse 1 (1941): 5-6 (under
      title "To David Lamson Awaiting Retrial in the Jail at
      San Jose"). Poems, GW, CP, CP(1960), CPYW.

354. "To Edwin V. McKenzie." Modern Verse 1 (1941): 4-5
      (under title "To Edwin V. McKenzie on His Defense of
      David Lamson"). Poems, AM, GW, CP, CP(1960),
      CPYW.

355. "A Winter Evening." NMQ 12 (1942): 205. GW, AW, CP,
      CP(1960), CPYW.

356. "A Testament: To One Now a Child." NMQ 12 (1942): 205-
6. GW, CP, CP(1960), CPYW. Reprinted in Perspectives USA, no. 15 (1956), pp. 102-3. Reprinted with
translation into French as "Testament pour un Être En-
core Enfant" in Profils, no. 15 (1956), pp. 20-21. Reprinted with translation into Italian as "Testamento a Uno
che ora è Bambino" in Prospetti, no. 15 (1956), pp. 128-
29. Reprinted with translation into German as "Ver-
mächtnis für einem, der noch ein Kind ist" in Perspektiven, no. 15 (1956), pp. 108-11.

357. "A Tentative Draft of an Academic Eclogue." NMQ 12
(1942): 206-7.

358. "For the Opening of the William Dinsmore Briggs Room."
NMQ 12 (1942): 339. GW, AW, CP, CP(1960), CPYW.

359. "Summer Noon, 1941." GW, CP, CP(1960), CPYW.

360. "To a Military Rifle." GW, WP, CP, CP(1960), MAP,
CPYW. Reprinted in Perspectives USA, no. 15 (1956),
pp. 101-2. Reprinted with translation into French as
"A un Fusil de Guerre" in Profils, no. 15 (1956), pp.
18-19. Reprinted with translation into Italian as "A un
Fucile da Guerra" in Prospetti, no. 15 (1956), pp. 126-
29.

361. "To Hawthorne in Concord a Hundred Years Ago: From the
San Francisco Peninsula." NMQ 14 (1944): 214.

362. "Aere Caliginoso." Poetry 65 (1944): 61-62.

363. "At the Site of the Murphy Cabin." Poetry 65 (1944): 62.

364. "Defense of Empire." Poetry 65 (1944): 59-60. CP,
CP(1960), CPYW.

365. "An Epitaph for the American Dead." Poetry 65 (1944): 60.

366. "Moonlight Alert." Poetry 65 (1944): 61. CP, CP(1960),
CPYW.

367. "Night of Battle: Europe: As Regarded from a Great Dis-
tance." Poetry 69 (1946): 140. CP, CP(1960), CPYW.
Reprinted in Stanford Today 1 (1962): n. p.

368. "A Song: From an Academic Bower." Poetry 69 (1946):
140-41. First stanza reprinted in SR 17 (1981): 708.

369. "To the Holy Spirit: From a Deserted Graveyard in the
Salinas Valley." Poetry 69 (1946): 138-39. ThP, Mod,
CP, MVE, CP(1960), MAP, PE, FOP, QR, VGW, PAM,
CPYW, PPO. Also separately published (see item 26).

Reprinted in Perspectives USA, no. 7 (1953), pp. 22-23. Reprinted with translation into French as "Au Saint Esprit: D'un Cimetière Abandonné dans la Vallée de Salinas" in Profils, no. 4 (1953), pp. 26-29. Reprinted with translation into German as "An Den Heiligen Geist: Von einem verlassenen Friedhof im Tale von Salinas" in Perspektiven, no. 4 (1953), pp. 22-25. Reprinted with translation into Italian as "Allo Spirito Santo: Da un Cimitero Abbandonato in Valle Salinas" in Prospetti, no. 4 (1953), pp. 48-53. Reprinted in Stanford Today 1 (1962): n. p.

370. "An Ode on the Despoilers of Learning in an American University." Poetry 71 (1947): 12-13. CP, Exp, CP(1960), SP, CPYW.

371. "A Song in Passing." ThP, CP, CP(1960), VGW, CPYW.

372. "A Fragment." ThP, CP, PE, CP(1960), CPYW.

373. "To Herman Melville in 1951." PS, no. 1 (1953), p. 21. CP, CP(1960), CPYW.

374. "To the Moon." PS, no. 1 (1953), p. 21. CP, CP(1960), HIP, CPYW. Reprinted in SR 17 (1981): 680.

375. "At the San Francisco Airport." HR 8 (1955): 57. CP(1960), HRA, Seq, FOP, QR, IP, RRHR, HIP, NOBA, CPYW, PPO. Reprinted in Stanford Today 1 (1962): n. p. Reprinted in Per Se 3 (1968): 40.

376. "A White Spiritual." Nation 185 (1957): 225.

377. "Two Old-Fashioned Songs" (I. 'Danse Macabre'; II. 'Dream Vision'). HR 10 (1957-58): 540-41. CP(1960), CPYW.

378. "To Herbert Dean Meritt, Professor of English Philology at Stanford University, on His Retirement." Philological Essays: Studies in Old and Middle English Language and Literature in Honour of Herbert Dean Meritt, Professor of English Philology, Stanford University. Edited by James L. Rosier. The Hague, Paris: Mouton, 1970, p. 7. CPYW. Quoted in SR 9 (1973): xxiii.

VI

POETRY TRANSLATIONS

379. "Ill-natured winter nights, Serpents of Alecto" (from the
     French of Pierre de Ronsard). Diadems and Fagots.
     Santa Fe, N. Mex.: privately printed, [1921], n. p.
     CPYW.

380. "Ah, long Winter nights, hang-women, give me now" (from
     the French of Pierre de Ronsard). Diadems and Fagots.
     Santa Fe, N. Mex.: privately printed, [1921], n. p.
     Poems, CPYW.

381. "Oh, why sleep, my soul, benumbed, with hidden face?"
     (from the French of Pierre de Ronsard). Diadems and
     Fagots. Santa Fe, N. Mex.: privately printed, [1921],
     n. p. CPYW.

382. "One has to leave his orchards and his gardens and his
     doors" (from the French of Pierre de Ronsard). Diadems
     and Fagots. Santa Fe, N. Mex.: privately printed,
     [1921], n. p. CPYW.

383. "A Sigh" (from the 19th Century French of Stéphane Mallar-
     mé). Forge 2 (1924): 9. Poems, CP, CP(1960), CPYW.

384. "Cossante" (from the 13th Century Gallician of Pero Meogo).
     Poetry 29 (1927): 302 (under title "Song of the Girl Who
     Tore Her Dress at the Spring"). Poems (under earlier
     title), CP, CP(1960), CPYW.

385. "Old Ballad" (from the Spanish). Poetry 29 (1927): 303.
     CPYW.

386. "The Skeleton Laborer" (from the 19th Century French of
     Charles Baudelaire). Gyr, [no. 2] (1929), p. 7. Poems,
     CP, CP(1960), CPYW. Reprinted in The Flowers of Evil:
     A Selection. Edited by Marthiel and Jackson Mathews.
     New York: New Directions, 1958, pp. 95, 97.

387. "The Lady's Farewell" (from the 13th Century Gallician of

Nuño Fernández Torneol). Gyr, [no. 3] (1929), p. 8.
Poems, CP, CP(1960), CPYW.

388. "Green" (from the 19th Century French of Paul Verlaine).
Roon 2 (1930): 25. Poems, CP, CP(1960), CPYW.

389. "Poem in Autumn" (from the French of Charles Baudelaire).
Hesperian, [no. 2?] (1930), n. p. CPYW.

390. "Rome (from the 16th Century French of Joachim du Bellay).
Hesperian, [no. 2?] (1930), n. p. Poems, CP, CP(1960),
CPYW.

391. "Threnody for Stéphane Mallarmé" (from the 19th Century
French of Francis Vielé-Griffin). Hesperian, [no. 2?]
(1930), n. p. Poems, CPYW.

392. "The Toad" (from the French of Tristan Corbière). Hesperian, [no. 2?] (1930), n. p. CPYW.

393. "Cantabria" (from the 19th Century Spanish of Antonio de
Trueba). Poems, CP, CP(1960), CPYW.

394. "Death's Warning" (from the 17th Century Spanish of Francisco de Quevedo y Villegas). Poems, CP, CP(1960),
CPYW.

395. "Marine" (from the 19th Century French of Arthur Rimbaud).
Poems, CP, CP(1960), CPYW.

396. "Poem" (from the 16th Century Spanish of Saint Theresa).
Poems, CP, CP(1960), CPYW.

397. "Reflections" (from the 17th Century French of Madame des
Houlières). Poems, CP, CP(1960), CPYW.

398. "Sonnet" (from the Spanish of Lupercio Leonardo de Argensola). PNR 5 (1978): 26. CPYW.

399. "The Nemean Lion" (from the French of José Maria de Heredia). PNR 5 (1978): 26. CPYW.

400. "Forgetfulness" (from the French of José Maria de Heredia).
PNR 5 (1978): 27. CPYW.

401. "Rondeau of Antique Love" (from the 16th Century French of
Clément Marot). CPYW.

402. "Song" (from the 16th Century French of Clément Marot).
CPYW.

403. "The Lost Secret" (from the 19th Century French of Marceline Desbordes-Valmore). CPYW.

VII

RECORDED READINGS

404. Twentieth Century Poetry in English: Recordings of Poets
Reading Their Own Poems. Library of Congress: PL 7.
1-12" LP, mono. Issued earlier as 1-12" 78 rpm: LC
1709. Recorded in 1945.
CONTENTS: "Sir Gawaine and the Green Knight"; "John
Sutter"; "Time and the Garden"; "The California Oaks. "

405. Yvor Winters Reading His Poems. Library of Congress:
LWO 2689, reel 11, 1-7", 7.5 ips. Recorded in 1945.
CONTENTS: "A Song of Advent"; "The Barnyard"; "The
Goatherds"; "Song of the Trees"; "To William Dinsmore
Briggs Conducting His Seminar"; "The Fall of Leaves";
"The Journey"; "Midas"; "Sonnet to the Moon"; "Heracles";
"The Old Age of Theseus"; "To David Lamson"; "John
Day, Frontiersman"; "John Sutter"; "The California Oaks";
"On Rereading a Passage from John Muir"; "The Man-
zanita"; "Sir Gawaine and the Green Knight"; "Much in
Little"; "An Elegy for the U.S.N. Dirigible Macon"; "Time
and the Garden"; "A Prayer for My Son"; "A Summer
Commentary"; "On a Portrait of a Scholar of the Italian
Renaissance"; "Summer Noon: 1941"; "To a Military
Rifle 1942. "

406. Yvor Winters Reads from His Own Works. Yale Series of
Recorded Poets. Jacket commentary by Alvin B. Kernan.
Carillon: YP 309. Decca 9136. 1-12" LP, mono.
CONTENTS: "The Cold"; "Quod Tegit Omnia"; "The Fall
of Leaves"; "Inscription for a Graveyard"; "The Slow Paci-
fic Swell"; "On a View of Pasadena from the Hills"; "A
Vision"; "On Teaching the Young"; "The Old Age of The-
seus"; "Lee Anderson and Yvor Winters" (an interview);
"The California Oaks"; "The Manzanita"; "Sir Gawaine
and the Green Knight"; "A Spring Serpent"; "Much in Lit-
tle"; "A Prayer for My Son"; "On the Portrait of a Scholar of the Italian Renaissance"; "Summer Noon: 1941";
"To a Military Rifle 1942"; "To the Holy Spirit"; "At the
San Francisco Airport. "

407. <u>Yvor Winters Reading His Poems</u>.   The Spoken Arts Treas-
     ury of 100 Modern American Poets.   Spoken Arts: SA
     1046, vol. 7.
     CONTENTS: "Before Disaster"; "Orpheus: In Memory
     of Hart Crane"; "John Sutter"; "Time and the Garden";
     "A Summer Commentary"; "To the Moon."

VIII.

REVIEWS

*   "An Orthodox Preacher." Review of The Solitary, by James Oppenheim. (Cited above as item 38.)

*   "A Cool Master." Review of Collected Poems, by Edwin Arlington Robinson. (Cited above as item 39.)

*   "A Distinguished Young Man." Review of The Living Frieze, by Mark Turbyfill. (Cited above as item 40.)

*   "A Woman with a Hammer." Review of The Contemplative Quarry and the Man with a Hammer. (Cited above as item 41.)

*   "Carlos Williams' New Book." Review of Sour Grapes, by William Carlos Williams. (Cited above as item 42.)

*   "Under the Tree." Review of Under the Tree, by Elizabeth Madox Roberts. (Cited above as item 43.)

*   "A Prejudiced Opinion." Review of Fringe, by Pearl Andelson. (Cited above as item 44.)

*   "Holiday and Day of Wrath." Review of Observations, by Marianne Moore. (Cited above as item 46.)

*   "Streets in the Moon." Review of Streets in the Moon, by Archibald MacLeish. (Cited above as item 48.)

*   "Hart Crane's Poetry." Review of White Buildings, by Hart Crane. (Cited above as item 50.)

*   "The Indian in English." Review of The Path on the Rainbow: An Anthology of Songs and Chants from the Indians of North America, edited by George W. Cronyn, and American Love Lyrics and Other Verse, selected by Nellie Barnes. (Cited above as item 51.)

* "Fugitives." Review of Fugitives: An Anthology of Verse. (Cited above as item 52.)

* "In Vindication of Poetry." Review of Mr. Pope and Other Poems, by Allen Tate. (Cited above as item 53.)

* "The Poetry of Louise Bogan." Review of Dark Summer. (Cited above as item 54.)

* "The Poetry of Malcolm Cowley." Review of Blue Juniata, by Malcolm Cowley. (Cited above as item 55.)

* "Edmund Wilson as Poet." Review of Poets, Farewell, by Edmund Wilson. (Cited above as item 61.)

* "Robinson Jeffers." Review of Dear Judas, by Robinson Jeffers. (Cited above as item 62.)

* "Foster Damon's Second Book." Review of Tilted Moons, by S. Foster Damon. (Cited above as item 63.)

* "Merrill Moore's Poems." Review of The Noise That Time Makes, by Merrill Moore. (Cited above as item 64.)

* "Recent Verse." Review of Selected Poems, by Conrad Aiken; O City, Cities!, by R. Ellsworth Larsson; and High Falcon, by Leonie Adams. (Cited above as item 65.)

* "The Progress of Hart Crane." Review of The Bridge, by Hart Crane. (Cited above as item 66.)

* "Major Fiction." Review of Flowering Judas, by Katherine Anne Porter. (Cited above as item 69.)

* "The Symbolist Influence." Review of L'Influence du Symbolisme Française sur la Poésie Américaine, by René Taupin. (Cited above as item 70.)

* "Traditional Mastery." Review of The Shorter Poems of Robert Bridges. (Cited above as item 71.)

* "Poets and Others." Review of Poems, 1928-31, by Allen Tate; Poems, by Wilfrid Owen; The Signature of Pain, by Alan Porter; Thrust at the Sky, by MacKnight Black; The Dark Land, by Kathleen T. Young; Thurso's Landing, by Robinson Jeffers; Mortal Triumph, by Selden Rodman; Now That the Hawthorne Blossoms, by Althea Bass; and The Flowering Stone, by George Dillon. (Cited above as item 72.)

* "The Objectivists." Review of An "Objectivists" Anthology. (Cited above as item 74.)

*   "T. Sturge Moore." Review of The Poems of T. Sturge Moore, vols. 1 and 2. (Cited above as item 75.)

*   "The Oxford Book of Sixteenth Century Verse." Review of The Oxford Book of Sixteenth Century Verse. (Cited above as item 76.)

*   Review of Collected Poems, by E. E. Cummings. (Cited above as item 90.)

*   "Poetry of Feeling." Review of The Complete Collected Poems, by William Carlos Williams. (Cited above as item 91.)

*   "In Plato's Garden." Review of In Plato's Garden: Poems 1928-1939, by Lincoln Fitzell. (Cited above as item 96.)

*   "The Poems of Theodore Roethke." Review of Open House, by Theodore Roethke. (Cited above as item 97.)

*   "Three Poets." Review of Losses, by Randall Jarrell; The Dispossessed, by John Berryman; and The Judge Is Fury, by J. V. Cunningham. (Cited above as item 107.)

*   "A Discovery." Review of The Cricket, by Frederick Goddard Tuckerman. (Cited above as item 111.)

*   "English Literature in the Sixteenth Century." Review of English Literature in the Sixteenth Century, by C. S. Lewis; Sixteenth Century English Poetry, edited by Norman E. McClure; and Sixteenth Century English Prose, edited by Karl J. Holzknecht. (Cited above as item 113.)

*   "The Poetry of Edgar Bowers." Review of The Form of Loss, by Edgar Bowers. (Cited above as item 114.)

IX

BRIEF NOTES, LETTERS TO PERIODICALS, MISCELLANEOUS

408. "A Poet's Handbook." Letter to the editor. <u>Poetry</u> 14
(1919): 346.
Suggests briefly that a handbook providing poets with basic
facts about natural science "would be of greater service to
the muse than the perpetuation of masterpieces!"

409. "Mr. Winters' Metrics." Letter to the editor. <u>SRL</u>, 4
October 1930, p. 188.
Replies briefly to William Rose Benet's request, in his review of <u>The Proof</u> (see item 485), for an explanation of the
metrical theory according to which Winters' free verse was
written. Explains free verse metrics in terms similar to
those used in <u>Primitivism and Decadence</u>. (See item 5.)

410. Letter to the editors. <u>H&H</u> 6 (1933): 323.
Replies to Basil Bunting's letter criticizing "Y. Winters'
flat verse" (see item 722) and Winters' review of the Objectivists (see item 74): "Mr. Bunting appears to offer me
some kind of challenge. I shall be glad to encounter him at
his own weapons--any kind of prose or verse--or, if he will
come to California, with or without gloves, Queensbury rules.
My weight is 180."

411. "Seven California Poets." <u>NR</u>, 7 November 1934, pp. 359-
60. A selection by Winters of poems by J. V. Cunningham, Howard Baker, Janet Lewis, Barbara F. Gibbs,
Don Stanford, Clayton Stafford, and Winters. Includes
by Winters: "John Day, Frontiersman."

412. Letter to the editor. <u>NR</u>, 2 June 1937, p. 104.
Replies to the editor's request for an explanation of his
poem, "Sir Gawayne and the Green Knight." Identifies the
knight as "a vegetation demon, a demon of growth (physical
growth), sense, nature in all its non-human signification,
tempting and trying a human, the human surviving more through
habitual balance than through perfect control at the height of
the temptation, but gradually recovering himself."

413. "Correspondence." SR 3 (1938): 829-30. Reply to Delmore Schwartz's review of PD.
Supports his earlier contention that Crane's verse is obscure through considering misinterpretations of the referent of the word, "numbers," in For the Marriage of Faustus and Helen. Had said earlier that it refers to numbers of people or to the mathematical abstractions of modern life. Schwartz had argued for the latter reading and another critic of Winters for the former. Neither is correct, and the word actually refers to "sparrow's wings." These misunderstandings validate the original objection to Crane's obscurity. (See items 649, 753.)

414. Reply to "Enquiry." Twentieth Century Verse, no. 12-13 (1938), p. 111.
Replies to three questions sent "to about twenty of the older poets": Is there a representative "American Poetry"? Or, "to put the question another way, do you think the American Renaissance of 1912 and the following years had permanent value?" Does the poet consider himself an American poet or a poet dissociated from nationality? Has American poetry during the last ten years shown any sign of development? Asserts that the restatement of the first question "is distinct from the first: the notion that [it] repeats the first displays lamentable ignorance," and goes on to describe briefly his own version of the history of nineteenth and twentieth century American poetry. (See items 5, 7.) Of the second question, states that "in so far as the question has meaning," he considers himself an American poet. In response to the third question, replies that most recent poets "are continuing the decay of the preceding two decades," and that the exceptions are "Howard Baker, Clayton Stafford, Allen Tate (in his more lucid moments), and J. V. Cunningham." Mentions also as "excellent poetry that doesn't fit into the scheme of the questions," some of the work of Agnes Lee, Adelaide Crapsey, and S. Foster Damon.

415. Reply to "Yvor Winters, Anatomist of Nonsense," by Thomas Howells. Poetry 63 (1944): 291-93. (See item 577.)
Replies to Howells that he has committed factual errors in his statements about the various versions of "Sunday Morning" and that he has not understood the underlying criticisms of determinism intended in the statements regarding Eliot and Adams.

416. Letter to the editors. AL 16 (1944): 221-22.
States that Oscar Cargill's review of The Anatomy of Nonsense (see item 498) is professionally irresponsible and merely a statement of unsupported opinions, and defends the derivation of Adams' thought from that of Ockham. (See items 417, 723, 732.)

417. Letter to Clarence Gohdes, managing editor. AL 16 (1944):

223-24.
Replies to Gohdes' letter (see item 732) that his criticisms
of Cargill's review are justified, that the editors of American
Literature were irresponsible in accepting the review for
publication, and that the original letter, Gohdes' letter, and
the present reply should be published.

418. Letter to William Rose Benét. Quoted in Benét's column,
"The Phoenix Nest," in SRL, 8 March 1947, p. 48.
Refers to Benét's objections to his reading of Robinson's
"The Whip" in his book, Edwin Arlington Robinson, quoted
in "The Phoenix Nest," SRL, 18 January 1947, p. 32. Acknowledges that Benét's reading may be correct but presents
objections to it.

419. "Problems of a Family Man." Letter to the editors. Poetry
72 (1947): 285-86.
Responds to the criticisms expressed in W. T. Scott's review of his book on Edwin Arlington Robinson. (See item
651.) To Scott's objection that the book contains numerous
minor errors, replies that he did not receive proof-sheets
and that his teaching job, his family, and his involvement in
community affairs, make it difficult for him to be a perfect
proofreader.

420. Letter to the editors of SRL, written 9 October 1949. Published in The Case Against The Saturday Review of Literature. Chicago: Poetry, 1949, pp. 69-71. Reprinted in
The Survival Years: A Collection of American Writings of
the 1940's. Edited by Jack Salzman. New York: Pega-
sus, 1969, pp. 225-33. (Salzman's note reads in part:
"His letter to The Saturday Review of Literature was never
printed.")
Objects to Robert Hillyer's article on the Bollingen award in
which Hillyer imprecisely identifies Winters and the Fellows
of the Library of Congress who made the award as New
Critics and accuses them of numerous moral and scholarly
shortcomings and of being Fascists. Demands that the editors
of The Saturday Review of Literature publish his letter and
provide a public statement of the evidence on which Hillyer's
charges are based.

421. "A Protest." AmS 19 (1950): 227-30. Concerns "The New
Criticism and the Democratic Tradition," by Robert Gor-
ham Davis (see item 516); Davis's rebuttal follows on pp.
230-31 of this issue (see item 726); further remarks by
Winters appear in the Summer 1950 issue (see item 422).
States that Davis is unjustified in arguing "that the writers
he mentions are fascists or potential fascists." Asserts that
Davis's essay is "a disgrace to The American Scholar, to
Phi Beta Kappa, and to American scholarship."

422. Further remarks relating to "The New Criticism and the

Democratic Tradition." AmS 19 (1950): 380, 382.
Asserts that "R. G. Davis' reply to my protest is as evasive
as his original article." (See item 516.) Insists that Davis's
meaning is that the authors whom he names are fascists, "in
spite of the fact that Davis used considerable tact in the matter of hinting rather than stating."

423.   Instruction sheet to dog owners, in response to Ordinance
       no. 33 of the City of Los Altos, Calif., adopted 7 July
       1953.
Instructs dog owners of their rights and obligations under
Ordinance 33 which relates to a licensing tax on dogs, the
powers and duties of poundmasters, the running at large of
animals, and the disposition of the bodies of dead animals.
Information itemized under two headings: "How to Take
Care of Your Dog," and "What Can Happen to Your Dog."

PART TWO

Secondary Sources

X

BOOKS AND COLLECTIONS OF ESSAYS

424. Baxter, John. Shakespeare's Poetic Styles: Verse into Drama. London, Boston, Henley: Routledge & Kegan Paul, 1980, passim.

425. Brady, Frank, John Palmer, and Martin Price, eds. Literary Theory and Structure: Essays in Honor of William K. Wimsatt. New Haven and London: Yale University Press, 1973, passim.

426. Brooks, Cleanth. The Well Wrought Urn: Studies in the Structure of Poetry. New York: Harcourt Brace, 1947, pp. 239-42.
Objects to Winters' view that poetry has paraphrasable content: "to refer the structure of the poem to what is finally a paraphrase of the poem is to refer it to something outside the poem." Similarly, Winters' view of the poem as an act of moral judgment "ties aesthetic values to a moral system: poetry tends to become the handmaid of religion or philosophy, whether Christian, Marxist, or some other."

427. Brooks, Van Wyck. Opinions of Oliver Allston. New York: E. P. Dutton, 1941, pp. 220-21, 242-44.
Refers briefly to Winters' critical evaluations and his analytical procedures, and objects to both.

428. Burke, Kenneth. Language as Symbolic Action: Essays on Life, Literature, and Method. Berkeley and Los Angeles: University of California Press, 1966, p. 486.
Mentions letter from Winters in which "Winters wrote me saying that he no longer puts much faith in either my terms or his as regards those early essays of ours."

429. Butterfield, R. W. The Broken Arc: A Study of Hart Crane. Edinburgh: Oliver & Boyd, 1969, passim.

430. Clark, David R., ed. Critical Essays on Hart Crane. Boston: G. K. Hall, 1982, passim.

431. Cosgrave, Patrick. The Public Poetry of Robert Lowell.
London: Victor Gollancz, 1970, passim.

432. Crane, Hart. The Letters of Hart Crane, 1916-1932.
Edited by Brom Weber. New York: Hermitage House,
1952, passim.

433. Crow, Charles L. Janet Lewis. Boise, Idaho: Boise
State University, 1980, passim.

434. Davie, Donald. Ezra Pound: Poet as Sculptor. New York:
Oxford University Press, 1964, pp. 217-18, 229-30.
Replies to Winters' assertion that, in reading Pound's
Cantos, "we have no way of knowing whether we have had
an idea or not" by stating that Pound was not attempting to
express ideas but to present "a state of mind in which ideas
as it were tremble on the edge of expression."

435. _____. Ezra Pound. New York: Viking Press, 1976,
p. 75.
Refers briefly and disapprovingly to Winters' criticism of
Pound's Lagorguian irony. Asserts that Winters' view that
ideas are propositional keeps him from perceiving the dy-
namic nature of ideas in the Cantos and leads to his being
bored by the poem.

436. _____. The Poet in the Imaginary Museum: Essays of
Two Decades. New York: Persea Books, 1977, passim.

437. Davis, Dick. Wisdom and Wilderness: The Achievement of
Yvor Winters. Athens, Ga.: University of Georgia Press,
1983.
Provides a detailed and sensitive reading of the entire body
of Winters' poetry and prose. Sees Winters' achievement in
terms of a fundamental dichotomy between being and finding,
between wilderness and wisdom, between "the evocation of
the American wilderness" and "the formulation of the nature
of human wisdom." Moving from the first half of this dichotomy to the second half, Winters also moved from poetry to
criticism. Throughout, Winters was essentially a poet, however. "I have treated Winters not as a critic who happened
to write poetry but as a poet who also wrote criticism."
(See items 514, 515.)

438. Denver Quarterly 2 (1967). An issue devoted to Alan Swal-
low, Winters' publisher.
Contains tributes, essays, and poems by Edgar Bowers, J.
V. Cunningham, Donald F. Drummond, Mark Harris, Gene
Lundahl, Thomas McGrath, Frederick Manfred, Anaïs Nin,
Martin Robbins, Alan Stephens, Allen Tate, Robert Penn
Warren, and Frank Waters, and essays and poems by Alan
Swallow.

439. Eastman, Max. The Literary Mind: Its Place in an Age of
      Science. New York and London: Scribner's, 1931, pp.
      111, 114-15.
      Describers Winters as a believer in poetry as a moral dis-
      cipline.

440. Fraser, G. S. Vision and Rhetoric: Studies in Modern Po-
      etry. London: Faber & Faber, 1959, pp. 254-59.
      States that "where romantic criticism usually starts with put-
      ting a main emphasis on the notion of the image, anti-
      romantic criticism tends to start with the notion of the state-
      ment." Objects to Winters' distinction between concept and
      motive (see item 99) and states that the language of poetry
      is not a matter of referent but is "language by itself."

441. Hamovitch, Mitzi Berger, ed. The Hound & Horn Letters.
      Foreword by Lincoln Kirstein. Athens, Ga.: University
      of Georgia Press, 1982, pp. 16-18 and passim.
      Recounts the details of Winters' relationship with the Hound
      and Horn, and describes the contents of his letters to Kir-
      stein. Winters' letters are not quoted, since a clause in his
      will forbids their publication until twenty-five years after his
      death. "One day, some fortunate editor will have access to
      Winters' letters, highly judgmental, at times vitriolic, always
      vigorous, and filled with his dogmatic and precise evalua-
      tions."

442. Hazo, Samuel. Hart Crane: An Introduction and Interpreta-
      tion. New York: Barnes & Noble, 1963, passim.

443. Horton, Philip. Hart Crane: The Life of an American Poet.
      New York: W. W. Norton, 1937, passim.

444. Isaacs, Elizabeth. An Introduction to the Poetry of Yvor
      Winters. Chicago; London; Athens, Ohio: Swallow Press/
      Ohio University Press, 1981.
      Summarizes Winters' life and maintains that most of his po-
      etic themes "are involved in one way or another with 'moral'
      attitudes." Winters' poetry constitutes a spiritual autobiog-
      raphy: the poet first perceives his "identity in the universe,"
      goes on to appraise the forces of "truth, wisdom, and jus-
      tice" as these are ranged against "evil, ignorance, and in-
      justice," recognizes the "relationship of man to nature,"
      develops stoic strength, engages in a "spiritual search for
      the ultimate mystery," and finally expresses his "desire for
      timelessness."
            Reviewed in Choice, 18 May 1981; NYTBR, 5 July
      1981; PNR 22 (1981); TLS, 16 August 1981; Antigonish Review,
      no. 48 (1982); Canadian Review of American Studies 13 (1982).

445. Janssens, G. A. M. The American Literary Review: A
      Critical History 1920-1950. The Hague, Paris: Mouton,
      1968, passim.

446. Jordan, Elijah. _Essays in Criticism._ Chicago: University of Chicago Press, 1952, passim.

447. Kermode, Frank. _Romantic Image._ New York: Macmillan, 1957, pp. 150-53, 156.
Summarizes, with qualified approval, Winters' objections to Eliot's defense of the romantic image and to Ransom's use of the terms, "structure" and "texture."

448. Krieger, Murray. _The New Apologists for Poetry._ Minneapolis: University of Minnesota Press, 1956, passim.

449. Leavis, F. R. _The Great Tradition._ London: Chatto & Windus, 1948, pp. 10-11.
Notes briefly that in _Maule's Curse_ Winters "brings out admirably" Henry James's relationship to the American tradition of Hawthorne and Melville.

450. Leibowitz, Herbert A. _Hart Crane: An Introduction to the Poetry._ New York: Columbia University Press, 1968, passim.

451. Lemon, Lee T. _The Partial Critics._ New York: Oxford University Press, 1965, passim.

452. Lewis, R. W. B. _The Poetry of Hart Crane: A Critical Study._ Princeton University Press, 1967, passim.

453. Lohf, Kenneth A. and Eugene P. Sheehy. _Yvor Winters: A Bibliography._ Denver: Alan Swallow, 1959.
Lists primary and secondary material; "aims to be complete through 1957, with some 1958 entries."

454. Magner, James E., Jr. _John Crowe Ransom: Critical Principles and Preoccupations._ The Hague, Paris: Mouton, 1971, pp. 41-45.
Replies to Winters' criticisms of Ransom's nominalism (see item 7) by saying that Ransom is only dispositionally a nominalist but is in practice, like Aquinas, a moderate realist. Nevertheless, "Winters has driven through a weak spot in the Ransom armor: Ransom's epistemology. And Winters' lance has been the strong weapon of his logic."

455. Meiners, R. K. _The Last Alternatives: A Study of the Works of Allen Tate._ Denver: Alan Swallow, 1963, passim.

456. O'Connor, William Van. _An Age of Criticism: 1900-1950._ Chicago: Henry Regnery, 1952, pp. 104-6.
Believes that much of Winters' theory of literature is fallacious, that _Primitivism and Decadence_ lacks an "exact center," that "motive does not exist until the poem is at least partly written," that Winters' scansions "do not allow

for the possibility of variant readings," and that "the source of Winters' assurances about moral issues is never made clear."

457. Parkinson, Thomas. Hart Crane and Yvor Winters: Their Literary Correspondence. Berkeley, Los Angeles, London: University of California Press, 1978.
Presents the surviving letters from Hart Crane to Yvor Winters along with an account of the probable content of Winters' side of the correspondence as it can be derived from the letters that Winters wrote to Allen Tate during the period of the correspondence with Crane, from discussions with Mrs. Janet Winters and others, from the evidence of Winters' publications, and from internal evidence in Crane's letters. The correspondence provides the necessary background for an understanding of Winters' largely negative response to The Bridge (see items 66, 104) in the review of 1930 and in the essay on Crane in In Defense of Reason. (See items 620, 621, 622, 665.)
Reviewed in AL 51 (1979); JEGP 78 (1979); SR 17 (1981).

458. Paul, Sherman. Hart's Bridge. Urbana, Chicago, London: University of Illinois Press, 1972, passim.

459. Pinsky, Robert. The Situation of Poetry: Contemporary Poetry and Its Traditions. Princeton: Princeton University Press, 1976, pp. 69-71. Dedicated to the memory of B. E. and of A. Y. W.
Discusses, as one of a number of modern poems that treat the natural universe as alien, Winters' "Sir Gawaine and the Green Knight."

460. Powell, Grosvenor. Language as Being in the Poetry of Yvor Winters. Baton Rouge and London: Louisiana State University Press, 1980.
Examines the poetry of Winters in the context of the traditions and philosophical issues pertinent to its appreciation. Shows that the issues that are resolved rationally in the criticism are also the central issues in the poetry. Winters thought of poetry as a discipline of contemplation and as a means of reeducating the human spirit and leading it away from romantic attitudes which he thought pernicious and which pervade our culture. (See items 630, 631, 632, 633, 634, 635.)
Reviewed in Library Journal, August 1980; TLS, 28 November 1980; PNR 22 (1981); SR 17 (1981); Journal of Modern Literature 8 (1981); JAS 16 (1982); Christianity and Literature, n. d.; Canadian Review of American Studies 13 (1982).

461. Press, John. Rule and Energy: Trends in British Poetry Since the Second World War. London: Oxford University Press, 1963, passim.

462. Pritchard, William H. Lives of the Modern Poets. New
       York: Oxford University Press, 1980, passim.

463. Rexroth, Kenneth. American Poetry in the Twentieth Cen-
       tury. New York: Herder & Herder, 1971, pp. 92-94.
       Regards Winters as "incomparably the best poet to have de-
       veloped in the post-war Chicago school centered in the Uni-
       versity," whose early Imagist poems "pushed the intense
       sensitivity of H. D. to the breaking point." His later and
       less impressive work is written in "a stark neo-classicism
       of his own invention."

464. Scott, Winfield Townley. A Dirty Hand: The Literary Note-
       books of Winfield Townley Scott. Austin and London:
       University of Texas Press, 1969, pp. 134-35.
       Dismisses Winters' criticism as "innocently dishonest, the
       work of a small writer who attempts to tear down all big
       writers and in the same process elevate a few other tiny
       writers. The real purpose is pathetic: to exalt by infer-
       ence his own value as a poet."

465. Sequoia 6 (1961). An Yvor Winters issue.
       Contains essays and poems by Steve Berry, J. V. Cunning-
       ham, Catherine Davis, Albert J. Guérard, Charles Gullans,
       Thom Gunn, Donald Hall, Philip Levine, Marianne Moore,
       Margaret Peterson, Judith Rascoe, Don Stanford, Alan
       Stephens, Alan Swallow, Allen Tate, Wesley Trimpi, and
       Yvor Winters.

466. Sexton, Richard J. The Complex of Yvor Winters' Criti-
       cism. The Hague and Paris: Mouton, 1973.
       Asserts that the "single purpose" of this study is "to pre-
       sent a comprehensive historical survey of the criticism of
       Yvor Winters.... The purpose of the study will be achieved
       if it serves as a basis for future explorations in depth of
       Winters." As a result of considering some one aspect of
       Winters' criticism instead of the total system, critics have
       misrepresented his position, Ransom labelling him a "logi-
       cal" critic, Wimsatt calling him "classical," Wellek "mod-
       ern," Hyman "evaluative," and O'Connor "analytical." The
       body of the books consists of an extended description of the
       contents of Winters' critical reviews, essays, and books.
              Reviewed in TLS, 3 August 1974; AL 46 (1975); SR
       11 (1975).

467. Smith, Bernard. Forces in American Criticism: A Study in
       the History of American Literary Thought. New York:
       Harcourt, Brace, 1939, passim.

468. Southern Review 17 (1981). An Yvor Winters issue.
       Contains essays and poems by Howard Baker, John Baxter,
       Ashley Brown, Turner Cassity, Terry Comito, Donald Davie,
       Dick Davis, Thomas D'Evelyn, Kenneth Fields, John Finlay,

Albert Guerard, Thom Gunn, David Levin, Raymond Oliver, Douglas Peterson, Helen Pinkerton, Grosvenor Powell, Steven Shankman, Donald E. Stanford, and Clive Wilmer.

469. Spears, Monroe K. Hart Crane. Minneapolis: University of Minnesota Press, 1965, passim.

470. Stanford, Donald E. In the Classic Mode: The Achievement of Robert Bridges. Newark: University of Delaware Press, 1978, passim.

471. Stoval, Floyd, ed. The Development of American Literary Criticism. Chapel Hill: University of North Carolina Press, 1955, passim.

472. Sutton, Walter. Modern American Criticism. Englewood Cliffs, N. J.: Prentice-Hall, 1963, pp. 127-35.
Asserts that Winters' moral and literary position is close to that of the theistic Humanist. Summarizes Winters' view of the nature and function of poetry and of the nature of the critical process. Objects that the act of judgment or evaluation in Winters' theory is "troublesome" and that Winters' standards are not always clear. In his treatment of specific writers to whom he objects, Winters' "view is too often a narrow one which fails to note compensating excellences and complexities that lie outside the scope of his interests." His criticism is valuable, however, "as a foil and a corrective to the theory and practice of the critics with whom he has identified himself."

473. Unterecker, John. Voyager: A Life of Hart Crane. New York: Farrar, Straus & Giroux, 1969, passim.

474. Van Deusen, Marshall. A Metaphor for the History of American Criticism. Essays and Studies on American Language and Literature, edited by S. B. Liljegren, no. 13. Lund: Carl Bloms Boktryckeri A.-B., 1961.
Summarizes the shifting relationships between language and reality in the history of ideas as it impinges on American literature from the Puritans through the New Critics. Acknowledges a debt to Winters' treatment of this material and emphasizes the same major writers: Emerson, Poe, Henry Adams, Babbitt, Cleanth Brooks, Ransom, Tate, and Blackmur. Concludes by agreeing with Winters that literature is a judgment of experience that is implicit within the literary work and not stated as an explicit system of moral values: "Winters knows that in art and life the final act of judgment is always a 'unique act,' and that it is enough for a system of values to be implicit in each judgment, measuring and checking the particular event, but in turn being modified and qualified by it."

475. Weber, Brom. Hart Crane: A Biographical and Critical Study. New York: Bodley Press, 1948, passim.

476. Wimsatt, W. K., Jr. The Verbal Icon: Studies in the Meaning of Poetry. Lexington, Ky.: University of Kentucky Press, 1954, passim.

XI

ESSAYS AND REVIEW-ARTICLES

477. Abood, Edward. "Some Observations on Ivor Winters."
    CR 11 (1957): 51-66.
    Examines the argument of "Problems for the Modern Critic
    of Literature." (See item 115.) Objects to Winters' un-
    fashionable critical judgments, to his distinction between
    prose and verse, and to his effort to arrange the various
    genres hierarchically. Argues that Winters puts undue em-
    phasis on language and does not consider the structural
    principles of the different forms. Winters' essay is, how-
    ever, "an attempt to cope with very real and persistent
    problems of literature."

478. Alvarez, A. "The Professional Critic." NS, 24 September
    1960, pp. 438-39. Reprinted as "Yvor Winters" in his
    Beyond All This Fiddle. London: Allen Lane, 1968:
    pp. 255-59.
    Contends that Winters is more impressive in his practice
    than in his theory. He was the first to show that Eliot's
    theories are Romantic and not Classical; and he praised
    Melville, James, Stevens, Crane, and Hawthorne before they
    were widely admired. Winters' insistence, however, on ra-
    tionality led him to reject the experimental in modern liter-
    ature and to prefer such undistinguished traditional poets as
    Robert Bridges, Adelaide Crapsey, Elizabeth Daryush, and
    T. Sturge Moore.

479. Andelson, Pearl. "One Poet Speaks for Himself." Poetry
    20 (1922): 342-44. Review of MS.
    States that "Yvor Winters is one of the rare American poets
    who are active critically, and whose theories are not laid
    by during the creative process."

480. Baker, Howard. "Yvor Winters' Stoicism." NR, 4 May
    1932, pp. 331-32. Review of J and Proof.
    Suggests that Winters' poems in traditional forms are an im-
    plicit criticism of romantic tradition. The poems are im-
    pressive technical accomplishments; their stoicism "comes

fundamentally from the Protestant tradition of the northern United States."

481. _____. "The Gyroscope." SR 17 (1981): 735-57.
Asserts that The Gyroscope "was the vehicle which Yvor Winters used to enunciate his abruptly matured thought and to demonstrate his equally decisive resolution of his own problems in writing poetry." Puts in the context of time and occasion Winters' objections to contemporary spiritual extroversion and emotionalism and his assertion of a classical frame of mind and the primacy of the rational in life and art. Discusses poems by such contributors as Winters, Janet Lewis, Grant H. Code, and Clayton Stafford. Describes experience as editor of the Magazine, an offshoot of The Gyroscope published between 1933 and 1935.

482. Barish, James A. "Yvor Winters and the Antimimetic Prejudice." NLH 2 (1971): 419-44.
Asserts that Winters cannot sympathize with mimesis "because he has from the outset declared the evaluation of experience, rather than experience itself, to be the valuable thing...." Winters' key terms are old-fashioned, belong to an obsolete faculty psychology, and are useless for the analysis of character. He fails to understand the conventions of drama and analyzes plays using only standards that he has established for analyzing poems.

483. Barrett, William. "Temptations of St. Yvor." KR 9 (1947): 532-51.
Defines Winters' moral theory as essentially a rejection of hedonism. Such a rejection cannot have meaning except as part of a religious position. Criticizes Winters' effort to find such a religious position in Thomism, and his effort to establish a moralistic position that does not derive in some sense from Plato. Raises questions as to how a poet's moral evaluation can arise from control of the details of form, and asserts that "moral evaluation, if it is there, must come as an explicit statement, or statements, about, or related to, the subject of the poem. This is what Winters must really mean...." Winters' particular judgments give an impression of startling idiosyncrasy and display his inability to appreciate the unpredictable ways in which forms develop historically. "Winters probably suffers most as a critic from a lack of this historical sense." (See items 60, 67, for Winters' discussion of morality and literature.)

484. Baxter, John. "Can Winters Mean What He Says?" SR 17 (1981): 833-50. Review of CPYW and Hart Crane and Yvor Winters: Their Literary Correspondence, by Thomas Parkinson.
Asserts, with reference to F. R. Leavis, that the question of a writers' sincerity is the central critical question. Vindicates Winters from the charge of insincerity through ex-

amining the complex texture of several of his poems. Maintains that, in the correspondence between Winters and Crane, it is Winters "who shows us what sincerity is by remaining true to the spirit of the correspondence as it has grown up between the two men, and it is Crane who violates it."

485. Benét, William Rose. "Round About Parnassus." SRL, 6 September 1930, p. 104. Review of The Proof.
Praises Winters' verse, but objects to arbitrariness of style and form: "his phrasing is often arresting, his impressions of natural things are sensitive, his metaphysics is interesting, but he often thwarts his effectiveness through mere singularity of presentation. Objects to the line divisions in the free verse of the first section of The Proof and asks a number of questions about details of punctuation and diction. "We ask to be informed. To us these matters seem arbitrary." (For Winters' response, see item 409.)

486. Blackmur, R. P. "A Critic and His Absolute." NR, 14 July 1937, pp. 284-85. Review of PD.
Objects to Winters' key evaluative terms on grounds that they are indefinable, but asserts that Winters is valuable when he ignores his critical standards and responds to poems in terms of his feelings. "When Mr. Winters is actually talking about the work of the American experimental poets, how it failed and even how it could have been improved, when he talks about meter and convention or any technical matter, he makes only normal mistakes and produces a great many pertinent and stimulating facts."

487. _____. "Note on Yvor Winters." Poetry 57 (1940): 144-52. Reprinted in his The Expense of Greatness. New York: Arrow Editions, 1940, pp. 167-75.
Maintains that Winters' insights into poetry and imaginative prose are extremely valuable, but that his systematization of these insights "makes an artificial barrier ... which obscures but does not touch the work he has actually performed." His greatest value lies in his deflating "the final value of poetry ... which fails to declare its subject."

488. _____. Review of IDR. Nation, 14 June 1947, pp. 718-19.
Describes Winters' criticism as "a very good reminder of the rational and formal qualities present, and highly valued, in every literature except our own."

489. _____. "John Wheelwright and Dr. Williams." Language as Gesture: Essays in Poetry. New York: Harcourt Brace, 1952, pp. 347-51.
Expresses skepticism as to the validity of Winters' attempt to scan the free verse of W. C. Williams: "I cannot follow the discussion myself, preferring to believe (until I can follow it) that Dr. Williams' astonishing success comes from

the combination of a good ear for speech cadence and for
the balance of meaning and sound, plus a facility for the
double effect of weight and speed." (See item 5 for a discussion of the scansion of free verse.)

490.   Bloom, Harold. "The Central Man: Emerson, Whitman,
        Wallace Stevens." Massachusetts Review 7 (1966): 23-42.
        Mentions Winters briefly as "too majestic a moralist to be
        accepted as a judicial [sic] critic," but one who did see
        Emerson, Whitman, Stevens, and Hart Crane as a continu-
        ous tradition and who saw all poetry in English since the
        mid-eighteenth century as essentially romantic. He de-
        scribes accurately and states his dislikes clearly.

491.   Bloomingdale, Judith. "Three Decades in Periodical Criti-
        cism on Hart Crane's The Bridge." Papers of the Bib-
        liographical Society of America 57 (1963): 360-71.
        Includes numerous references to Winters' critical reactions
        to The Bridge.

492.   Bogan, Louise. Review of GW. NY, 22 July 1944, pp. 57-
        58. Reprinted as "Yvor Winters" in Selected Criticism:
        Poetry and Prose. New York: Noonday Press, 1955,
        pp. 269-71.
        Praises Winters as a poet of "untouchable probity and dis-
        tilled power."

493.   Brooks, Cleanth. "Cantankerous and Other Critics." KR 6
        (1944): 282-88. Review of AN.
        Describes Winters as logically rigorous, intelligent, and
        cantankerous. Winters has stated the negative case against
        Henry Adams well, but his treatment of Wallace Stevens,
        T. S. Eliot, and John Crowe Ransom is damaged by his
        refusal to "exert that effort of imaginative comprehension
        which he possesses ... in trying to understand what the
        critic is saying."

494.   _____. "Implications of an Organic Theory of Poetry."
        English Institute Essays. New York: Columbia University
        Press, 1958, pp. 53-79.
        Categorizes Winters as a critic who believes that poetry is
        cognitive and that the content of feeling in a poem is con-
        trolled by the rational content. Asserts that Winters' in-
        sistence on the dualism of form and content makes it doubt-
        ful that he can maintain as well a theory of organic form,
        although Winters' belief that poetry provides more than prop-
        ositional truth and is unified on the level of feeling implies
        such a theory.

495.   Brown, Ashley. "The Critical Legacy of Yvor Winters."
        SR 17 (1981): 729-34.
        Discusses question of the usefulness of Winters' criticism to
        the contemporary critic and poet. He was a precocious poet

who, at the age of twenty-one, "was as alert as anyone to
the new ways of writing poetry in the 1920's," and he was
a precocious critic who recognized a year before the first
publication of Harmonium the merits of Wallace Stevens.
He went on to develop beyond modernism in both mediums.
He made valuable contributions in the theory of meter and
form and in the application of the history of ideas to the
understanding of literature. He "based his entirely consistent view of English poetry on a certain historical development: the decline of traditional structure based on logic, in
favor of the structure of revery or association."

496.   Campbell, Gladys. "Some Recollections of the Poetry Club
         at the University of Chicago." Poetry 107 (1965): 110-17.
       Refers briefly to Winters' involvement with the Poetry Club.

497.   Campbell, Harry M. "Academic Criticism on Henry Adams:
         Confusion about Chaos." Midcontinent American Studies
         Journal 7 (1966): 3-14.
       Maintains that Winters often misread Henry Adams as when
       he asserts that Adams' morality "aims at loss of balance"
       where Adams had been simply stating his disillusionment with
       modern psychology as a possible source of unity. Identifies
       Winters' theory "which determines truth by what it promises
       toward insuring our sanity" with Pragmatism and says that
       Adams would have scorned such a view. Since Adams some-
       times defends his preferences, he is not, as Winters main-
       tains, a relativist. (See item 7 for Winters' discussion of
       Adams.)

498.   Cargill, Oscar. Review of AN. AL 15 (1944): 432-34.
         (See item 416 for Winters' reply; see also items 417,
         723, 7.)
       Objects that Winters, in defending himself from Ransom's
       criticisms, does not evaluate "from a recognizably moral
       point of view," that he is journalistic, that he should not
       compare Wallace Stevens to W. C. Bryant or derive the
       thought of Henry Adams from that of William Ockham.

499.   Carruth, Hayden. "The University and the Poet." Poetry
         75 (1949): 89-93. (See item 109 for Winters' reply.)
       Takes issue with Winters' contention in the "Post Scripta" to
       The Anatomy of Nonsense that the academic profession is an
       appropriate one for poets and one that will improve the qual-
       ity of the poetry produced. (See item 7.) Argues that there
       are a large number of poets in the universities not because
       these men feel a strong academic vocation but merely be-
       cause their particular bookish talents are only marketable
       within the universities. Academic duties deprive the poet
       of the intellectual solitude that he requires, and the academic
       institution is likely to prove an unhealthy sanctuary from en-
       gagement with life. Although "the university may profit from
       the poet, the poet can derive little benefit from the univer-
       sity."

500. _____. "A Location of J. V. Cunningham." MQR 11
(1972): 75-83.
Argues that, although Winters and Cunningham shared certain principles regarding the form and structure of poetry,
the latter was not a disciple of the former. "In styles,
tones, modes of feeling, and topical preoccupations, the two
are not only distinct but far apart." Whereas Winters was
principally influenced by nineteenth century French poetry,
Cunningham derives largely from Latin and Renaissance literature and the Jonsonian epigram.

501. Casey, John. "Reason Defended: Yvor Winters and the Nature of Criticism." The Language of Criticism. London:
Methuen, 1966, pp. 120-39.
Regards as central to Winters' thought the "idea of the sev-
erance of things which, if they are to make sense ... should
be intimately connected." Morality is dissociated from the
Aristotelian-Thomistic tradition that alone can give it meaning, emotions are separated from concepts, and ethical
choice detached from manners. Considers this approach the
"fundamental fallacy" in Winters' thought. On the highest
level of abstraction, it leads Winters to the "idea that particular judgements, if they are to be objective, have to be
deduced from general principles." Believes that there are
no general laws that can serve the function of providing
critical absolutes: "to defend a judgment of a poem, one
has to go on describing it, relating it to other poems and
so on, until the person one is trying to convince is satis-
fied." (See item 99 for Winters' defense of absolutes.)

502. Cassity, Turner. "Notes from a Conservatory." SR 17
(1981): 694-706.
Describes his experience as a student in Winters' writing
class and of Winters as a practical teacher, concerned with
the difficulty and importance of poetry, undogmatic and in-
tent on teaching the craft of metrical writing. Regarding
structure, Winters taught that every detail must be functional.
This emphasis on perfection of language and structure led,
in the work of his students, to an exploration of the traditional subjects of lyric poetry, self and nature, rather than
the wider ranges of prosaic material made available by the
plain style. Winters' concern with metrical precision,
"something to give every syllable an exact weight, and only
that weight," produced rhetorical intensities that were balanced, however, by the virtues of plainness. "The best
piece of advice he gave is that poetry is not a career."

503. Comito, Terry. "Winters' 'Brink.'" SR 17 (1981): 851-72.
Suggests that "Winters wrote only one story because he had
only one story to write." Winters' concern is not with the
merely psychological; he is concerned with the place of human consciousness and will within a universe of matter. "If
force or matter is indeed, as Winters sometimes appeared

to suggest, a kind of deity, then man defines himself in Promethean opposition." The something that tries to possess the narrator in the story is "demonic because it is not more than human but less." Concludes that the transcendence of the Emersonian mystic is a solipsistic merging with this demonic element and a loss of the human self. "The hallucinatory appearance of the face in the window suggests that at such moments of Emersonian transcendence the 'self' becomes as insubstantial as the world, mere line and shadow, the intersection of two bright voids." (See item 630.)

504. Cunningham, J. V. "Obscurity and Dust." Poetry 40 (1932): 163-65. Review of J.
Notes that, in The Journey, Winters has escaped the limitations of a poetry of pure ecstasy of the sort one finds in Crane and Hopkins through adopting the heroic couplet, a form that makes possible a more inclusive subject matter and more prosaic effects. Winters has a talent for "adopting a poetic form, realizing the experience it offers, and deliberately choosing another and different one."

505. _____. "The 'Gyroscope' Group." Bookman 75 (1932): 703-8.
Describes the members of the group associated with the mimeographed quarterly, The Gyroscope, and the effect of their personal association as a group. The members of the group were in agreement on critical principles and questions of style and in their rejection of romantic and modernist attitudes but were not committed as a group to a political program or a particular subject matter. The principal writers discussed are Janet Lewis, Howard Baker, Achilles Holt, and Yvor Winters.

506. Davie, Donald. "Editorial." PNR 4 (1977): 1-2.
Mentions Winters as a writer who "even in his lifetime enjoyed a better press over here than in his native U.S.A., rather surprisingly, since he never visited these shores, and in his assessment of nineteenth-century poetry he conspicuously slighted the British performance in favour of the Americans."

507. _____. "On a Wrong Track." PNR 4 (1977): 46-48.
Review of Ten English Poets, edited by Michael Schmidt. Objects to the influence of Winters on the diction of some of the poets included in Ten English Poets. (See item 752.)

508. _____. "The Poetry of Yvor Winters." PNR 5 (1978): 24-26. Reprinted as the introduction to CPYW. (See item 30.)
Regards Winters as essentially a poet for whom poetry is considered rather than unconsidered utterance, but believes nevertheless that it is important to ignore Winters' critical

statements in approaching his poetry. One of Winters'
strongest poetic impulses is "the Virgilian _pietas_" towards
one's native or adopted land, a powerful feeling that finds
no justification in his criticism. Because Winters "is so
much a poet of his nation, his region, and his time," he
would not be "a good model for young poets of today to
emulate."

509. _____. "Winters and Leavis: Memories and Reflections."
SewR 87 (1979): 608-18. Reprinted in part in his These
the Companions: Recollections. Cambridge: Cambridge
University Press, 1982, pp. 108-16.
Recalls in some detail two meetings with Winters, one in
Santa Barbara in 1958 and one in Los Altos in 1967, the
summer before Winters' death. Finds in the work of both
Winters and Leavis a "theological" energy; both are puritan-
ical in their commitment to artistic--more than to intellectual
or religious--values.

510. _____. "John Peck's Shagbark." Trying to Explain.
Ann Arbor: University of Michigan Press, 1979, pp.
174-78.
Refers briefly to Peck's "The Upper Trace," which is in-
scribed "for Y.W." Speaks of Winters "as on the whole a
poet of stone or of the lapidary effect" and states that "poem
after poem by Winters enacts a drama in which the precarious solidity of stony land is threatened and undermined by
ocean, destructively fluid."

511. _____. "Homage to Cowper." PNR 6 (1980): 21-24.
Refers briefly to Winters' discussion of "the plain style" in
English poetry.

512. _____. "F. W. Bateson--in Memoriam." PNR 7 (1980):
10-12.
Quotes Winters' praise in Forms of Discovery of Bateson's
English Poetry: A Critical Introduction, and moves associ-
atively from his memories of Bateson to his memories of
Winters. Asserts that Winters, "as politically naive as only
a Rooseveltian liberal of his generation could be," practiced,
without knowing what he was doing, "the stratagem of seem-
ing to exalt poetic utterance, by detaching it from the socio-
political context in which it was uttered." It is partly to
this failure to recognize the social nature of language that we
can attribute Winters' "elevating the history of ideas into a
privileged status above all other kinds of history--above social, political, economic history."

513. _____. "Yvor Winters and the History of Ideas." SR 17
(1981): 723-28.
Objects to Winters' approach to literary forms through the
history of ideas because this approach has "done more to
empty literary forms of moral significance than social history

has." Assumes that Winters' evaluation of British poets is based on the same scheme as that applied to American literature, and criticizes him for applying the history of ideas as it has developed in America to the evaluation of poets in England where ideas have developed differently. Winters' critical formulas are too simple because they do not mention the particulars to which they refer. Forms of Discovery "is grotesque, a disaster" and the value judgments therein expressed represent aberrations of Winters' old age. As an American, Winters is only competent to judge the poetry of his own country.

514. Davis, Dick. "Limits: An Essay on Yvor Winters and Ludwig Wittgenstein." PNR 4 (1977): 21-25.
Argues that both Winters and Wittgenstein underwent a similar intellectual and spiritual development. Both, in their early work, expressed a solipsistic mysticism in an elliptical and private language. Both abandoned this early position and turned to a more public language expressing a distrust of mysticism and a rejection of transcendental meanings behind phenomena. For both, the world is "real" and means itself.

515. _____. "Turning Metaphysician: Winters' Change of Direction." SR 17 (1981): 781-802.
Suggests that the stylistic changes occurring in Winters' poetry after 1928 resulted from a psychological crisis that is chronicled in "The Brink of Darkness." Winters rejected solipsistic mysticism and affirmed an Aristotelian-Thomistic metaphysical position that protected him from the "metaphysical horror of modern thought" projected by the earlier position. Discusses "Statement of Purpose" and, in great detail, "The Extension and Reintegration of the Human Spirit Through the Poetry Mainly French and American Since Poe and Baudelaire." (See items 56, 60.)

516. Davis, Robert Gorham. "The New Criticism and the Democratic Tradition." AmS 19 (1949-50): 9-19.
Argues that the New Criticism is part of an international conservative movement extending over at least two centuries that is fascistic and anti-American in its opposition to liberal tradition. (See items 421, 726.)

517. Deutsch, Babette. "Poets and Some Others." Bookman 67 (1928): 441-43. Review of BH.
States of Winters' poetry that there is "an integrity about it which derives from the poet's metaphysical passion--a passion colored by sharp apprehension of physical things, and having its issue in a profound disenchantment with the world."

518. D'Evelyn, Thomas. "The Brink of Darkness: Mallarmé and Winters." SR 17 (1981): 887-906.
Argues that Winters "felt the full horror of the symbolist

state of mind and, through his post-symbolist method, left
it completed for us to enter. In completing he has judged
it. The morality of poetry lies in the power of words to go
beyond expression to evaluation--to, in fact, do both simultaneously. A complete poem is one that exploits this double
force of language, the structure which allows language to
comment on itself. "

519. Dickey, James. Review of CP(1960). SewR 70 (1962): 496-
99. Reprinted as "Yvor Winters" in Babel to Byzantium:
Poets and Poetry Now. New York: Farrar, Straus &
Giroux, 1968, pp. 182-86.
Regards Winters as "the best example our time has to show
of the poet who writes by rules, knows just what he wants to
do when he begins a poem, and considers himself compelled
to stick to his propositions in everything he sets down. "
Prefers Winters' early poems to those written after 1928.
The early poems are influenced by Williams but are "better
than any poem Williams has ever written. "

520. _____. "The Winters Approach." The Suspect in Poetry.
Madison, Minn. : Sixties Press, 1964, pp. 12-15.
Reviews Donald Drummond's The Battlement and Ellen Kay's
A Local Habitation. Finds in both books the influence of
Winters essentially a negative one.

521. Dickinson-Brown, Roger. "The Art and Importance of N.
Scott Momaday." SR 14 (1978): 30-45.
Discusses briefly Momaday's employment of the post-Symbol-
ist method. (See item 15.)

522. Donahue, Charles. "Philosophy vs. Literature." Comm, 10
February 1939, p. 442. Review of MC.
Argues that Winters' approach to literature through the history of ideas is misunderstood because the poet normally
"expresses the accepted philosophical or theological doctrine
of his age. " Winters' insistence on reading modern literature through reference to the entire history of Western
thought is resisted as a curtailment of artistic freedom, but
"is of great interest. "

523. Donoghue, Denis. "The Black Ox. " NYRB 10 (1968): 22-24.
Review of FD.
Regards "The Brink of Darkness" as the clearest expression
of Winters' central preoccupation: an obsession with the invasion of disorder and oblivion that continually threatens life.
Winters' criticism is an impressive defense of the literary
values that support life in this struggle. Forms of Discovery
is a major contribution to this defense but is weakened by the
extreme nature of some of the judgments, the failure to consider large numbers of important poets, and the author's frequent lack of objectivity.

524. _____. "The Will to Certitude." TLS, 30 August 1974,
pp. 917-18. Review of UER and of The Complex of Yvor
Winters' Criticism, by Richard J. Sexton.
Suggests that the moment-by-moment need to maintain mental
coherence through an act of will is the essential attitude ly-
ing behind all of Winters' work: "the mind is alone in an
alien world; the dominant feeling is dread to be contained
only by the power with which it is understood." Traces this
attitude as it appears in Winters' poetry and in his critical
judgments.

525. Drew, Elizabeth. Review of PD. MLR 32 (1937): 627.
Describes with approval Winters' view that the perfect poem
is "a complete act of the spirit, calling upon the full life of
the spirit in both reader and writer" and his view of contemporary poets "as limiting and weakening their art by a
deliberate exclusion of an essential part of that spirit."

526. Drummond, Donald F. "Yvor Winters: Reason and Moral
Judgment." AQ 5 (1949): 5-19.
States that critics who object to Winters misunderstand his
use of the term moral, and describes that morality as the
effort, through poetry, to arrive at a full understanding of
the human condition so as to improve the capacity for judging accurately. (See items 60, 67 for Winters' discussion
of morality and literature.) The artist is a man learning
to live more completely. Discusses, as illustration of Winters' merits as a poet, "The Old Age of Theseus," "On
Teaching the Young," and "The Invaders." Describes Stanley
Hyman's misrepresentations of Winters in The Armed Vision.
(See item 579.)

527. Elman, Richard M. "A Word for Yvor Winters." Comm,
14 July 1961, pp. 401-3. Review of CP(1960).
Asserts that Winters is capable of strong, aphoristic statement and of massive elevation within the severe limitations
of method that he has imposed on himself as a poet. If his
apparent humorlessness is regarded as a weakness, then
it is one shared with such masters as Herbert, Pope, Dickinson, and Milton.

528. England, Eugene. "Tuckerman's Sonnet I:10: The First
Post-Symbolist Poem." SR 12 (1976): 323-47.
Refers briefly and approvingly to Winters' discussions of
Tuckerman and of post-Symbolist imagery. (See item 15
for Winters' discussion.) When using this kind of imagery,
the poet "is not thinking about something but rethinking it by
way of selected and empowered verbal images; it is the most
mature form of expression of a mature poet, experiencing
and creating for us a new realization of combined idea and
emotion."

529. Fields, Kenneth. "The Free Verse of Yvor Winters and

William Carlos Williams." SR 3 (1967): 764-75. Review
of EP.
Considers Williams and Winters as Imagist masters and regards Winters as the more complex of the two.

530.   _____. "Introduction." Quest for Reality: An Anthology
of Short Poems in English. Edited by Yvor Winters and
Kenneth Fields. Chicago: Swallow Press, 1969, pp. 1-9.
States that "our best writers live fully in the knowledge that
language is at once personal and public; they know that only
by precisely controlling the public medium of language can
they realize private experience." Most readers look for
the distinguishing mannerism of a poet rather than for unmannered excellence. "The kind of poetry which we are
trying to exemplify does not consist in a specific subject
matter or style, but rather in a high degree of concentration
which aims at understanding and revealing the particular subject as fully as possible."

531.   _____. "Forms of the Mind: The Experimental Poems
of Yvor Winters." SR 17 (1981): 938-63.
Describes the skeptical foundations of early twentieth century
literary theory and the fining down of human perception to the
arbitrary juxtaposition of things and to the observation solely
of relationships. Discusses the resulting techniques of exclusion and elimination in the early poems.

532.   Finlay, John. "N. Scott Momaday's Angle of Geese." SR
11 (1975): 658-61.
Identifies Momaday as a post-Symbolist poet in Winters' sense
of the word and refers to Winters' discussion of Momaday in
Forms of Discovery. (See item 15.)

533.   _____. "The Unfleshed Eye: A Reading of Yvor Winters'
'To the Holy Spirit.'" SR 17 (1981): 873-86.
Regards "To the Holy Spirit" as "a summary of Winters'
entire poetic career, one which began in free verse, imagism, and atheistic relativism and which ended in traditional
meter, classicism, and theistic absolutism." Maintains that
Winters' "unqualified theism is still intellectual to the core.
Instead of extracting the divine essence out of God and set-
ting it up as concept, Winters now leaves that divine essence
within God, but eliminates everything else from Him, so that
He becomes whatever that essence is defined as being, which,
in Winters' case, is 'pure mind'."

534.   Fitzell, Lincoln. "Western Letter." SewR 55 (1947): 530-35.
Comments on the work of major American writers of the
West including Winters, who is praised for his "exciting use
of traditional verse forms" and his "plain speaking in criticism."

535.   _____. "The Sword and the Dragon." South Atlantic

Quarterly 50 (1951): 214-32.
Discusses Winters' poetry briefly: it is "more often heroic,
lyric, pastoral, and satiric than tragic, but a close reading
of Winters's work yields lines that dissect the tragedy of
this age." Quotes as an example "The Prince."

536. Fitzgerald, Robert. "Recent Poetry." H&H 4 (1931): 313-16.
Review of Proof.
States that Winters' poems fall into two categories: those in
which he is "trying to create a sensuous reality" and "those
in which he is trying to 'express an idea'." Some of the
poems are marred by the "suggestion of false grandiloquence
and aimlessness," others by "having lines or words obviously
dictated by metrical exigency," and others by "forced intensity." In the best poems, "the poet has wrought a texture
sustained, luminous, and moving. It is more than virtuosity;
it is the work of an artist; it is good to read."

537. _____. "Against the Grain." Poetry 50 (1937): 173-77.
Review of PD.
Traces briefly Winters' poetic career and derives his critical
principles from the transition from experimentalist to tradi-
tionalist. The narrowness of Primitivism and Decadence
"occurs in the application of Winters' principles rather than
in the principles themselves."

538. Flint, Frank Cudworth. "A Critique of Experimental Poetry." VQR 13 (1937): 453-57. Review of PD.
Summarizes with approval the analytical machinery in Primitivism and Decadence, but asserts that Winters' "system of
values seems timid" and that his preferences among twentieth
century poets represent "strange aberrations." Winters'
critical approach imprisons poetry in conventionality. Regards the terms, primitivism and decadence, as pejorative
terms. (For Winters' use of the terms, see item 89.)

539. Fowler, Helen. "The Eliot of Yvor Winters." Approach,
no. 10 (1954), pp. 2-8.
Maintains that the basic assumption on which Winters' theory
rests, "that in his poem the poet fuses feeling and reason so
that the poem emerges with the weight of the poet's whole
personality behind it, not just one or more of its sundered
parts," is extremely valuable, but that Winters wastes himself in forensics. Instead of analyzing the fundamental weakness in Eliot's critical theory, that "it reduces poetry to the
kind of automatic writing which is produced when an emotion
or image takes over the field of consciousness," Winters
merely repeats his theory. In discussing Eliot's poetry,
Winters concentrates on the bad influence of Ezra Pound and
Henry Adams, but does not discuss what Eliot owes to Pound,
"the rediscovery and the adaptation of the rhythm used in
Anglo-Saxon prosody," a rhythm that made possible Eliot's
discovery and exploration of much of his subliminal material.

Winters' defensiveness and sense of martyrdom make it "improbable that his thought will have the beneficial results it might otherwise have had." (See item 95 for Winters' discussion of T. S. Eliot.)

540. Fraser, John. "A Great American Critic." Graduate Student of English 1 (1957): 24-29. Review of FC.
Regards Winters as the most important critic now writing: he is concerned with the final cause of literature, the relationship between literature and morality, and the importance of ideas in literature. His faults are sins of omission: he discusses only American critics and very few non-American novelists. He treats genres other than the short poem superficially. His discussion of such key subjects as the relationship between reason and emotion and the role of syllogistic reasoning in human thought is oversimplified.

541. _____. "Leavis and Winters: A Question of Reputation." Western Humanities Review 26 (1972): 1-16.
Asserts that Leavis and Winters have been received negatively because they challenge the profession of English studies to examine its basic assumptions, and this has caused offense. Both exhibit an intense commitment to the discipline and an insistence that the ideas embodied in literature and criticism have moral implications.

542. _____. "Leavis and Winters: Professional Manners." Cambridge Quarterly 5 (1970): 41-71.
Defends Leavis and Winters from the charge that they are ill-mannered. Their forthrightness results from a direct engagement with particular fellow academics in defense of the moral necessity for accepting the consequences in the world of action of one's scholarly and literary position: "if academic studies are to be rationally defensible as significant intellectual enterprises the defense has to be in terms of the general good of society."

543. _____. "Leavis, Winters, and 'Concreteness.'" Far-Western Forum 1 (Berkeley, Calif., 1974): 249-66.
Maintains that Leavis and Winters, despite differences in assumptions, authors whom they discuss, and judgments at which they arrive, share basic attitudes towards language, reality, and human value. Leavis develops in part from Coleridge and Winters from classicism. Leavis praises and Winters disparages Wordsworth, Blake, Hopkins, and Eliot. Leavis avoids metrical analysis; Winters engages in it. Both believe that literary language gains its power from its connection with idiomatic speech. Figurative language for both "should in some sense take one outward into a coherent physical world of things and actions charged with the properties attributed to them." Both believe that abstract perceptions must be grounded in a firm apprehension of commonsense reality and that literature has ethical implications.

544. _____. "Leavis, Winters, and Poetry." <u>Southern Review</u> 5 (Adelaide, 1972): 179-96.
States that Leavis and Winters differ in their particular judgments and in their attitudes towards technique. Leavis does not discuss the truth of a literary statement nor the degree of formal mastery exhibited. Winters feels that a literary statement must tell the literal truth and that the form is important as a tool of definition. Leavis is unsympathetic with the analysis of technique; Winters feels that such analysis is essential. Fraser agrees hesitantly that Winters is in the right.

545. _____. "Leavis, Winters, and Tradition." <u>SR</u> 7 (1971): 963-85.
Suggests that Leavis and Winters have been rejected by academics for having attacked the avant-garde from a traditional position that is regarded as no more than timid conservatism. Although the ideas of these two critics are not reducible to one another, they are expressions of a redefinition of tradition as a living application and adjustment of our Christian past to the problems of adapting to our industrial, post-romantic, and technologically controlled present.

546. _____. "Winters' <u>Summa</u>." <u>SR</u> 5 (1969): 184-202. Review of <u>FD</u>.
Asserts that Winters, in <u>Forms of Discovery</u>, is very largely "right in his general view of the history of poetry in English, and right in a great many of his particular judgments." The book presents Winters' full system and the evidence for his positive judgments and serves to render comprehensible Winters' earlier negative judgments and the incomplete argumentation of <u>Primitivism and Decadence</u> and of <u>The Function of Criticism</u>. (See items 5, 10.)

547. _____. "Yvor Winters: The Perils of Mind." <u>Centennial Review</u> 14 (1970): 396-420.
Discusses Winters' academic career as it exhibits his character and the value that he placed on the academic profession. Despite lack of encouragement and the hostility of traditional scholars, Winters did not turn against the profession but regarded academic discipline and scholarship as essential to the discipline of poetry. His own poetry exhibits a full engagement with the life of his place and time.

548. Freer, Agnes Lee. "A Poet Philosopher." <u>Poetry</u> 32 (1928): 41-47. Review of <u>BH</u>.
Describes the philosophy of <u>The Bare Hills</u> as one in which Deity is identified with the Universe which is defined as limitation, forces in relationship in time. Eternity is infinity or nothingness, the absence of limitation and relationship. Mind is simply the form of the changes in time and ceases when motion ceases. The poems express this view of things with seriousness and economy.

549. Fussell, Edwin. "The Theory of Modern Traditional: Some Doubts and Reservations." Tal, no. 8 (1955-56), pp. 58-65.
Replies to essays by Irmgard Johnson, Robert Greenwood, and Alan Swallow that are concerned with defining "Modern Traditional Poetry." (See items 557, 677.) Sees these critics as followers of Winters who lack his "highly developed historical sense and moral earnestness." Johnson leaves out of account "such aspects of romantic theory as are of continuing interest" and implies "that the process by which a poem may be criticized is the same as the process by which it must be written." Greenwood discusses usefully the "reduction of abstraction" and techniques of direct statement, but is overly general and dogmatic in his approach to critical and poetic problems. Both Greenwood and Swallow make the mistake of regarding all poetry before the twentieth century as traditional and of thereby oversimplifying the term. Swallow's subject is metrics and he "somewhat dutifully" follows Winters' defense of standard meters. (See items 5, 112, for Winters' treatment of meter.)

550. Gioia, Dana. "An Interview with Donald Davie." Seq 22 (1977): 20-27. Reprinted in Davie's Trying to Explain. Ann Arbor: University of Michigan Press, 1979, pp. 203-13.
Interviews Donald Davie who states that the critical views that Winters held in his old age were "too narrow and too strict for me to agree with" and that Winters was "at his best both as a poet and a critic when he was younger." Hopes that his own teaching of poetry and writing at Stanford "is a loyal and natural development out of Winters' legacy."

551. Glicksberg, Charles Irving. "Yvor Winters (1900-   )." American Literary Criticism, 1900-1950. New York: Hendricks House, 1951, pp. 533-36.
Provides brief summary of Winters' life and brief description of the contents of In Defense of Reason. Associates Winters with the New Humanism of Irving Babbitt. Asserts that Winters considered his own critical position invariably right and other positions wrong and that he confused aesthetic and philosophical values. Claims that poetry can not be judged by standards derived from philosophy since one cannot judge the relative validity of different philosophical systems, and states that a poet might well choose to avoid acceptance of any metaphysical system on the grounds that such acceptance imposes limitations on the poet.

552. Gomme, Andor. "The Rationalist Ideal." Attitudes to Criticism. With a preface by Harry T. Moore. Carbondale and Edwardsville: Southern Illinois University Press, 1966, pp. 66-100.
Contends that Winters' defense of his critical position is a philosophical argument that derives from his judgments of

individual works. Winters' moral absolutism is a deduction from his own experience, and "absolute" is used as a synonym for "objective." His understanding of the place of morality in poetry, however, is more consistent and penetrating than that of such critics as Kenneth Burke and John Crowe Ransom, but he is inconsistent when he objects to didacticism since his own evaluations are essentially didactic.

553. Graff, Gerald. "Attitudes to Criticism." SR 3 (1967): 525-28. Review of Attitudes to Criticism, by Andor Gomme.
Asserts that Gomme fails to recognize the nature of Winters' rationalism: "Winters' criterion of fitness between motive and emotion is a restatement of the ancient classical rhetorical principle of decorum, the theory that a writer's manner of speaking ought to correspond to what he has to set forth, that the emotional tone suggested by his style ought to be appropriate to his ideas." (See item 552.)

554. _____. "Yvor Winters of Stanford." AmS 4 (1975): 291-98. Reprinted in Masters: Portraits of Great Teachers. Edited by Joseph Epstein. New York: Basic Books, 1981, pp. 140-54.
Recounts personal experience of Winters as a teacher. Winters was within a modernist tradition: his history of poetry is like other theories of romantic decline, and his theory of impersonal formal reading is consistent with the modernist defense of impersonality. Winters differed from other teachers of literature in that he "presented a model of intense, almost priestly, seriousness about literature" and defined his critical position clearly and absolutely, thus forcing his students to define their own positions.

555. Greenbaum, Leonard. "The Hound & Horn Archive." Yale University Gazette 39 (1965): 137-46.
Provides a history of the Hound & Horn based on the letters preserved by the editor, Lincoln Kirstein, and deposited at Yale. The collection contains many letters from Winters to Kirstein that reveal Winters as "blunt, opinionated, and honest." As a contributing editor, his role was to explain and argue for his own critical standards.

556. _____. "Yvor Winters and the Pacific Writers." The Hound & Horn: The History of a Literary Quarterly. London, Paris, The Hague: Mouton, 1966, pp. 160-88.
States that "a mutually profitable relationship existed between The Hound & Horn and Yvor Winters." Although Winters published relatively little in the magazine, he did publish there his major critical statements of the early thirties: the reviews of Robert Bridges and of T. Sturge Moore and the review of the Oxford Book of 16th Century Verse. (See items 71, 75, 76.) Recounts, with quotations from letters in the files of The Hound and Horn, the history of Winters'

activities as regional contributing editor for the Pacific sea-board.

557. Greenwood, Robert. "Techniques in Modern Traditional Poetry." Tal, no. 6 (1954), pp. 55-69.
Describes under such headings as "Rhyme and Meter," "Metaphor," "Conceit," "Reduction of Abstraction," and "Direct Statement," the characteristics of modern traditional poetry, poetry that makes use of traditional resources instead of deriving itself exclusively from the experimental innovations of Pound and Williams. "One would expect, nevertheless, to find a great deal of difference between, say, the Elizabethan lyric and the Modern Traditional lyric. Not only will the contemporary poet's attitude toward his subject be different, but also the diction will be different." Discusses examples from the work of J. V. Cunningham, Lincoln Fitzell, Robert Frost, Yvor Winters, Janet Lewis, and Mark Van Doren. (See items 549, 657, 677.)

558. Gregory, Horace. "Of Vitality, Regionalism, and Satire in Recent American Poetry." SewR 52 (1944): 572-93. Review of TP and GW.
Objects that Winters and the poets associated with him confused "the desire to employ traditional forms in verse" and "the desire to impose a rigidly and naively formed convention" upon poetry.

559. Guerard, Albert J. "The Brink of Darkness." Seq 6 (1961): 25-30.
Describes the narrator of "The Brink of Darkness" as a victim of "mild paranoid schizophrenia." Places the story in a tradition that includes Conrad's "The Secret Sharer" and "The Shadow-Line" and James's "The Turn of the Screw," and sees it as an account of psychological disturbance rather than of demonic possession. Believes that the narrator's inability to define the invading power is evidence of "still lingering paranoid delusion" and is a weakness in the story: the narrator "is a man who is now quite sane, and who is capable of definition." (See item 503 for another discussion of the story.)

560. _____. "The Voice of Passionate Control." SR 17 (1981): 716-22.
Asserts that Winters is not a detached and wholly intellectual writer but one intimately involved in a personal struggle with disorder and the irrational. "His poetry is concerned with measuring and controlling demons; it is concerned with the dangers of traffic with the subhuman or inhuman ... or such demons, in the criticism, as Whitman, Eliot, and Hart Crane." The dramatic qualities in his prose develop from this same struggle.

561. Gunn, Thom. "[Arthur] Yvor Winters." The Concise Ency-

clopedia of English and American Poets and Poetry.
Edited by Stephen Spender and Donald Hall. London:
Hutchinson, 1963, p. 359.
Summarizes briefly the essential facts of Winters' career
and poetic development. "The discipline of his style does
not reject experience--rather it is a means of simultaneously
conveying it, in all its richness and variety, and evaluating
it, since the conveying has little meaning without the evaluating."

562. _____. "A Critical 'Discovery': At the Heart of Good
Poetry." San Francisco Sunday Examiner & Chronicle,
17 March 1968, "This World," p. 36. Review of FD.
Summarizes approvingly Winters' history of the short poem
in English. Winters' great virtue is "that he is concerned
with poetry as poetry, not as evidence of a Zeitgeist any
more than as proof of an academic theory. His definition
of poetry arises from specific poems, which he is prepared
to analyze in detail." Praises the book very highly:
"Forms of Discovery is a book of the greatest importance.
I know of no other prose work from which one can learn so
much about poetry, how it actually works, what makes it
valuable. Winters never forgets why a man wants to write
poetry in the first place, for 'the exploration and understanding of experience' is a pursuit in which the intellect and the
passions are fully occupied. Their activity is so full that it
amounts to a form of love, a love concentrated almost to the
point of obsession."

563. _____. [Statement]. Per Se 3 (1968): 40.
Comments briefly on the significance of his year as a writing
fellow studying at Stanford with Winters: "It was certainly
the most important single year of my writing life: Winters
constantly encouraged me to extend myself, to take risks.
At the same time I was learning (as I took them) the nature
of those artistic risks and how closely they related to risks
in my life."

564. _____. "The Openness of Donald Davie." Seq 22 (1977):
30-32.
States that Davie "started considering the ideas of both Winters and Olson before the English had deigned to recognize
the name of either."

565. _____. "My Life Up to Now." Thom Gunn: A Bibliography, 1940-1978. Compiled by Jack W. C. Hagstrom
and George Bixby. London: Bertram Rota, 1979, pp.
11-26. Reprinted in his The Occasions of Poetry: Essays in Criticism and Autobiography. Edited with an introduction by Clive Wilmer. London: Faber and Faber,
1982, pp. 169-88.
Includes references to his studies with Winters.

566. _____. "On a Drying Hill." SR 17 (1981): 681-93.
Recalls his association with Winters during the year 1954-
55 as a poetry fellow at Stanford and subsequently. Praises
him as a remarkable teacher with a passion for poetry. He
"was one of the few people I have ever come across" who
could define the nature of meter and its relationship to poetic meaning. As a teacher of the writing of poetry, he
had "the knack--the genius perhaps--of divining your intentions, even if the poem was so obscurely or clumsily car-
ried out that those intentions had become hidden."

567. Gurian, Jay. "The Possibility of a Western Poetic." Colorado Quarterly 15 (1966): 69-85.
Discusses briefly, as part of a general consideration of
Western American verse, Winters' poetry as "clean lyricism,
in a classic and pastoral manner," but does not fully accept
the high estimate of that poetry expressed by Alan Swallow
in "Poetry of the West" (see item 680).

568. Hammond, Karla H. "A Conversation with Ann Stanford."
SR 18 (1982): 314-37.
Interviews Ann Stanford who refers briefly to Winters as an
Imagist and as a teacher: "Yvor Winters, as you know, is
the great traditional poet. But he was an Imagist when he
started and that's what I picked up from him: the sense of
order, the sense of criticism, the sense of not being senti-
mental--in that you thought before you wrote. Possibly all
of these qualities are what you've found, or others have
found, classical in my work."

569. Hamovitch, Mitzi Berger. "My Life I Will not Let Thee Go
Except Thou Bless Me: An Interview with Janet Lewis."
SR 18 (1982): 299-313.
Interviews Janet Lewis who refers briefly to her life with
Yvor Winters.

570. Hass, Robert. "World Was Not Enough." Review of An Introduction to the Poetry of Yvor Winters, by Elizabeth
Isaacs. NYTBR, 5 July 1981, pp. 6, 15-16.
Describes the young Winters as "not the fierce old curmud-
geon of Palo Alto" but as "a tubercular boy, just beginning
to read the moderns ... in a New Mexico sanitarium." Discusses sympathetically the early poems in which Winters
"had, with admirable fidelity and discipline, taken the imagist poem to one of its limits," and discusses with admiration
but less sympathy the later poetry: "what is damaging about
the later work is that, in addition to adopting the forms and
themes of the English poets, he adopted their diction."

571. Hobsbaum, Philip. "The Critics at the Harmonium: Blackmur and Winters on Stevens." Bulletin of the British Association for American Studies, no. 11 n. s. (1965), pp. 43-57.
Compares Blackmur's textural and linguistic approach to Wal-

lace Stevens with Winters' thematic approach and emphasis
on ideas and subject matter. In discussing "On the Manner
of Addressing Clouds," Blackmur claims that such an unusual
word as funest can only be understood in its context, but analyzes this and other words with little reference to the particular context. Winters' approach seems more satisfactory
since it allows him to see the precious diction as a means
of conveying an ironical attitude toward subject matter. In
discussing "The Comedian as the Letter C," Blackmur discusses language but has little to say about the subject matter that gives the language a function. Winters sees the
language as a means of conveying an attitude toward the subject of the poem: the plight of the romantic artist who finally sees his art as superfluous to life. Analyzes, with similar results, discussions by Blackmur and Winters of "Sunday
Morning."

572. _____. "The Discovery of Form." MQR 12 (1972):
        235-42.
Suggests that Winters may be "one of the two or three greatest critics ever to have written in the English language."
Maintains that the greatest literary critics are creative writers who justify and analyze their own craft. Winters'
achievement gains force and authority from his accomplishment as a poet. Winters' advocacy of relatively neglected
poets such as Charles Churchill, Jones Very, and his own
students is not a weakness; these poets are impressive writers. In Forms of Discovery, "a literary masterpiece in its
own right," Winters not only dismisses poets whose reputa-
tions are in excess of their accomplishment (Gray, Wordsworth, and Shelley), but demonstrates the merits of little
known poets. "Winters' criticism ... is not an act of destruction; it is an act of piety.

573. Hofheins, Roger and Dan Tooker. "A Conversation with
        Janet Lewis." SR 10 (1974): 329-41.
Includes very brief reference to Winters as a teacher.

574. Holloway, John. "The Critical Theory of Yvor Winters."
        Critical Quarterly 7 (1965): 54-68.
Reduces Winters' theory of poetry to three assertions: a
poem is about a human experience, a poem is a rational apprehension of its subject, and a poem communicates the degree of feeling appropriate to that apprehension. Objects
that the first assertion is too limited, that the second is
incomprehensible, and that the third is untrue.

575. Honig, Edwin. "The Mind's Immortal, but the Man Is Dead."
        Poetry 65 (1944): 43-47. Review of GW.
Asserts that Winters' poetry is deadened by its dependence
on outmoded models and antiquated ideas and that it is, at
the same time, a development from the Imagist experiments
of the early twentieth century. When Winters writes in this

Imagist tradition and not from his intelligence, he can write
well.

576. Horton, Philip. "The California Classicism." Poetry 51
    (1937): 48-52. Review of TP.
    Describes the principal aim of the poets included in Twelve
    Poets of the Pacific as "spiritual control" achieved through
    a control of the stylistic details and techniques of traditional
    form. Asserts that this aim is usually achieved in the po-
    ems of Winters, Janet Lewis, and J. V. Cunningham but not
    of the other poets represented.

577. Howells, Thomas. "Yvor Winters, Anatomist of Nonsense."
    Poetry 63 (1943): 86-96. (See item 415 for Winters' re-
    ply.) Rejoinder by Howells in Poetry 63 (1944): 293-94.
    Summarizes unsympathetically the argument of The Anatomy
    of Nonsense, with particular reference to the degree of he-
    donism present in the various versions of "Sunday Morning,"
    to Eliot's view of the relationship between ideals and feelings,
    and to Henry Adams' determinism. (See item 7 for Winters'
    argument.)

578. Humphries, Rolfe. "Foreword, with Poems." Poetry 45
    (1935): 288-91. Review of BD.
    Notes that Winters asks too much of his readers in the way
    of background reading to his poems and that his "formalism
    cannot be called truly classical, for it stems from his aware-
    ness of its absence in his fellow citizens." Praises the tech-
    nical accomplishments in Winters' verse but feels that the
    verse lacks intensity, suspecting that Winters' critical intel-
    ligence has inhibited his poetic productivity.

579. Hyman, Stanley E. "Yvor Winters and Evaluation in Criti-
    cism." The Armed Vision: A Study in the Methods of
    Modern Literary Criticism. New York: A. A. Knopf,
    1948, pp. 49-72.
    Asserts that Winters' critical judgments are self-evidently
    absurd. Winters is in a moralistic tradition and exhibits the
    defects of dogmatism and bad judgment that characterize Ry-
    mer, Dennis, Johnson, and Landor. Although Winters' goal
    is the correction of opinion, this "is a more or less point-
    less form of activity." Winters' use of terms is confusing:
    the term "moral" is used in many different ways and finally
    means "any work or attitude that Winters likes." The terms
    "primitivism" and "decadence" are used arbitrarily as terms
    of abuse. Winters is finally "an excessively irritating and
    bad critic of some importance." (See items 60, 67, for
    Winters' discussion of morality in literature, and item 89
    for the meaning of the terms primitivism and decadence.)

580. Inglis, Fred. "A 'Reactionary' American Critic: Yvor
    Winters." Listener 76 (1966): 322-23.
    Summarizes approvingly Winters' views on the relationship

between romanticism and relativism and the necessity for countering modern relativism with critical absolutism. Praises Winters for his insistence that literature is about life and has moral consequences and for his "readiness to say what he thinks, to quote what he finds unintelligible, to expose himself to fire." Notes that Winters' criticism provides a context for his poems. "It defines the moral tradition which shapes the poems."

581. Jarrell, Randall. "The Morality of Mr. Winters." KR 1 (1939): 211-15. Review of MC.
Asserts that the history of ideas developed in Maule's Curse is weak because it neglects science and philosophy and confines itself to theology, and because "a disproportionate importance is given to causes that were certainly partial." Objects to a number of Winters' unfashionable value judgments, but concludes that "Maule's Curse is the best book on American literature I ever read, and I make so great a point of its author's vices only because his virtues are apparent and indeed overwhelming."

582. _____. "Fifty Years of American Poetry." Prairie Schooner 37 (1963): 1-27.
Suggests that joining doctrinaire groups is bad for poets and provides as examples such groups as the beatniks and "the beatniks' opposite, the followers of Yvor Winters."

583. Johnson, Carol. "Yvor Winters: Poetics of Rectitude." Reason's Double Agents. Chapel Hill: University of North Carolina Press, 1961, pp. 91-103.
Contends that Winters' moral position is qualified and justified by his aesthetic perceptions and that his apparent exclusiveness is only a rejection of vagueness, impressionism, and adolescent responses. Within his own poetry, Winters resolves critical questions as questions of style; the elements of feeling included in his poetry are those of which the mind has a firm grasp and are realized through "the search for substantial form."

584. Kaye, Howard. "Yvor Winters: 1900-1968." NR, 2 March 1968, pp. 31-33.
Asserts that Winters' mature poetry was an effort to escape insanity and achieve wisdom through discipline and that his criticism "aimed at nothing less than a revolution in taste."

585. _____. "The Tougher Poets." SR 6 (1970): 824-29. Review of QR.
States that Quest for Reality is compiled on two principles: that of providing a collection of the greatest poems in English and American literature and that of preserving a body of minor but distinguished poetry that might otherwise disappear from view.

586.   . "The Post-Symbolist Poetry of Yvor Winters."
     SR 7 (1971): 176-97.
     Shows that Winters' early poetry is composed of sensory
     images without rational content and that some of his later
     poetry is written wholly in the abstract language of concepts.
     Describes Winters' post-Symbolist poetry as a merging of
     the two methods in which "sensory details are present in
     language which also conveys philosophical ideas." Such po-
     etry can be distinguished from Symbolist poetry in which
     concrete detail and abstract meaning are inseparable, but
     the abstract meaning is connotative rather than denotative;
     and it can be distinguished from much Renaissance poetry
     in which the concrete detail is decoration of a conceptual
     meaning from which it can be separated. (See item 15 for
     Winters' discussion of post-Symbolist imagery.)

587. Kermode, Frank. "Counter-Revolution." Spectator, 1 July
     1960, pp. 25-26. Review of IDR.
     Suggests that Graham Hough and Winters are critics who
     "may be inaugurating one of those periodic reappraisals of
     literary history which normally accompany some major alter-
     ation of taste."

588. Kimbrough, Robert. "Discipline the Saving Grace: Winters'
     Critical Position." Ren 15 (1963): 62-67.
     Summarizes briefly the theistic, linguistic, and moral ideas
     that inform Winters' absolutism. Objects that the rational
     discipline that Winters proposes is too uncompromising and
     difficult for most men and that greater charity is needed in
     passing moral judgments than Winters exhibits. (See items
     60, 67, for Winters' discussion of morality.)

589. Kunitz, Stanley J. and Howard Haycraft, eds. "Yvor Win-
     ters." Twentieth Century Authors: A Biographical Dic-
     tionary of Modern Literature. New York: H. W. Wilson,
     1942, pp. 1534-35.
     Details the facts of Winters' biography and publications. In-
     cludes statement by Winters that reads in part: "Whatever
     the virtues of my poetry, past or present, absolutely con-
     sidered, I think one may reasonably say the later work sur-
     passes the earlier and will probably prove, in the long run,
     of greater value than my criticism."

590. Lemon, Lee T. "Winters as Critic." Prairie Schooner 42
     (1968): 277-78.
     Asserts that Winters "is a critic who states his position so
     clearly and so forcefully that readers are shocked into
     thought; and his theoretical position is so strong that, in
     disagreeing honestly with him, one is forced to think about
     literature widely and deeply."

591. Levin, David. "Yvor Winters at Stanford." VQR 54 (1978):
     454-73.

Describes a little-known side of Winters' contribution to letters: his attractiveness, generosity, and responsibility as a colleague.

592. _____. "A Historical Reconsideration of Maule's Curse."
SR 17 (1981): 803-13.
Summarizes and praises Winters' analysis of New England Puritanism in Maule's Curse, but maintains that recent scholarship enforces some qualification of Winters' conclusions. Winters, while emphasizing logical and historical developments, fails to note that the Puritans were concerned with difficult and subtle moral choices. While treating Emerson as a relativist and a pantheist, he fails to do justice to Emerson's conception of Reason and the distinction between Reason and Understanding. Describes Winters' analysis of reversals in the logic of literary representation within American literature. (See item 6.)

593. Le Vot, André. "La Voix de Frost." Langues Modernes
59 (1965): 93-100.
Repeats, with the implication that they are clearly indefensible, Winters' objections to Frost's poetry. (See item 106.)

594. Lowell, Robert. "Yvor Winters: A Tribute." Poetry 98
(1961): 40-43.
Praises Winters as poet and critic: "Winters is a writer of great passion, one of the most steady rhetoricians in the language, and a stylist whose diction and metric exemplify two hundred years of American culture."

595. McDonnell, Thomas P. "Criticism and Belief: The Life of
the Catholic Critic." Ren 11 (1959): 59-64.
States that, despite his moral position and his admiration for Aquinas, Winters' criticism cannot be incorporated into a Christian critique of literature because he has drawn his absolutes from literature rather than from theology. Compares Winters unfavorably with Charles Du Bos, who derives his absolutes from theology and then applies them to literature.

596. _____. "Hopkins as a Sacramental Poet: A Reply to
Yvor Winters." Ren 14 (1961): 25-33, 41.
Objects to Winters' view that Hopkins is not one of the major poets of his time. Winters' Horatian view that poetry is a commentary on experience rather than an involvement in experience leads to his failure to appreciate the theological implications of Hopkins' poetry. Justifies Hopkins through reference to the doctrine of the immanence of God in the world, but asserts that Winters does not "come in full contact with the doctrine."

597. McKean, Angus Keith Ferguson. "Yvor Winters and the
Neo-Humanists." University of Kansas City Review 22
(1955): 131-33.

Argues that Winters "is primarily the critic who stays strictly with art and holds to a conception of the creative act which allows him to deal with the whole poem in moral terms," whereas Irving Babbitt "is primarily a moralist who freely illustrates his discussions with the materials of literature." Winters' original insight is that "the act of artistic creation is essentially an ethical experience, because it is one in which the artist must shape, evaluate, and, in effect, control the experience he tries to portray." It is an act that resembles the adjustment to reality and control of feelings that is required in everyday life.

598. _____. "Introduction." On Modern Poets, by Yvor Winters. New York: Meridian Books, 1959, pp. 7-10. States that, although Winters shares with such neo-humanists as Irving Babbitt a concern with the moral implications of literature, he is primarily concerned with poetry as an art. (See item 67.) For Winters, a poem has a rational structure, which is paraphrasable, and a feeling content, which is largely non-paraphrasable. Winters' emphasis on morality derives from his insistence that literature has meaning, and meaning necessitates judgment. Winters' critical theories "tend to carry him directly to the work. If the rational structure of a poem is obscure, then there can be no appropriate emotion; or, if the emotion is not clearly motivated by the meaning, then again we have obscurity."

599. _____. "Yvor Winters." The Moral Measure of Literature. Denver: Alan Swallow, 1961, pp. 98-125. Asserts that the key concept in Winters' criticism is balance. In this it differs from the ethical and literary criticism of such neo-humanists as Babbitt and Paul Elmer More in which the key concept is control by the "higher will" or by an "inner check." Winters' concept of balance determines his view of the relationship between motive and emotion in a poem and the relationship between meter and rhythm. Other distinctions in Winters' criticism--such as that between the primitive and the decadent--are also the means of determining the presence or absence of balance in the elements that enter into literature. Primitivism and Decadence is concerned mainly with style and experimental techniques in twentieth century poetry. Subsequent books concentrate on individual writers as they exhibit the effects of intellectual traditions of the last several centuries and particularly of the romantic movement.

600. McWilliams, Carey. "The Writers of California." Bookman 72 (1930): 352-59. Chronicles California literary history with brief mention of Winters as editor of The Gyroscope: "of late Palo Alto has come to life. I attribute this largely to the presence of Mr. Yvor Winters."

601.   Marsh, Robert. "Observations on the Criticism of Yvor
       Winters." Spectrum 4, no. 2 and 3 (1960), pp. 116-18
       and 146-62 respectively.
       Distinguishes between the New Critical belief that "poetry is
       a natural substance ordered and ordained by deeper forces
       than the mere actions of men" and Winters' insistence "that
       poems are the product of human artistry, not of natural
       mechanisms." Praises Winters' defense of free will and
       conscious skill, but objects to his view that poetry is essen-
       tially statement. Asserts that poems should be regarded as
       mimetic and demonstrates the limited applicability of Win-
       ters' term to Gray's "Elegy." Suggests that Winters' own
       poem, "The Marriage," can be described as imitation rather
       than statement.

602.   Matthiessen, Francis Otto. "A Review of Recent Poetry."
       SR 3 (1937): 368-91. Review of TP.
       Asserts that Twelve Poets of the Pacific presents an illumi-
       nating practice of the theory developed in Primitivism and
       Decadence: "in reversal of the usual order, the practice
       excels his critical exposition in lucidity and coherence."
       Singles out Ann Stanford, Janet Lewis, Howard Baker, and
       Winters himself for particular praise. Winters' poetry,
       despite its impressiveness, "yields the dominant impression
       of being studied and willed" and does not appear to rise
       "from emotional levels deeper than conscious thought."

603.   _____. "American Poetry Now." KR 6 (1944): 683-96.
       Reprinted as "Four American Poets, 1944." Responsibil-
       ities of the Critic: Essays and Reviews. New York:
       Oxford University Press, 1952, pp. 116-28. Review of
       GW.
       Argues that Winters is a weak judge of poetry but good at
       "articulating his conception of a poem." His own poetry is
       usually stiff, dry, and lacking in humor. Occasionally, how-
       ever, his small subjects are enlivened "through recognition
       of the violence by which all balance is threatened."

604.   Maxeiner, Tom. "The Poetry of Yvor Winters: Part I."
       Seq 12 (1966): 29-45.
       Discusses solipsism, nominalism, and the various conven-
       tions that function within the early poems. Describes the
       virtues and limitations of the kind of poetry that Winters
       wrote during the first phase of his career. In his early
       work, Winters "is confined to a limited approach to experi-
       ence; he is deprived of the areas that demand a greater com-
       prehension and more complete context of experience, from
       understanding the history that motivates a human relationship,
       for example."

605.   _____. "The Poetry of Yvor Winters: Part II." Seq
       12 (1967): 37-47.
       Contrasts the conventions and subject matter of the later

poems with the more limited approach in the early poems
(see item 604). Discusses, in the later work, "the function
that is given to the poem and the new stance that is acquired
to the problem of knowledge." In the early work, the function of the poem was the recovery of the particular experience; in the later, the poem becomes an act of generalization,
definition, and evaluation. Having developed beyond the
nominalistic world of the early poems, the poet can now entertain the possibility of knowledge; the later poetry "assumes that knowledge is possible and may be improved, but
perfection cannot be reached."

606. Mayo, Alberto Porqueras. "El 'New Criticism' de Yvor
Winters." Historia y Estructura de la Obra Literaria.
Madrid: Consejo Superior de Investigaciones Cientificas,
1971, pp. 57-63.
Regards Winters as the Unamuno of the New Critics, T. S.
Eliot being the Ortega. Outlines Winters' basic principles
as these are presented in In Defense of Reason and The
Function of Criticism. The former book is described as at
once conservative and original and as one of the great hu-
mane documents of our century.

607. Meiners, R. K. "Yvor Winters and the Possibilities of a
Rational Criticism." Papers of the Midwest Modern Language Association 1 (1969): 1-7.
Notes that Winters' key critical assumptions are that a poem
is a statement and that it should establish a clear relationship between motive and feeling. Winters' insistence on
critical judgment and the importance of reason at first seems
impressive but gradually comes to seem less so.

608. Middleton, David. "'Men in Dark Times': Three New British Poets." SR 15 (1979): 585-604.
Asserts that Dick Davis, Robert Wells, and Clive Wilmer
are concerned with questions of identity and value that derive
from romanticism and modernism, but that they are influenced, in their rejection of modernist procedures, by Winters' poetry and criticism.

609. Mizener, Arthur. Review of AN and GW. Accent 4 (1944):
185-87.
Praises Winters' "skill, consistency, and inclusiveness" as a
critic, but maintains that the price he pays for this consistency
is that he cannot fully explain everything that he knows about
literature. In verse, he demonstrates that the poet can free
himself from the limitations of the age and can write with
skill and distinction while doing so.

610. _____. "Three Critics." SewR 52 (1944): 597-604. Review of AN.
Regards Winters' insistence that concept motivate feeling as
a preference for a poetry of statement. Winters' value is

that he points out the narrowness of the twentieth century
preference for less rational procedures.

611.   Monroe, Harriet. "Youth and the Desert." Poetry 18 (1921):
       339-43. Review of IW.
       States, of Winters' early poetry, that "youth is so prone to
       prolixities and sentimentalities that the opposite excess is
       something of a relief."

612.   Mudrick, Marvin. "Three Stanford Poets." Lugano Review
       1 (1965): 83-94.
       Ridicules the poetry of Winters and those poets associated
       with him at Stanford. Singles out, for particular attention,
       the work of Winters himself, J. V. Cunningham, and Edgar
       Bowers. Accords Cunningham some praise for possessing
       "the special obstinate talent which could absorb what it
       needed, and eventually discard what it had no use for."
       Characterizes Winters as a teacher who "looks a cold mad
       feary father ... but has a soft heart and eats none of his
       trusting limbless children."

613.   Munson, Gorham. "The Classicism of Robert Frost."
       Modern Age 8 (1964): 291-305.
       Disapproves of Winters' denial that Frost is a classical poet
       and his definition of Frost as an Emersonian romantic. As-
       serts that Winters' criticisms of Frost are based on a series
       of misreadings. (See item 106 for Winters' discussion.)

614.   _____. "A Comedy of Exiles." Literary Review 12
       (1968): 41-75.
       Recounts origins and history of Secession, in which appeared
       Testament of a Stone. (See item 1.)

615.   Murphy, Francis. "Introduction." UER. (See item 16.)
       Places Winters within the generation of critics that profited
       from the example of Pound and Eliot and made literary
       criticism "one of the chief glories of American literature."
       Winters' name is associated with controversy. In a rela-
       tivistic age, he insisted on the importance of meaning in lit-
       erature and of evaluation in criticism. He was among the
       first to recognize that romanticism and modernism are es-
       sentially the same movement, but he was unable to recognize
       the criticism of romanticism that appears within that tradi-
       tion, as, for example, in the later work of Emerson and
       Whitman. Despite occasional narrowness of perspective, "at
       his best, and that is very often indeed, Winters was one of
       the great discoverers."

616.   Nilsen, Helge Normann. "The Quest for Reality: A Study
       in the Poetry of Wallace Stevens." Americana Norvegica:
       Norwegian Contributions to American Studies. 2. Edited
       by Sigmund Skard. Philadelphia: University of Pennsyl-
       vania Press, 1968, 219-98.

Refers briefly and with approval to Winters' discussion of
the nominalism and hedonistic aestheticism that keeps Stevens
from appreciating the element of moral judgment in poetry:
"there is no doubt that Stevens' lack of moral engagement ...
is largely responsible for his defaults as a poet." (See item
100.)

617.   Nist, John. "In Defense of Yeats." AQ 18 (1962): 58-65.
States that Yeats has not damaged the style of younger writers as Winters claims, since younger writers have not been
influenced by him. Winters is wrong in his objections to the
conceptual limitations of Yeats's work since Yeats's genius
transcends his conceptual limitations. Winters' objections to
Yeats's ignorance are unfounded since Yeats prayed for ignorance. Winters' essay is an example of "condescension in
tone, peevish pomposity of manner, question-begging in argument, oversimplification in interpretation, misapplication of
extrinsic knowledge to intrinsic meaning, picayunishness in
attack, pedanticism in style, lack of proper examples in illustration, and falsification in choice of material."

618.   Ohmann, Richard. "Ordeal by Parenthesis." Audit 1 (1960):
4-8.
Discusses briefly Winters as one of those critics who dismiss
major writers by way of name-calling and guilt by association
without first engaging in the critical act of understanding.

619.   Oliver, Raymond. "Yvor Winters and the English Renaissance." SR 17 (1981): 758-80.
Argues that many of Winters' poems in standard meter "are
written in something closely akin to the plain style of the
English Renaissance and were in many ways modeled on that
style." Summarizes Winters' "doctrine of traditional poetry,"
shows its correspondence with his description of plain style
poems and the accuracy of that description for his own poems. Discusses the contempt for the world and the stoic
acceptance of common sense reality that characterizes poems
in the Renaissance plain style and poems by Winters. Lists
also "some points of nonresemblance, lest I give the invidi-
ous impression that Winters did indeed 'slavishly imitate' his
predecessors." (See item 92 for Winters' discussion of the
plain style; see item 628.)

620.   Parkinson, Thomas. "The Hart Crane-Yvor Winters Correspondence." Ohio Review 16 (1974): 5-24.
Traces aspects of the relationship between Crane and Winters
as revealed in Crane's side of the correspondence with emphasis on the meeting of the two that took place during the
Christmas week of 1927. (See item 457.)

621.   _____. "Hart Crane and Yvor Winters: A Meeting of
Minds." SR 11 (1975): 491-512.
Presents a reconstruction of the facts of Winters' biography

during the fall of 1926 and commentary on letters of Crane
to Winters during this period. (See item 457.)

622. _____. "Hart Crane and Yvor Winters: White Buildings."
SR 12 (1976): 232-45.
Details the circumstances surrounding the publication of
White Buildings in 1927 and of Winters' review of the book.
Provides commentary on letters of Crane to Winters during
this period. (See item 457.)

623. Payne, Basil. "Debunking Yeats." Irish Times, 31 March
1962, p. 9.
Claims that Winters was right in denying that Yeats was a
great Irish poet.

624. Pearce, Roy Harvey. "Romantics, Critics, Historicists."
HR 10 (1957): 447-57. Review of FC.
States that "The Function of Criticism is not one of Mr.
Winters' major works." Believes that in judging literary
works, which are historical phenomena, Winters distorts
history: "Mr. Winters would discover that absolutist rational morality expressed in the very continuum of history
whose artistic productions he would judge by means of it."

625. Pearson, Gabriel. "The Defeat of Yvor Winters." The
Review, no. 8 (1963), pp. 3-12. Reprinted as "Yvor
Winters" in The Modern Poet: Essays from the Review.
Edited by Ian Hamilton. London: MacDonald, 1968, pp.
64-73. Review of CP(1960).
Identifies Winters' poems as those of a restrained neoclas-
sicist with little to restrain. The motive of the poems is
peace and quiet, and the tone is elegiac: "elegies sung
over himself and the situations with which he has failed to
cope and opted out of." The most frequent symbolic pattern is a contrast of land and sea; he habitually presents the
sea or any water as a dissolving and eroding agent attacking
dry, firm land. He is good at landscape, because he can
plausibly put his allegory across while doing a straightfor-
ward job of description." Compares Winters' attitude towards
experience with Arnold's: "Winters's is an extreme version,
almost a parody, of the Arnoldian rigor mortis."

626. Pemberton, Vivian H. "Hart Crane and Yvor Winters,
Rebuttal and Review: A New Crane Letter." AL 50
(1978): 276-81.
Presents the text of Crane's letter to Winters of June 4,
1930, in which he expresses his indignation at Winters' review of The Bridge and defends the poem from Winters'
criticisms. (See items 66, 104, 457.)

627. Peterson, Douglas. "Yvor Winters' 'By the Road to the
Air-Base'." SR 15 (1979): 567-74.
Analyzes "By the Road to the Air-Base" as an example of

post-Symbolist imagery and of the mature style that Winters developed during the 1930's and '40's. Within the poem, physical details are realized fully but in such a way that they imply the intellectual concepts that give them meaning. Key words that are, on one level, descriptive, convey the gradual evolution of life and consciousness and the conflict between nature and human order. This mature style "is skillful, accomplished, informed by a lifetime of study, and sufficiently flexible to accommodate an extraordinarily wide range of experience." (For post-Symbolist method, see item 15.)

628. _____. "The Poetry of Yvor Winters: The Achievement of a Style." SR 17 (1981): 907-37.
Traces from Winters' early free verse through his mature work in traditional forms the gradual escape from solipsistic nominalism. The limitations of Winters' early technique were appropriate to the limited subject matter that could be realized within his early view of the nature of human experience. The adoption of a more inclusive technique made possible the realization of an external world extending beyond the isolated mind, a world that included other people and public concerns and traditions. On the level of technique, the separation of mind and external world is finally resolved in the post-Symbolist method, in terms of which "specific actions and scenes, as well as particular objects, are intelligible because they are particular instances of generic concepts that are immanent in physical things and their interactions." Discusses a number of instances of the post-Symbolist method in the later poetry. (For post-Symbolist method, see item 15.)

629. Pinsky, Robert. "The Interest of Poetry." PNR 7 (1980): 34-35.
Refers briefly to the separation of writing poetry and studying literature in the universities and to "Yvor Winters, a noble figure grumpily situated exactly at the juncture of writing and literature, defending the juncture, and making us student-writers assume that it existed."

630. Powell, Grosvenor. "Mythical and Smoky Soil: Imagism and the Aboriginal in the Early Poetry of Yvor Winters." SR 11 (1975): 300-17.
Asserts that Winters believed, during his formative years as an Imagist and a romantic mystic, that the poet alters his consciousness by fusing it with the image. Winters saw two ways in which such fusion could be understood: as an expansion of consciousness in which the poet identifies himself with the universe and as an invasion of consciousness in which demonic forces decrease the being of the poet who has evoked them (for another discussion of demonic possession, see item 503.) Winters believed that the first is an illusion and that the second is a dangerous reality that has to be mastered

through poetry considered as a technique of contemplation. He found in American Indian poetry and the French Symbolists the relevant techniques. In shifting to the formalism of his later work, he retained the evocative technique of his early poetry but added to it a technique of definition. (See item 460.)

631. _____. "Some Key Terms in the Poetry of Yvor Winters." SR 11 (1975): 838-54.
Shows that the most important line of development in Winters's poetry can be defined through a consideration of the following terms: Intuition, Mind, Purity, and Being. These concepts relate to being or its absence in the Aristotelian and Thomistic senses of the word. Intuition and Purity are characteristic forms of modern deprivation of being: Intuition is an incomplete mode of perception and Purity the characteristic of certain deprived kinds of experience. Mind is the means to recovery and to the realization of human potentiality. These concepts expose a development from a romantic view of Being to a Thomistic one. (See item 460.)

632. _____. "Being, Poetry, and Yvor Winters' Criticism." DQ 10 (1975): 54-66.
Argues that all of Winters' thought, both in verse and prose, must be understood in terms of the Thomistic notion of good as fullness of being and of evil as absence of being. Discusses the absence of being in twentieth century conceptions of life and the parallel absence of being in twentieth century poetry. Explains these conceptions and defines the poetic tradition that Winters sees as a remedy for the modern situation. (See item 460.)

633. _____. "Quantity and the Meters of Yvor Winters." DQ 10 (1975): 38-53.
Describes principles of free verse as Winters understood them and shows that the weakness of such verse lies in the limited range of feeling that it can express. The necessarily fragmented nature of the elements counterpointed leads to a necessarily fragmented syntax as the only appropriate structure for the meaning expressed in the poem. In turning to an accentual-syllabic meter, Winters adopted a form that allowed him to retain the virtues of free verse while reintroducing into his poetry the full potentialities of the language and of the conceptualizing mind. (See items 5, 112 for Winters' discussion of meter; see item 460.)

634. _____. "Solipsism and the Absolute in Yvor Winters' Poetry." Compass 1 (1977): 44-59.
Asserts that the two major themes of Winters' early poetry, solipsism and invasion of being, are the two halves of the romantic experience. This solipsism and fear of invasion had their roots deep in Winters' personality. He cured himself of a kind of madness encouraged by romantic doctrine

by thinking his way into an opposing doctrine, the Aristotelian-Thomistic position of his later years, but the early attitudes persisted. The cure had to be continually reinforced,
and this reinforcement became the function of poetry.

635.   . "Yvor Winters' Greek Allegories." SR 14 (1978):
          262-80.
          Describes Winters' exploration of the possibilities of poetic
          narrative as a vehicle for his major themes. Winters be-
          lieved that the short poem is essentially expository in struc-
          ture and that poetry is not the appropriate medium for long
          narrative. The compactness and intensity of poetic language
          leads to overstatement when applied to the description of an
          action. Narrative should only appear in poetry by way of
          summary or allusion to known myth. By using Greek my-
          thology in place of natural detail, he brings post-Symbolist
          imagery into poems that have a narrative base. (See item
          460.)

636.   . "Yvor Winters: A Poet Against Grammatology."
          SR 17 (1981): 814-32.
          Traces the unfortunate consequences of pursuing an ever-
          retreating immediacy of experience in Derrida's deconstruc-
          tion and in Structuralist and post-Structuralist literary criti-
          cism. The indeterminacy of meaning that results from this
          effort is regarded as a positive quality in modern criticism.
          Winters opposes these tendencies and argues for a kind of
          poetry that "can serve as a technique for circumscribing and
          realizing the essentially unformulable" in human experience.
          Poetry remains, however, an art of feeling and not the
          wholly rational art that some critics have accused Winters
          of defending.

637.   Powell, Neil. "What Is Traditional Poetry?" PNR 4 (1977):
          31-37. Reprinted in his Carpenters of Light: Some Con-
          temporary English Poets. Manchester: Carcanet New
          Press, 1979, pp. 1-18.
          Demonstrates that Graham Hough, Donald Davie, and Yvor
          Winters each finds the quest for clarity to be the defining
          characteristic of traditional as opposed to modernist theory,
          but that each defines the term in a different way: "Hough's
          clarity is largely a matter of tone, to be found in the con-
          ventional lyric poem; Davie's a matter of syntax and econ-
          omy, to be found in the Augustans and elsewhere; and Win-
          ters's a matter of reasoned intellect, to be found in the
          Renaissance and in the twentieth century."

638.   Pritchard, John Paul. "New Criticism: Yvor Winters."
          Criticism in America. Norman: University of Oklahoma
          Press, 1956, pp. 261-65.
          Contends that Winters' interest in the logical structure,
          ethical significance, and paraphrasable content of poems
          separates him from such New Critics as Ransom and Brooks.

639. Ramsey, Paul. "Yvor Winters: Some Abstractions Against
      Abstraction." SewR 73 (1965): 451-64.
      Praises Winters as "a distinguished poet and an important
      and valuable critic," but accuses him of oversimplifying the
      key terms in his theory: rational statement, motivated feel-
      ing, denotation, connotation, realism, and nominalism. An-
      alyzes and praises Winters' poems, "On Rereading a Pas-
      sage from John Muir," "Sir Gawaine and the Green Knight,"
      and "A Summer Commentary," to show that his poetry con-
      tains virtues that are not accounted for by his theory and is
      marred by the presence of statements asserting a belief in
      the primacy of the rational.

640. Ransom, John Crowe. "Yvor Winters: The Logical Critic."
      The New Criticism. Norfolk: New Directions, 1941, pp.
      211-75.
      Examines Primitivism and Decadence with reference to his
      own distinction between structure and texture. Describes
      Winters' analyses of organizational methods and of metrical
      structure, maintaining that Winters' theories account for
      structure but not for texture in a literary work. Asserts,
      in contrast to Winters, that the relationship between struc-
      ture and texture is arbitrary. Winters' criticism is damaged
      by his moral position, although the moralism deserves our
      respect for its sincerity. (For Winters' response, see item
      101.)

641. Rao, E. Nagaswara. "A Note on the Poetry of Yvor Win-
      ters." Journal of English Studies, no. 4 (Warangal,
      1974), pp. 364-68.
      Recounts the facts of Winters' poetic career and discusses
      favorably Winters' achievement in traditional meters. As-
      serts that Winters' principal theme is "the ultimate mystery
      of human experience." Although a rationalist, he "has a
      profound realization of the mystery itself."

642. Rascoe, Judith. "Winters of Stanford." Seq 6 (1961): 13-16.
      Describes Winters' manner and procedures as a teacher at
      Stanford. Recounts briefly the facts of his biography and
      lists his major publications.

643. Read, Herbert. "The Intangibility of Poetic Style." Style
      1 (1967): 15-28.
      Objects to Winters' view that words are primarily conceptual,
      asserting, instead, that words were originally symbolic.
      States that the shortcomings that Winters finds in Hopkins'
      'The Windhover"--its mysticism, its metrical unsoundness,
      and the obscurity of the central comparison--are not blem-
      ishes but poetic assets.

644. Ringrose, C. X. "F. R. Leavis and Yvor Winters on G. M.
      Hopkins." English Studies 55 (Amsterdam, 1974): 34-42.
      Argues that the differences between F. R. Leavis and Winters

are as important as their similarities, and discusses their
assessments of Gerard Manley Hopkins. For Leavis, Hopkins bears "no relation to Shelley or to any nineteenth century poet," whereas, for Winters, he is a product and continuation of romanticism. "Winters' placing of Hopkins ...
is more significant than Leavis' ... in that it leads us to
examine important defects in his work."

645. Robson, W. W. "The Literary Criticism of Yvor Winters."
    Cambridge Quarterly 5 (1973): 189-200. Reprinted in his
    The Definition of Literature and Other Essays. Cambridge:
    Cambridge University Press, 1982, pp. 246-59. Review
    of FD.
Regards Winters as a Platonic realist for whom art equals
technique. Objects that Winters does not define the short
poem and that his value judgments are self-evidently absurd.
Praises Winters' prose style and suspects that he may be a
better critic of prose than of verse.

646. _____. "Yvor Winters: Counter-Romantic." Essays in
    Criticism 25 (1975): 168-77. Reprinted in The Defini-
    tion of Literature and Other Essays. Cambridge: Cam-
    bridge University Press, 1982, pp. 259-67. Review of
    UER.
Asserts that Winters' short reviews are disappointing; his
most successful formulations are in his essays and books.
Although his particular judgments are narrow and eccentric,
he is important as the critic who has challenged the usual
twentieth-century view that poetry has no truth value.

647. Rodker, John. "In the October Number." LR 6 (1919):
    42-43.
Objects briefly to inconsistencies in diction and meaning in
Winters' note criticizing Jessie Dismorr. (See item 36.)

648. Ross, Morton L. "Alan Swallow and Modern Western Amer-
    ican Poetry." Western American Literature 1 (1966): 97-
    104.
Discusses the difficulties that the Western writer faces in his
struggles against the Eastern establishment and Swallow's
efforts to define the Western sensibility. Winters' critical
views, and particularly his treatment of the relationship between technique and morality, influenced Swallow in his own
critical pronouncements.

649. Schwartz, Delmore. "Primitivism and Decadence." SR 3
    (1938): 597-614. Reprinted in Selected Essays of Delmore
    Schwartz. Edited by Donald A. Dike and David H. Zuck-
    er. Chicago and London: University of Chicago Press,
    1970, pp. 332-50. Subsequent correspondence by Winters
    and Schwartz appears in SR 3 (1938): 829-31. (See items
    413, 753.)
Describes Primitivism and Decadence as a book that contains

remarkable insights: Winters shows that Hart Crane's and Robinson Jeffers' feelings toward nature lead logically to suicide; he extends our taste so that it includes such writers as Charles Churchill and John Gay; and he is the first to show the ways in which meter, morality, structure, and meaning are interrelated. But the book contains serious flaws: his view of morality is too narrow; his philosophical observations are inexact; his assumption that the meter of a poem indicates moral character is unconvincing; his analysis of poetic structures is largely polemical; and his rejection of determinism places both poet and poem in a cultural void.

650. _____. "A Literary Provincial." PR 12 (1946): 138-42. Review of AN.
Contends that Winters is mistaken in regarding the lyric poem as superior to other types of literature and that he exaggerates the importance of moral evaluation. In defending these views, Winters frequently misunderstands the authors whom he quotes, and, in particular, misunderstands T. S. Eliot's use of the term "autotelic."

651. Scott, Winfield Townley. "Great and Austere Poet." Poetry 70 (1947): 94-98. Review of EAR.
Praises Winters for understanding Robinson better than had earlier critics and for his sensitivity to the poetry. Although he is more stringent in his judgment, his admiration of Robinson's best achievements is not less than the most fervid." Asserts that Winters' "essentially technical approach is more rewarding than the ideological would have been," and that "Winters' book comes brilliantly near to outlining, if not establishing, the Robinson canon." Objects to the absence of quotations from Robinson's verse and the fact that the reader is instead referred by page and line number to the Collected Poems. Points out misprints and minor errors of fact. (For Winters' response, see item 419.)

652. Shankman, Steven. "Rationalism Ancient and Modern." SR 17 (1981): 972-82.
Contrasts rationality, "the constant attempt by the consciousness to achieve a balance between intentionality and mystery," and rationalism, the belief "in the virtually unlimited power of the pragmatic reason." Treats Winters' "An Elegy (for the U. S. N. Dirigible, Macon)" as an indictment of rationalism that parallels a similar indictment to be found in "the powerful analysis of Athenian rationalism made by Sophocles and Thucydides."

653. Skard, Sigmund. "E. A. Robinson: 'Eros Turannos,' A Critical Survey." Americana Norvegica: Norwegian Contributions to American Studies. 1. Edited by Sigmund Skard and Henry H. Wasser. Philadelphia: University of Pennsylvania Press, 1966, 286-330.
Discusses the text, critical reception, and classical back-

> ground of "Eros Turannos" with frequent references to Winters' analysis and evaluation of the poem. (See item 8.)

654. Smith, Susan Sutton. "Introduction." The Complete Poems and Collected Letters of Adelaide Crapsey. Edited with an Introduction and Notes by Susan Sutton Smith. Albany: State University of New York Press, 1977, pp. 28-29.
Quotes approvingly Winters' praise of Crapsey's work.

655. Spencer, Theodore. Review of Words for Music Perhaps and Other Poems. H&H 7 (1933): 164-74. Reprinted in Theodore Spencer: Selected Essays. Edited by Alan C. Purves. New Brunswick, N.J.: Rutgers University Press, 1966, pp. 295-307.
Objects to Winters' preference for T. Sturge Moore over Yeats (see item 75), and identifies Yeats's later work with the poetry of immediacy and Yeats's early work, along with T. S. Moore's work generally, with the poetry of revery. In the poetry of immediacy, "the poet has put the reader in the midst of the action; the subject is not considered and contemplated from outside; the matter has been so vividly an essential part of the poet's experience, that it becomes ... an equally vivid part of the reader's experience too." In the poetry of revery, the effect on the reader "will be to lull rather than to excite, to describe or even lament, as beautifully as possible, rather than to assert or protest." (For Winters' discussion of the distinction, see item 95.)

656. Stafford, William. "Indirections of Reason." Poetry 105 (1965): 262-64.
Regards Cunningham as a member of the Yvor Winters group, the defining characteristic of which is its concern with reason.

657. Stanford, Ann. "Metrics and Meaning." Tal, no. 8 (1956), pp. 66-71.
Takes issue with Alan Swallow's assertions that the perception of rhythm is a perception of meaning, that line length in free verse is determined syntactically, and that metrical verse is more valuable than free verse because it provides a norm that makes possible the perception of variation. (See item 677.) Maintains that Swallow's equation of rhythm and meaning stretches the terms: "to push the equivalence too far is to become imprecise and to render meaning meaningless." Line endings in free verse are a means of achieving rhythmical effects; no "poet of quality would found his rhythm ... on the merely syntactic." The abandonment of traditional meter makes possible the ordering of material by other means. (See item 549.)

658. Stanford, Donald E. "The Classicism of Yvor Winters." KR 3 (1941): 257-59. Review of Poems.
States that the publication of Winters' first collected volume

is important because of the intrinsic value of the poems and
also because the poems illustrate the abandonment of the
purely experimental procedures of Imagism and the adoption
of a method that combines experimental methods with the
traditional accentual-syllabic line and rational modes of organization. The reasons for the change are set forth in
Winters' criticism (See items 60, 67, 5.) Through this
combination of the experimental and the traditional, Winters
achieved "that hard, dry classicism which T. E. Hulme
said, over thirty years ago, was just around the corner, that
classicism which Ezra Pound and H. D. thought they were
achieving in the Imagist movement."

659.   . "A Note on Yvor Winters." Tal, no. 9 (1956),
         pp. 38-46.
Presents what has come to be the accepted view of Winters'
development as a poet. His career falls into three phases:
experimental, transitional, and reactionary. Winters shifted
from the presentation of experience in free verse forms to
the understanding of experience in predominantly iambic
forms. "The shift marked a radical departure from the
aesthetic of the experimentalists to a traditional aesthetic;
it marked the change from Winters as a minor poet to Winters
as a major poet. It was a change which led away from mystical madness toward wisdom and sanity; it was a change for
which his contemporaries have never forgiven him." Traces
this development with reference to passages quoted from the
several phases.

660.   . "Mr. Winters' Recent Criticism." Poetry 91
         (1958): 393-95. Review of FC.
Asserts that "Winters' criticism (and some of his poems)
will remain as solid accomplishments" when the excitement
of twentieth-century experimentation has subsided and that
"young poets who wish to be ahead of their time" should read
him.

661.   . "The Language and the Truth." Seq 6 (1961):
         20-23.
Puts Winters' development as poet and critic in the context
of Saint-Beuve's claim that "the good critic should be able
to recognize and evaluate at first glance new poetry by un-
established writers" and Baudelaire's statement that "the best
critic is the poet who has, as the result of a spiritual crisis,
felt the need to discover the obscure laws underlying the art
of poetry." Winters is both the critic who has recognized
major poets before they have been generally recognized and
the poet whose search for the laws underlying his art led
him from an antirational Imagism to the merging of sensory
detail and abstract language in the later verse.

662.   . "Yvor Winters: 1900-1968." SR 4 (1968): 861-63.
Summarizes Winters' accomplishment as critic, poet, and

teacher: his insistence that "a poem is an act of contemplation rather than an expression of personal feeling," his post-
Symbolist synthesis of "rational content and structure ...
with that peculiarly modern awareness of the sensory world,"
and his "greatness as a teacher of young poets."

663. _____. "Classicism and the Modern Poet." SR 5 (1969):
475-500.
Questions the legitimacy of Eliot's designation of himself as
a classicist through examining the essentially romantic, rev-
olutionary, and nihilistic views of the writers whom Eliot
presents as instances of the classical ideal: T. E. Hulme,
Georges Sorel, and Charles Maurras. Finds equally non-
classical views in the thought of Eliot's associates, Ezra
Pound and Wyndham Lewis. Refers to Winters' analysis of
the contradictions in Eliot's thinking and of Eliot's assertion
of both classical and romantic presuppositions. (See item
95.) Discusses as writers within a genuine classical tradition, Robert Bridges, E. A. Robinson, Yvor Winters, J. V.
Cunningham. The pattern that emerges from a consideration
of these writers can be described as follows: "in politics
the position of these poets is moderate, favorably disposed
towards constitutional democracy, both British and American.
In religion, there is considerable skepticism about Catholi-
cism, or indeed about all forms of dogmatic Christianity,
and, in art a theory of poetry that is rational as opposed to
the irrationalism of the Hulme-Pound school."

664. _____. "The Short Short Poem." SR 9 (1973): xix-xxiii.
Quotes, as examples of the short short poem, works by J. V.
Cunningham, Burma Shave, Robert Bridges, and Yvor Win-
ters.

665. _____. Review of Hart Crane and Yvor Winters: Their
Literary Correspondence, by Thomas Parkinson. AL 51
(1979): 285-87.
Praises Parkinson's recreation of the Crane-Winters correspondence and the circumstances surrounding it as "an even-
handed, intelligent critique of Crane's aesthetic convictions
and also of Winters' intellectual position, not only during the
period of this correspondence, but afterwards." The book
"presents for the first time a fully informed and sympathetic
treatment of Winters' side of a friendship which ended in
disruption."

666. _____. "Yvor Winters in the Academic Bower." SR 17
(1981): 711-15.
Discusses Winters' evaluations of the poetry of his friends
and students. "I have never met a person who took poetry
more seriously. If I wrote four lines of verse he liked I was
his friend--until I wrote a few lines he didn't like, and then
he made me feel as if I had committed a major crime."
Summarizes Winters' critical principles, and points out that

his belief in the value of language and the existence of objective meaning places him philosophically at an opposite extreme from the distrust of language and subjective denial of meaning characteristic of most twentieth century critics and maintained in a radical form by the Yale Deconstructionists.

667.   _____. "Yvor Winters (1900-1968)." Revolution and Convention in Modern Poetry. Newark, Del.: University of Delaware Press, 1983, pp. 191-244.
Regards Winters as "the only important poet of the century to go from experimental to traditional poetic technique" and as "the only critic of the twentieth century who formulated a coherent theory of poetry at the same time he was practicing it." Discusses in great detail Winters' development as a theorist and as a poetic technician, with particular reference to the function of meaning in poetry, the theory of the Image developed in The Testament of a Stone, the style of the early poems, the theoretical necessities that led to the abandonment of the early style, the nature and expressive possibilities of the accentual-syllabic line, and the characteristics of post-Symbolist imagery. Examines most of Winters' characteristic poems and analyzes in detail a number of the major poems. Demonstrates that Winters achieves, in Yeats's phrase, "unity of being": the "proper relationship between the heart and the head, between emotion and thought."

668.   Stein, Robert A. "The Collected Poems and Epigrams of J. V. Cunningham." Western Humanities Review 27 (1973): 1-12.
Mentions association of Winters' name with Cunningham's and states that the relationship is one of "congruence" rather than "influence." Winters derives from late nineteenth century France and Cunningham from the Latin epigrammatists and Ben Jonson. Cunningham seems "far more directly personal, more consistently moving and engagingly less assured about final things" than Winters.

669.   Stephens, Alan. Review of CP. Tal, no. 3 (1953), pp. 12-15.
Discusses Winters' management of the free verse line, his translations, and his traditional verse: "the form of a poem by Winters has its own inviolable identity; it is impenetrable to particular influences. It is traditional for this reason." Winters is concerned with "the relation of the realms of matter and of spirit." The clarity and simplicity of his treatment of such an elemental issue may seem platitudinous but is, in fact, economical and subtle. (See item 670.)

670.   _____. "Apologia." Tal, no. 4 (1953), p. 43.
Apologizes for an error of fact in his review of the Collected Poems in Talisman, no. 3. (See item 669.)

671.   Stephens, Alan. "The Collected Poems of Yvor Winters."
        TCL 9 (1963): 127-39.
        Regards the Collected Poems as the tale of "a conscious-
        ness that is solitary, that refrains from believing and re-
        flecting, that is confined in the moment and sustained only
        by the given." The tale proceeds as this consciousness as-
        similates time, other consciousnesses, and abstract ideas.
        The poems do not suggest that one gains wisdom in order to
        live but that one lives in order to gain wisdom and that the
        gaining of wisdom is fatal. Winters uses an overly limited
        and specialized vocabulary and, when he employs the post-
        Symbolist method, writes poems of sharply realized vehicle
        but unclear tenor whose meaning is available only to an inner
        circle of readers. In comparison with the work of W. C.
        Williams, Hart Crane, and Wallace Stevens, a poem by Win-
        ters has a definitive quality: "there is a dignity in that
        definiteness which makes Winters's best work persist in the
        mind." (For Winters' response, see item 120.)

672.   Stone, Geoffrey. "Morals and Poetry: A Defense of Both."
        AR 9 (1937): 58-79. Review of PD.
        Discusses attempts by I. A. Richards, T. S. Eliot, Allen
        Tate, Stephen Spender, Irving Babbitt, and Yvor Winters to
        provide a theory of value for poetry. States that Winters
        has provided "a statement of Babbitt's doctrines in their
        relation to the more concrete issues of the poet's craft."
        Summarizes approvingly and accurately Winters' critical
        position as it is developed in Primitivism and Decadence.
        (See item 5.)

673.   Swallow, Alan. "The Sage of Palo Alto." RMR 4 (1940):
        1-3. Reprinted in his An Editor's Essays of Two Dec-
        ades. Seattle and Denver: Experiment Press, 1962, pp.
        194-201.
        Discusses Winters as a critic who applies his critical judg-
        ments to his own creative work and is widely disliked for
        standing outside of fashionable cliques. The key terms in
        Winters' system are moral and obscurantism. The first
        refers to the necessity for any poet to write as a whole man
        whose work relates to life, and the second is used to de-
        scribe the characteristic failure of American writers to re-
        late major abstractions and experience meaningfully to one
        another.

674.   _____. Review of Poems. NMQ 11 (1941): 241-43.
        Praises the diversity and sustained impressiveness of Win-
        ters' verse: "I do not think there are three other poets
        writing in English today who have equaled it; perhaps over
        the last thirty years only Hardy and Yeats have bettered it."

675.   _____. "An Examination of Modern Critics: 6. Yvor
        Winters." RMR 9 (1944): 31-37. Reprinted in his An
        Editor's Essays of Two Decades. Seattle and Denver:

Experiment Press, 1962, pp. 202-14.
Argues that Winters is "the greatest critic of the recent
critical renaissance." Winters' books are part of an overall
design and must be read in conjunction with one another:
Primitivism and Decadence examines the failures of method
in experimental poetry, Maule's Curse the ideational background for modern obscurantism, and The Anatomy of Nonsense the critical position of major critics and an alternative
position of his own. The essay on sixteenth century poetry
is the beginning of Winters' history of a better tradition of
method and idea than the modern one.

676. _____. "Winters' 'A Summer Commentary.'" Explicator
9 (1951): 6-8. Reprinted in his An Editor's Essays of
Two Decades. Seattle and Denver: Experiment Press,
1962, pp. 215-19.
Examines word-placement, scansion, rhythm, and imagery
of "A Summer Commentary" to illustrate Winters' skill and
the view that several of his poems contain "the richest sen-
suousness, the greatest evocation of sensory detail" to be
found in modern poetry.

677. _____. "An Essay in the Theory of Traditional Metrics."
Tal, no. 7 (1955), pp. 29-38.
Outlines in terms similar to those employed by Winters, the
characteristics of quantitative meter, accentual meter, syllabic meter, accentual-syllabic meter, and free verse.
States that poems in free verse "are almost certain to be
minor poems, for the resources of the versification available to the use of the poet are, by number or variety of effectiveness, simply less than those of traditional metres."
Emphasizes the simplicity of means in traditional meter and
the inexhaustibility of the rhythmical patterns that can
emerge. (See items 5, 112, 549, 557, 657.)

678. _____. "Story of a Publisher." NMQ 36 (1966): 301-24.
Recounts details of his life as a publisher.

679. _____. "Yvor Winters: A Publisher's Comment." Seq
6 (1961): 7-10.
Praises highly Winters' critical and poetic achievement and
recounts his experiences as the publisher of Winters' work.
Winters' criticism has been underrated because critics have
not troubled to read the relatively unknown poems that Winters has championed, and his poetry has been disregarded
because most of it remained out of print until the Collected
Poems of 1952.

680. _____. "Poetry of the West." South Dakota Review 2
(1964): 77-87.
Asserts that the large number of significant poets living in
the western United States cannot be defined as a group
through reference to any common subject matter or approach.

In variety and quality, however, the region has produced
more impressive poetry since 1920 than has any other region of the country. Discusses Winters as "the most influential poet in the West," and as the poet who founded the
school of poets whose work is represented in Twelve Poets
of the Pacific. These poets agree in their opposition to the
obscurantism of contemporary poetry, in their belief that
feeling should be comprehensibly motivated, and that style
should be pure and free from mannerism. Discusses, as
well, other groups of poets that have arisen in the West.

681.   Tate, Allen. "Clarity, Elegance, and Power." NR, 2
            March 1953, pp. 17-18. Review of CP.
        Asserts, of Winters' poetic accomplishment, that "among
        American poets who appeared soon after the first war he is,
        Crane being dead, the master." He has initiated "a poetic
        revolution all his own that owes little or nothing to the earli-
        er revolution of Pound and Eliot."

682.   _____. "Homage to Yvor Winters." Seq 6 (1961): 2-3.
        Recalls his acquaintance with Winters and praises him as
        one of the three major poets of his generation. In his criti-
        cism, Winters created a technical apparatus that made pos-
        sible perceptions and discoveries that could not otherwise
        have been achieved.

683.   _____. "Poetry Modern and Unmodern: A Personal
            Recollection." HR 21 (1968): 251-62. Reprinted in his
            Essays of Four Decades. Chicago: Swallow Press, 1968,
            pp. 222-36.
        Discusses the usefulness of Winters' fallacy of imitative form
        as a tool that "gives us a way of understanding the anti-
        poetry of our time as no other insight does; but it also al-
        lows him a too literal application of his theory." Objects to
        Winters' identification of imitative form and qualitative pro-
        gression, and maintains that Winters misapplies the term
        pseudo-reference in his discussion of Eliot's "Gerontion":
        "It is not Eliot, it is Winters, who has withheld the meaning
        of the entire passage." Winters has withheld the context that
        gives significance to the gestures of the characters within the
        poem. (See item 5 for a discussion of imitative form, quali-
        tative progression, and pseudo-reference.)

684.   _____. "A Note on Paul Valéry." VQR 46 (1970): 461-
            70. Reprinted in his Memoirs and Opinions, 1926-1974.
            Chicago: Swallow Press, 1974, pp. 128-39.
        Refers to Winters' "brilliant commentary" on "L'Ebauche
        d'un Serpent." Winters states the theme of the poem so as
        to exhaust its paraphrasable content. Objects to Winters'
        statement that the theme of the poem is the theme of tragedy:
        "I am inclined to doubt that this is true, in the sense that I
        doubt that tragedy ever quite exhibits a theme as such apart
        from tragic action. What Winters describes as the theme of

tragedy seems to me to be merely the historic paradox of
imperfection and evil existing in a world that we can imagine
only if we assume that it was created by a perfect being."

685.   Thompson, Lawrance. "A Background for Modern Poetry."
        Antioch Review 2 (1942): 90-102.
        Traces throughout the history of poetry two attitudes roughly
        equivalent to a doctrine of art-for-art's sake and a doctrine
        of art-for-wisdom's sake.   Remarks briefly that Winters'
        theories, as expressed in Primitivism and Decadence, repre-
        sent "perhaps the most successful reconciliation of the op-
        posed positions.   Mr. Winters points out that the confusion
        and inadequateness of much modern poetry arises from its
        wilful attempt to stumble along without subject matter."
        Despite Winters' sympathy with experimental poetry, he re-
        asserts the traditional conviction that poetry should enrich
        human experience through strengthening "the moral temper
        sensitized by ethical thinking and feeling."

686.   Van Deusen, Marshall. "In Defense of Yvor Winters."
        Thought 32 (1957): 409-36.
        Asserts that Winters is "alone among modern critics in hav-
        ing a clear notion of a final cause for poetry" and that the
        final cause is the statement of truth: "all the formal proper-
        ties of poetry ... are only the means the good poet uses to
        render his statements more subtle, more true." Examines
        pronouncements of T. S. Eliot, John Crowe Ransom, R. P.
        Blackmur, and Allen Tate, to show that each avoids assert-
        ing that poetry should aim at truth.   Rejects Winters' as-
        sertion that the presence of feeling distinguishes a literary
        statement from a scientific one, but believes that this objec-
        tion does not damage his basic position.   Winters' criticism
        is characterized by a common sense that has been widely in-
        fluential even on critics who have not acknowledged his influ-
        ence or who are opposed to his position.

687.   Veeder, William and Robert Von Hallberg.   "A Conversation
        with James McMichael." CR 26 (1975): 154-64.
        Interviews McMichael who recounts experience of studying at
        Stanford with Winters in the early 1960's.

688.   Von Hallberg, Robert. "Yvor Winters." American Writers.
        Supplement II, Part 2.   New York: Charles Scribner's
        Sons, 1981, pp. 785-816.
        Considers Winters principally as a poet rather than as a
        critic.   Recounts his life and analyzes the several phases
        of his career with particular reference to the variety of
        styles and procedures employed.   Examines in detail char-
        acteristic poems from each phase.   Asserts that "Winters'
        major subject as a poet was the extent to which the intelli-
        gence can open itself to turbulent, meaningless experience,
        on the one hand, and to the vacancy of solitude, on the oth-
        er."   Describes briefly Winters' treatment of the essential

issues in twentieth-century poetic criticism: the relationship
between sign and referent, the function of poetic convention,
and the importance of the history of ideas. While acknowledging that Winters wrote well of his own time, regards as a
weakness his emphasis on relatively timeless issues and his
disinterest in articulating the values and experience of an entire culture. The poets who have attempted to express their
age fully, Homer, Vergil, Dante, Shakespeare, and, in our
time, Pound, Eliot, and Crane, "took risks and suffered
failures that Winters did not, and their accomplishments can
be distinguished in kind from his."

689.   Weber, Brom. "Allen Tate, Yvor Winters, and Hart Crane."
         Poetry 92 (1958): 332-35.
         Disagrees with Oscar Cargill's claim in The Nation for 15
         February 1958 that Allen Tate and Yvor Winters conspired to
         damage Hart Crane's reputation as a poet.

690.   Weir, Charles, Jr. Review of Jones Very, Emerson's
         Proud Saint," by William Irving Bartlett. New England
         Quarterly 15 (1942): 734-35.
         Mentions briefly "Winters's brilliant essay ... which hails
         Very as a major American writer ... and which has pointed
         the way that will have to be followed" by future students of
         Very's poetry. (See item 81.)

691.   Weiss, Theodore. "The Nonsense of Winters' Anatomy."
         QRL 1 (1944): 212-34, 300-318. Review of AN.
         Asserts that Winters has "overestimated the significance of
         the intellectual." Objects to Winters' absolutism by assert-
         ing that truth and taste are relative. If a position or mode
         of experience exists, the writer has no other responsibility
         than to express that position or mode. States that Winters
         misunderstands Aquinas's separation of reason and revelation
         and that he is not an Aristotelian, as he maintains, but a
         Platonist. Quotes numerous passages from The Anatomy of
         Nonsense to which he objects and offers his own interpreta-
         tions. (See item 102.)

692.   Wellek, René. "Concepts and Structure in Twentieth Century
         Criticism." Neophilologus 42 (1958): 2-11.
         Mentions Winters briefly as a New Critic who, like John
         Crowe Ransom and Allen Tate, has relapsed into the "ancient
         dualism" of form and content. The dualism appears in Ran-
         som's distinction between "texture" and "structure" and in
         Tate's distinction between "intension" and "extension." Win-
         ters equates form with the moral order that the poet imposes
         on matter, which is equated with content.

693.   _____. "Cleanth Brooks, Critic of Critics." SR 10
         (1974): 125-52.
         Summarizes briefly and approvingly Brooks's evaluation of
         Winters' criticism, that it is excessively rational and stoical.
         (See items 493, 494.)

694. _____. "Yvor Winters Rehearsed and Reconsidered."
DQ 10 (1975): 1-27.
Lists and rejects Winters' pronouncements on the following
subjects: the definition of poetry, the nature of criticism,
the source of value in life and art, the meaning of key
critical terms, and the relative importance of the various
genres. Outlines Winters' version of the history of English
poetry. Describes Winters' reactions to the major twentieth
century critics. Asserts that Winters' critical values rest
finally on nothing beyond his own literary taste and that the
basis of this taste remains obscure. "We cannot, finally,
believe in Winters' rewriting of the history of English poetry
and thus accept his contradictory concept of poetry. Winters
does not reconcile his moralism and rationalism with his
actual taste."

695. West, Ray Benedict. "The Language of Criticism." RMR
8 (1943): 12-13, 15. Review of AN.
Asserts that Winters' main thesis in The Anatomy of Nonsense, that the lack of philosophical justification in modern
criticism leads to hedonism, is an accurate statement with
regard to Henry Adams and Wallace Stevens but is less accurate as applied to John Crowe Ransom and T. S. Eliot.

696. White, Gertrude M. "Robinson's 'Captain Craig': A Rein-
terpretation." English Studies 47 (1966): 432-39.
Attempts to correct a number of critical views of Robinson's
"Captain Craig," including Winters' view that it "is a character study, not a didactic piece." Asserts, instead, that
it is "a drama, the theme of which is self-realization."

697. Whittemore, Reed. "The Principles of Louise Bogan and
Yvor Winters." SewR 63 (1955): 161-68. Reprinted in
The Fascination of the Abomination: Poems, Stories, and
Essays. New York: Macmillan, 1963, pp. 321-29.
States that Louise Bogan and Winters derive stylistically from
work of earlier centuries and that this impulse is like the
romantic yearning for far away places. Objects that, for
both poets, style and rhetoric are more important than subject matter. Praises their professional craftsmanship.

698. Williams, Miller. "Yvor Winters or How to Measure the
Wings of a Bumblebee." Nine Essays in Modern Literature. Edited by Donald E. Stanford. Baton Rouge:
Louisiana State University Press, 1965, pp. 159-79.
Argues that Winters' ideal of morality is too vague and limiting, that he is too fond of paraphrase, that the poets whom he
most admires are not impressive writers, and that the virtues for which he looks in a poem are those of a well-
written essay.

699. Wilmer, Clive. "Definition and Flow: A Personal Reading
of Thom Gunn." PNR 5 (1978): 51-57.

Discusses briefly, in the context of Gunn's qualification of
the position, Winters' view of the poem as a statement whose
object is an understanding of human experience and of ideas
as essentially conceptual in nature. (See item 99 for Winters' definition of a poem.)

700. _____. "Adventurer in Living Fact: The Wilderness in
Winters' Poetry." SR 17 (1981): 964-71.
Examines Winters' use of the American frontier as a representation of an inimical reality apart from human association
and culture. Regards the frontiersman as a figure who, like
the poet, explores this alien world. The wilderness possesses the same symbolic meaning as does the sea in "The
Slow Pacific Swell" and in Winters' essay on Melville.

701. Wimsatt, W. K., Jr. "Wimsatt on Winters." Prairie
Schooner 32 (1958-59): 254-57. Review of FC.
Identifies Winters as a rationalist who believes in the need
for a clear relationship between motive and emotion and as
a critic who is neither a classicist nor a romanticist and
who rejects the classical doctrine of imitation in all of its
forms, whether Aristotelian, Augustan, or Chicagoan. Winters believes, instead, that a great poem is not narrative
in structure but rational and expository. Expresses admiration for and qualified agreement with Winters' position.

702. Woodson, Thomas. "Robert Lowell's 'Hawthorne,' Yvor
Winters and the American Literary Tradition." American
Quarterly 19 (1967): 575-82.
Suggests that Lowell's paraphrase of Septimius Felton in his
poem, "Hawthorne," may be based on a quotation from
Maule's Curse rather than on the work itself. Winters'
comments on Hawthorne's text help to clarify ambiguities
in Lowell's poem.

703. Yueh, Norma N. "Alan Swallow, Publisher, 1915-1966."
Library Quarterly 39 (1969): 223-32.
Recounts the details of the publishing activities of Winters'
publisher.

704. Zabel, Morton Dauwen. "A Poetry of Ideas." Poetry 37
(1931): 225-30. Review of Proof.
Asserts that Winters' development as a poet has been a consistent development of principles present from the beginning
of his career. This development is impeded by "an emotional and expressive inadequacy which continues to loom as
the chief impediment to Mr. Winters' full success as a
poet." He is, nevertheless, "one of the most serious and
courageous intelligences now observable in American literature."

705. Zaniello, Thomas A. "The Early Career of Yvor Winters:
The Imagist Movement and the American Indian." Studies

in the Humanities 6 (1977): 5-10.
Traces Winters' development from his early belief in the
adequacy of perception unsupported by rationality as it is
found in Imagism and American Indian poetry to his mature
view that physical perception and intellectual concept are
interrelated.

706. Zimmerman, Michael. "The Pursuit of Pleasure and the
Uses of Death: Wallace Stevens' 'Sunday Morning,'"
University Review 33 (Kansas City, 1966): 113-23.
Offers a corrective to Winters' view that "Sunday Morning"
recommends the "cultivation of the emotions as an end in
itself." Such a view does not do justice to Stevens' devo-
tional intention and to his recommendation that we worship
the divinity within ourselves.

XII

REVIEWS

*   The Immobile Wind (cited above as item 17.)
      1.   Monroe, Harriet. Poetry 18 (1921): 339-43.

*   Diadems and Fagots (cited above as item 18.)
      1.   Lee, Muna. Poetry 23 (1923): 113-14.

*   The Magpie's Shadow (cited above as item 19.)
      1.   Andelson, Pearl. Poetry 20 (1922): 342-44.
      2.   Littel, Robert. NR, 9 August 1922, pp. 313-14.

*   The Bare Hills (cited above as item 20.)
      1.   Deutsch, Babette. Bookman 67 (1928): 441-43.
      2.   Dial 84 (1928): 522.
      3.   Freer, Agnes Lee. Poetry 32 (1928): 41-47.

*   The Proof (cited above as item 21.)
      1.   Baker, Howard. NR, 4 May 1932, pp. 331-32.
      2.   Benét, William Rose. SRL, 6 September 1930, p. 104.
      3.   Fitzgerald, Robert. H&H 4 (1931): 313-16.
      4.   Gregory, Horace. New York Herald Tribune Books, 7 September 1930, p. 14.
      5.   Hutchison, Percy. NYTB, 14 December 1930, p. 22.
      6.   Schappes, M. U. New York Evening Post, 20 December 1930, p. 4d.
      7.   Troy, William. Bookman 72 (1930): 190.
      8.   Walton, E. L. Nation, 17 December 1930, pp. 679-80.
      9.   Zabel, Morton Dauwen. Poetry 37 (1931): 225-30.

*   The Journey (cited above as item 22.)
      1.   Baker, Howard. NR, 4 May 1932, pp. 331-32.
      2.   Cunningham, J. V. Poetry 40 (1932): 163-65.

*   Before Disaster (cited above as item 23.)
      1.   Cunningham, J. V. Comm, 5 October 1934, pp. 538-39.
      2.   Humphries, Rolfe. Poetry 45 (1935): 288-91.

* Primitivism and Decadence (cited above as item 5.)
    1. Blackmur, Richard P. NR, 14 July 1937, 284-85.
    2. Drew, Elizabeth. MLR 32 (1937): 627.
    3. Fitzgerald, Robert. Poetry 50 (1937): 173-77.
    4. Flint, F. C. VQR 13 (1937): 453-57.
    5. Gregory, Horace. New Masses, 2 March 1937, pp. 22-23.
    6. Guerard, Albert, Jr. New York Herald Tribune Books, 4 April 1937, p. 24.
    7. Schwartz, Delmore. SR 3 (1938): 597-614.
    8. SRL, 14 August 1937, p. 18.
    9. Stone, Geoffrey. AR 9 (1937): 58-79.
    10. TLS, 7 August 1937, p. 572.
    11. Troy, William. Nation, 20 February 1937, p. 216.
    12. Walton, E. L. NYTB, 2 May 1937, p. 23.

* Twelve Poets of the Pacific (cited above as item 31.)
    1. Benét, William Rose. SRL, 5 June 1937, p. 19.
    2. Coblentz, Stanton A. NYTB, 29 August 1937, p. 2.
    3. Gregory, Horace. SewR 52 (1944): 572-93.
    4. Holmes, John. Boston Transcript, 10 July 1937, p. 5.
    5. Horton, Philip. Poetry 51 (1937): 48-52.
    6. Lechlitner, Ruth. New York Herald Tribune Books, 29 August 1937, p. 12.
    7. Matthiessen, Francis Otto. SR 3 (1937): 368-91.
    8. Morse, Samuel F. Reading and Collecting, 1 November 1937, p. 23.
    9. Time, 28 June 1937, p. 67.
    10. Walton, E. L. Nation, 17 June 1937, p. 76.

* Maule's Curse (cited above as item 6.)
    1. Blackmur, Richard P. Boston Transcript, 26 November 1938, p. 3.
    2. Carpenter, Frederick I. New England Quarterly 12 (1939): 558-59.
    3. Donahue, Charles. Comm, 10 February 1939, p. 442.
    4. Follett, William. NYTB, 4 December 1938, p. 36.
    5. Hatcher, Harlan. AL 12 (1940): 258-60.
    6. Jarrell, Randall. KR 1 (1939): 211-15.
    7. Thornbury, E. M. SRL, 24 December 1938, p. 20.

* Poems (cited above as item 24.)
    1. Aiken, Conrad. NR, 21 April 1941, pp. 539-40.
    2. Blackmur, Richard P. SR 7 (1941): 187-213.
    3. Bogan, Louise. NY, 17 May 1941, pp. 77-78.
    4. Stanford, Donald E. KR 3 (1941): 257-59.
    5. Swallow, Alan. NMQ 11 (1941): 241-43.
    6. Wallis, Charles Glenn. Contemporary Poetry 1 (1941): 17.

* The Anatomy of Nonsense (cited above as item 7.)
    1. Brooks, Cleanth. KR 6 (1944): 282-88.

2. Cargill, Oscar. AL 15 (1944): 432-34.
3. Daniel, Robert. SewR 51 (1943): 602-6.
4. Hume, Robert A. South Atlantic Quarterly 43 (1944): 210-12.
5. Mayberry, George. NR, 12 July 1943, pp. 51-52.
6. Mizener, Arthur. Accent 4 (1944): 185-87.
7. _____. SewR 52 (1944): 597-604.
8. Nation, 18 September 1943, p. 332.
9. NY, 3 July 1943, p. 64.
10. Schwartz, Delmore. PR 12 (1946): 138-42.
11. Swallow, Alan. NMQ 13 (1943): 371-72.
12. Weiss, Theodore. QRL 1 (1944): 212-34.
13. West, Ray Benedict. RMR 8 (1943): 12-13, 15.
14. Wright, Cuthbert. Comm, 30 July 1943, p. 374.
15. Zink, Sidney. Journal of Aesthetics 3 (1944): 92-93.

* The Giant Weapon (cited above as item 25.)
  1. Bogan, Louise. NY, 22 July 1944, pp. 57-58.
  2. Gregory, Horace. SewR 52 (1944): 572-93.
  3. Honig, Edwin. Poetry 65 (1944): 43-47.
  4. Humphries, Rolfe. NYTB, 23 April 1944, p. 24.
  5. Matthiessen, F. O. KR 6 (1944): 683-96.
  6. Mizener, Arthur. Accent 4 (1944): 185-87.
  7. Tobin, James Edward. Spirit 11 (1944): 56-57.

* Edwin Arlington Robinson (cited above as item 8.)
  1. Bunker, Robert. NMQ 17 (1947): 382-83.
  2. Dauner, Louise. AL 19 (1947): 189-91.
  3. _____. New England Quarterly 20 (1947): 427-29.
  4. New York Herald Tribune Weekly Book Review, 11 May 1947, p. 35.
  5. NY, 8 February 1947, p. 98.
  6. Quirk, Charles J. Thought 23 (1948): 729-30.
  7. Ransom, John Crowe. NYTB, 19 January 1947, p. 7.
  8. Scott, Winfield Townley. Poetry 70 (1947): 94-98.
  9. Snell, George. San Francisco Chronicle, 13 April 1947, p. 20.
  10. Time, 6 January 1947, p. 96.
  11. United States Quarterly Book List 3 (1947): 14.
  12. Wilson, Milton. Canadian Forum 26 (1947): 286.

* In Defense of Reason (cited above as item 9.)
  1. Alvarez, A. NS, 24 September 1960, pp. 438-39.
  2. Barrett, William. KR 9 (1947): 532-51.
  3. Blackmur, Richard P. Nation, 14 June 1947, pp. 718-19.
  4. Bunker, Robert. NMQ 17 (1947): 382-83.
  5. Cruttwell, Patrick. Essays in Criticism 12 (1962): 75-81.
  6. Gunn, Thom. London Magazine 7 (1960): 64-66.
  7. Jarrell, Randall. NYTB, 24 August 1974, p. 14.
  8. Kermode, Frank. Spectator, 1 July 1960, pp. 25-26.
  9. Ross, Malcolm. Canadian Forum 27 (1947): 94.

10. Snell, George. San Francisco Chronicle, 15 June 1947, p. 16.
11. TLS, 23 September 1960, p. 610.

* Poets of the Pacific (cited above as item 32.)
   1. Caldwell, J. R. SRL, 22 October 1949, p. 31.
   2. Eberhart, Richard. NYTB, 10 July 1949, p. 10.
   3. Ferril, Thomas H. San Francisco Chronicle, 18 September 1949, p. 18.
   4. NY, 15 October 1949, p. 139.
   5. Parker, John W. Voices 140 (1950): 43-44.

* Collected Poems (cited above as item 28.)
   1. Carruth, Hayden. Poetry 82 (1953): 151-57.
   2. Ciardi, John. NYTB, 15 February 1953, p. 24.
   3. Cole, Thomas. Voices, no. 153 (1954), pp. 47-48.
   4. Cunningham, J. V. VQR 29 (1953): 633-37.
   5. Daiches, David. Yale Review 42 (1953): 628.
   6. Humphries, Rolfe. Nation, 14 February 1953, p. 152.
   7. Justice, Donald. Western Review 18 (1954): 167-71.
   8. McDonald, Gerald D. Library Journal, 15 March 1953, p. 525.
   9. Morgan, Frederick. HR 6 (1953): 134-36.
  10. Nemerov, Howard. KR 16 (1954): 149-50.
  11. Stephens, Alan. Tal, no. 3 (1953), pp. 12-15.
  12. Tate, Allen. NR, 2 March 1953, pp. 17-18.
  13. United States Quarterly Book Review 9 (1953): 302.
  14. Warren, Austin. PR 21 (1954): 109-10.
  15. Whittemore, Reed. SewR 63 (1955): 161-68.

* The Function of Criticism (cited above as item 10.)
   1. Bateson, F. W. Listener, 8 March 1962, pp. 432, 435.
   2. Fraser, John. Graduate Student of English 1 (1957): 24-29.
   3. Hochmuth, Marie. Quarterly Review of Speech 43 (1957): 314.
   4. Kermode, Frank. NS, 16 March 1962, p. 382.
   5. Kirby, John Pendy. VQR 33 (1957): 631-35.
   6. Merwin, W. S. NYTB, 21 July 1957, p. 10.
   7. Pearce, Roy Harvey. HR 10 (1957): 447-57.
   8. Stanford, Donald E. Poetry 91 (1958): 393-95.
   9. Tanner, Tony. Spectator, 2 March 1962, p. 279.
  10. TLS, 30 March 1962, p. 219.
  11. Wimsatt, Jr., W. K. Prairie Schooner 32 (1958-59): 254-57.
  12. Yates, Peter. Coastlines 12 (1959): 10-14.

* Four Poets on Poetry (cited above as item 116.)
   1. Donoghue, Denis. Poetry 96 (1960): 382-87.

* The Poetry of W. B. Yeats (cited above as item 12.)
   1. Moore, John R. SewR 71 (1963): 123-38.
   2. TLS, 18 February 1965, p. 126.

* Collected Poems. Rev. ed. (Cited above as item 28a.)
  1. Dickey, James. SewR 70 (1962): 496-99.
  2. Elman, Richard M. Comm, 14 July 1961, pp. 401-3.
  3. Kaufman, Wallace. Agenda 3 (1963): 15-16.
  4. Kunitz, Stanley. Harper's Magazine, September 1960, p. 98.
  5. Pearson, Gabriel. The Review, no. 8 (1964), pp. 3-12.
  6. Stephens, Alan. TCL 9 (1963): 127-39.
  7. Sullivan, Nancy. Voices, no. 175 (1961), pp. 43-48.

* The Early Poems of Yvor Winters 1920-28 (cited above as item 29.)
  1. Elman, Richard M. Comm, 20 October 1967, p. 90.
  2. Fields, Kenneth. SR 3 (1967): 764-75.
  3. TLS, 9 February 1967, p. 108.

* Forms of Discovery (cited above as item 15.)
  1. Brown, Merle E. Criticism 10 (1968): 355-58.
  2. Cardwell, Guy. Phi Beta Kappa Reporter 33 (1968): 85.
  3. Childs, Barney. AQ 24 (1968): 265-67.
  4. Cruttwell, Patrick. HR 21 (1968): 413-16.
  5. Donoghue, Denis. NYRB 10 (1968): 22-24.
  6. Fraser, John. SR 5 (1969): 184-86.
  7. Goode, John. PR 35 (1968): 462-66.
  8. Gunn, Thom. San Francisco Sunday Examiner & Chronicle, 17 March 1968, "This World," p. 36.
  9. Hough, Graham. NS, 5 January 1968, pp. 15-16.
  10. Jeffares, Norman. Review of English Studies 20 (1969): 390.
  11. Lemon, Lee T. Prairie Schooner 42 (1968): 277-78.
  12. Løsnes, Arvid. English Studies (Amsterdam) 50 (1969): 314-17.
  13. McAuley, James. Journal of the Australian Universities Language and Literature Association 30 (1968): 254-56.
  14. McMichael, James. MQR 9 (1970): 140-41.
  15. Robinson, Fred C. Comparative Literary Studies 5 (1968): 489-92.
  16. Robson, W. W. Cambridge Quarterly 5 (1973): 189-200.
  17. Rosenthal, M. L. Poetry 114 (1969): 116-21.
  18. Stepanchev, Stephen. New Leader, 4 December 1967, pp. 25-28.
  19. TLS, 1 February 1968, p. 106.

* Quest for Reality (cited above as item 34.)
  1. Choice 7 (1970): 388.
  2. Kaye, Howard. SR 6 (1970): 824-29.
  3. Library Journal, 1 September 1969, p. 2931.
  4. Prairie Schooner 44 (1970): 184.

5. Taylor, Henry. <u>Western Humanities Review</u> 23 (1969): 367.

*   <u>Edwin Arlington Robinson.</u> Rev. ed. (Cited above as item 8a.)
    1. <u>Library Journal</u>, 1 January 1972, p. 62.
    2. Murray, Philip. <u>Poetry</u> 120 (1972): 234-35.

*   <u>Uncollected Essays and Reviews</u> (cited above as item 16.)
    1. Bromwitch, David. <u>NYTB</u>, 19 May 1974, p. 36.
    2. <u>Choice</u> 11 (1974): 264.
    3. Donoghue, Denis. <u>TLS</u>, 30 August 1974, pp. 917-18.
    4. James, Clive. <u>NS</u>, 21 February 1975, pp. 243, 246.
    5. Kaye, Howard. <u>SR</u> 11 (1975): 652-55.
    6. <u>Library Journal</u>, 1 December 1973, p. 3563.
    7. Robinson, Ian. <u>Spectator</u>, 31 August 1974, p. 277.
    8. Robson, W. W. <u>Essays in Criticism</u> 25 (1975): 168-77.

*   <u>The Collected Poems of Yvor Winters</u> (cited above as item 30.)
    1. Baxter, John. <u>SR</u> 17 (1981): 833-50.
    2. Bromwitch, David. <u>TLS</u>, 24 November 1978, pp. 1363-65.
    3. <u>Choice</u> 18 (1980): 251.
    4. <u>Observer</u>, 20 May 1979, p. 36.
    5. Parkinson, Thomas. <u>Georgia Review</u> 34 (1980): 671-77.
    6. Rallis, G. <u>Library Journal</u>, July 1980, pp. 1521-22.

XIII

DISSERTATIONS

707.   Channing, Michael Denis. "The Representation of Nature in Twentieth-Century American Poetry." Ph. D. dissertation, Stanford University, 1974.

Discusses, in the chapter entitled "The Unmoved Landscape of Yvor Winters," the development in Winters' poetry from the early position that the poet and his perception of nature are identical to the later position that the mind must maintain its precarious independence from immersion in nature. In the early poetry, the poet's thoughts are his sensory perceptions and the mind has no independent existence. In the later poetry, the beauty of nature is acknowledged, but a discontinuity between the human mind and nature is maintained. The self-conscious human mind, not nature itself, is seen as the source of nature's meaning. Discusses in detail the following poems from the later work: "The Slow Pacific Swell," "On a View of Pasadena from the Hills," "The Journey," On Rereading a Passage from John Muir," "Sir Gawaine and the Green Knight," "A Summer Commentary," and "The Manzanita."

708.   Fields, Kenneth Wayne. "The Rhetoric of Artifice: Ezra Pound, T. S. Eliot, Wallace Stevens, Walter Conrad Arensberg, Donald Evans, Mina Loy, and Yvor Winters." Ph. D. dissertation, Stanford University, 1967.

Discusses, in the chapter entitled "Yvor Winters, Adventurer in Living Fact," the large variety of rhythmical and imagistic techniques to be found in Winters' early poetry, the dissolution of self in this early work, and the various stategies whereby Winters escaped the limitations of this work in his later work. Winters is a poet who has enriched the existing tradition through incorporating into it the work of modern poets outside the tradition. "In Winters one may see an extremely rare combination of the theoretical and sensitive minds, and he has worked long and hard to show that they ought properly to be inseparable as functions of a civilized sensibility."

709.   Finlay, John Martin. "The Unfleshed Eye: A Study of In-
       tellectual Theism in the Poetry and Criticism of Yvor
       Winters." Ph. D. dissertation, Louisiana State University
       and Agricultural and Mechanical College, 1980.
       Describes Winters' early attitude toward human experience
       as a kind of naturalistic mysticism based on mechanistic and
       deterministic theories that denied the possibility of moral and
       intellectual values. Winters' later affirmation of moral dis-
       tinctions and intellectual order necessitated a theistic posi-
       tion. His instinctive fear of the supernatural led him to af-
       firm theism reluctantly. He defined God as existentially
       neutral and as non-providential in relation to humanity. He
       thought of God as Pure Mind or Perfect Concept and as the
       absolute standard of judgment in life and poetry. Examines
       "To the Holy Spirit" as a full summary of the themes asso-
       ciated with Winters' theism.

710.   Fraser, Shirley Sternberg. "Yvor Winters: The Critic as
       Moralist." Ph. D. dissertation, Louisiana State University
       and Agricultural College, 1972.
       Distinguishes between moralism and didacticism, and asserts
       that Winters' work exemplifies the one but not the other.
       Relates Winters to the moral tradition in literature epitomized
       by Plato, Sidney, Samuel Johnson, Arnold, Babbitt, and
       More; concludes that Winters, like Johnson, can be placed
       in the moral tradition but is essentially independent of liter-
       ary schools. Describes the moral-ethical basis of Winters'
       thought as Aristotelian and Thomistic, but notes that Winters
       felt himself a reluctant theist. Applies Winters' moralistic
       and evaluative approach to a consideration of various value
       systems: Romanticism, Deism, determinism, Calvinism,
       Unitarianism, and classicism. Discusses Winters' approach
       to the poetry of Yeats, Stevens, Very, Robinson, T. S.
       Moore, Hopkins, T. S. Eliot, the post-Symbolists, and J. V.
       Cunningham. Concludes that, despite widespread objections
       to Winters' critical position, it "is in the mainstream of
       Anglo-American letters and his approach has much to offer
       modern times."

711.   Geier, Norbert Joseph. "The Problem of Aesthetic Judgment
       and Moral Judgment of Literary Value in the Critical The-
       ories of Irving Babbitt, Paul Elmer More, Yvor Winters,
       and T. S. Eliot." Ph. D. dissertation, University of Wis-
       consin, 1964.
       Discusses, in the chapter entitled "Yvor Winters: The Moral-
       ity of Literary Form," Winters' effort to fashion a unified
       literary theory in which moral value is an essential part.
       Winters is in the New Humanist tradition of Babbitt and
       More, but he differs from these two scholars in giving pri-
       macy to the reason rather than the will and in regarding both
       Babbitt and More as incompetent judges of literature. Win-
       ters' theory is one in which literary form itself conveys the
       moral content of a literary statement. Form, for Winters,

is the quality of order detectable in a poem and consists of "the rational structure, the rhythmical progression, and the equation of motive and feeling." Examines in detail "Problems for the Modern Critic of Literature" (see item 115), concluding that Winters' argument assumes what it tries to prove and that there is no necessary connection between the conceptual nature of language and the necessity that literature be evaluative.

712.   Harvey, Gordon Charles. "Yvor Winters and Modern Poetry: Toward an Understanding of 'Post-Symbolist Imagery'." Master's Thesis, University of Alberta, 1979.
Explores the significance and usefulness of Winters' notion of post-Symbolist imagery. Sensory detail in Renaissance poetry is usually subordinate to thought. The sensory exists in Imagism and Mallarméan Symbolism to the exclusion of rationality. Presents Winters' account of post-Symbolist imagery as a fusion of concrete and abstract, of symbol and figure. Uses Winters' notion as an analytical tool in examining passages in modern poetry and in poetry exhibiting the romantic theme of communion with nature.

713.   Kaye, Howard Joel. "The Poetry of Yvor Winters." Ph.D. dissertation, Columbia University, 1968.
Recounts the development of Winters' poetry from the early work in a reductive modernist tradition through the later work that combines the stylistic virtues of the first phase with a fuller use of the potentialities of the language and of the human mind. Comments fully on Winters' post-Symbolist method of writing poems in which "sensory details are presented in language that implies a consistent abstract meaning." The mature poetry "is concerned with the horrifying effects of an alien universe, change, and death on man, who desires stability. The only bulwark against madness is reason, which issues ultimately in a kind of massive wisdom, but there is a great price--life itself--to pay for the perfection of wisdom."

714.   Linger, Sarah McCordic. "Yvor Winters and John Crowe Ransom: A Study of a Critical Controversy." Master's thesis, Ohio State University, 1974.
Asserts that the "conflict between Winters and Ransom centers upon the importance of logic and sensibility in poetry, the importance of morality in poetry, and whether art is an imitation or an experience." Ransom believes that "true reality does not exist in an abstract principle but in the experience and objects of this world," whereas Winters "maintains that matter does not exist apart from the rational form and that the only means of knowing particulars is through knowledge of universals."

715.   McKean, Angus Keith Ferguson. "Ethical Judgments in the Criticism of Irving Babbitt, Paul Elmer More, and Yvor Winters." Ph.D. dissertation, University of Michigan,

1949.
(For annotation, see item 599.)

716. Mugerauer, Robert William, Jr. "The Autonomy of Literature: Toward the Reconciliation of the Intrinsic and Extrinsic Dimensions with Special Reference to the Work of Northrop Frye and Yvor Winters." Ph.D. dissertation, University of Texas, 1973.
Considers the two extreme views of the nature of literary value and meaning: that literature is autotelic, self-referential, and finds its value only in itself, and that literature refers to an external world of "real" experience and is valuable as a comment on that world. Identifies the first position with modern critical theory and the critical position of Northrop Frye, and the second with classical critical theory and the critical position of Yvor Winters. Concludes that literature is, at one and the same time, self-referential and extra-referential and that the dilemma resulting from the conflict of the two positions can only be met in a position that encompasses both.

717. Mundt, Whitney Robert. "Yvor Winters and His Critics." Master's thesis, Louisiana State University and Agricultural and Mechanical College, 1961.
Examines Winters' criticism as it is illuminated by the critical objections to it. Critics "who have criticized Winters because his position is inimical to their own or who have criticized him because his judgments differ from conventional opinion have not judged him on relevant grounds"; critics "who have criticized him on the basis of his theory have judged him on relevant grounds, and significantly, their criticism has been the most favorable."

718. Schaffner, Sister Bonita. "Three Studies in English: Paradise Lost; Woolf: Between the Acts; An Allen Tate Letter." Master's thesis, Pennsylvania State University, 1969.
Quotes two unpublished letters, dated 24 June 1961 and 3 December 1961, from Winters to Donald Carroll, editor of The Dubliner, for insights that they provide into the relationship between Winters and Allen Tate.

719. Sexton, Richard J. "The Complex of Yvor Winters' Criticism." Ph.D. dissertation, Fordham University, 1965.
(For annotation, see item 466.)

XIV

MISCELLANEOUS

720.   Barth, R. L.   "The Jeweler: For the Memory of A. Y. W."
       SR 15 (1979): 1009.   Reprinted in his Looking for Peace.
       [Florence, Ky.]: [Robert L. Barth], 1981, p. 23.

721   Bryant, Marjorie.   "For Yvor Winters."   Recall the Poppies.
       Limited Edition.   Portola Valley, Calif.:   No Dead Lines,
       1979, p. 20.

722.   Bunting, Basil.   Letter to the editors.   H&H 6 (1933): 322-
       23.
       Objects to the printing of Winters' review of the Objectivists
       (see item 74), "the vomit of a creature who ... found his
       own name omitted from an anthology that proposed to sample
       everything at this moment alive in poetry."   (For Winters'
       reply, see item 410.)

723.   Cargill, Oscar.   Letter to the editors.   AL 16 (1944): 225-
       26.
       Asserts, in response to Winters' letter objecting to his re-
       view of The Anatomy of Nonsense, that the principal weak-
       ness of Winters' book is facile generalization.   (See items
       7, 416, 417, 498.)

724.   Coxe, Louis D. "Winters on Eliot." KR 3 (1941): 498-500.
       Objects that Winters, in his criticism of Eliot's determinism
       and his notion that lyric poetry is dramatic, does not take
       sufficiently into account Eliot's own qualifications of his po-
       sition.

725.   Dale, Peter.   "Ivor Winters."   Agenda 20 (1982): 95.

726.   Davis, Robert Gorham.   "A Reply."   AmS 19 (1950): 230-31.
       Argues that Winters' excessive emphasis on the word fascist
       leads to "a willful misinterpretation of all that I wrote."
       (See items 421, 422, 516.)

727.   Day, A. Grove.   The Sky Clears: Poetry of the American

Indians. New York: Macmillan, 1951. Dedication for Yvor Winters, Singer of Power.

728. Drummond, Donald F. The Drawbridge. Denver: Alan Swallow, 1958. Dedicated to Yvor Winters.
Acknowledges in the Preface his debt to Winters and his belief that "there can be no better word by word, line by line, structure by structure critic of verse in our time. He is among the finest poets."

729. _____. "To Yvor Winters." No Moat No Castle. Denver: Alan Swallow, 1949, p. 41.

730. Finlay, John. "Two Poems in Memory of Yvor Winters: Odysseus; Audubon at Oakley." SR 18 (1982): 356-57.

731. Franklin, H. Bruce. The Wake of the Gods: Melville's Mythology. Stanford: Stanford University Press, 1963. Dedicated to Yvor Winters.

732. Gohdes, Clarence. Letter to Yvor Winters. AL 16 (1944): 222-23.
Requests, as managing editor of American Literature, that Winters reconsider his letter objecting to Oscar Cargill's review of The Anatomy of Nonsense, and withdraw it. (See items 416, 417.)

733. Guérard, Albert, Jr. Robert Bridges: A Study of Traditionalism in Poetry. Cambridge: Harvard University Press, 1942. Dedication for Arthur Yvor Winters, "A great teacher and a dear friend."

734. Gullans, Charles. Arrivals and Departures. Minneapolis: University of Minnesota Press, 1962. Dedicated to Yvor Winters, magister ludi.

735. _____. "In Memoriam: A.Y.W." Marilyn 1 (1975): 20.

736. Gunn, Thom. "To Yvor Winters, 1955." The Sense of Movement. London: Faber & Faber, 1957, pp. 44-45. Reprinted in Seq 6 (1961): 4-5.

737. Kay, Ellen. A Local Habitation. Denver: Alan Swallow, 1958. Dedicated to Jinx Rule and Yvor Winters.

738. _____. "Ars Artis: To Y.W." A Local Habitation. Denver: Alan Swallow, 1958, p. 9.

739. Laurel, Archaic, Rude: A Collection of Poems Presented to Yvor Winters on His Retirement by the Stanford English Department. Stanford, Calif.: Department of English, Stanford University, 1966.
CONTENTS: One poem each by the following poets:

Howard Baker, J. V. Cunningham, Catherine Davis, Donald F. Drummond, Kenneth Fields, Lee Gerlach, Charles Gullans. Thom Gunn, Donald Hall, Elizabeth Harrod, Ann Hayes, Ellen DeYoung Kay, Philip Levine, Fred Levy, Janet Lewis, Michael V. Miller, N. Scott Momaday, Raymond Oliver, Margaret Peterson, Helen Pinkerton, Clayton Stafford, Ann Stanford, Don Stanford, Alan Stephens, Wesley Trimpi.

740.   Lee, Agnes. Under One Roof. Chicago: Ralph Fletcher Seymour, n. d. Dedicated to Yvor Winters.

741.   Levin, David. "To a Moral Navigator, Observed on His Way to Class." SR 1 (1965): 427.

742.   Lewis, Janet. Poems/1924-1944. Denver: Alan Swallow, 1950. Dedicated to Yvor Winters.

743.   Mellers, Wilfrid Howard. The Happy Meadow: Cantata for Speaker, Children's Voices, Recorder Consort, Glockenspiel, Xylophone and Percussion. To poems by Robert Duncan and Yvor Winters. London: Novello, 1964.
Sets to music six poems by Winters: "The Goatherds" (under title "The Goatherd"); "Song" (Where I walk out; under title "The Goldfinches"); "José's Country" (under title "A Pale Horse"); "April" (under title "April Goat Dance"); "Song for a Small Boy Who Herds Goats" (under title "Goatherd's Song"); "The Upper Meadows" (under title "Epilogue: The Upper Meadow").

744.   Moore, Marianne. "To Yvor Winters." Seq 6 (1961): vi. Reprinted in Seq, 20th Anniversary Issue, 1956-1976, p. 1961.

745.   Peck, John. "The Upper Trace: For Y. W." Shagbark. Indianapolis, New York: Bobbs-Merrill, 1972, pp. 21-22.

746.   Pinkerton, Helen. "Autumn Drought: Stanford University 1976: To the Memory of A. Y. W." SR 17 (1981): 983.

747.   Pinsky, Robert. "Essay on Psychiatrists," Sadness and Happiness. Princeton: Princeton University Press, 1975, pp. 57-74. Section XX of this poem, 'Peroration, Concerning Genius,' contains a description of Winters as a teacher of poetry.

748.   Rexroth, Kenneth. "A Letter to Yvor Winters." In What Hour. New York: Macmillan, 1940, p. 31.

749.   _____. "The Giant Weapon." The Signature of All Things. New York: New Directions, 1949, pp. 45-46.

750.   Roberts, Elizabeth Madox. The Time of Man. New York: Viking Press, 1926. Dedicated to J. L. L. and A. Y. W.

751. Sachs, David. "Concerning Yvor Winters, Who Foretold Hart Crane's Death." Furioso 3 (1948): 44.

752. Schmidt, Michael. "Introduction." Five American Poets: Robert Hass, John Matthias, James McMichael, John Peck, Robert Pinsky. Manchester: Carcanet, 1979, pp. ix-xii.
Suggests that it might be tempting to regard the poets represented in the anthology as "the 'last generation' of Wintersians, but this would be an error. To an extent they shared an apprenticeship, but they fell under the influence of the old man in different ways and to different extents, and as their work matured they moved beyond his influence, and away from one another."

753. Schwartz, Delmore. "Correspondence." SR 3 (1938): 830-31. Reply to Winters' objections to Schwartz's review of PD.
Reaffirms his original reading, arguing that the total context of the poem supports it. (See items 413, 649.)

754. Snodgrass, W. D. "In Praise of Reason." In Memoriam, Yvor Winters. QRL 10 (1960): 140.

755. Stafford, Clayton. "A Word to Critics: With a Copy of Yvor Winters' 'Before Disaster.'" The Swan and the Eagle and Other Poems. San Francisco: Privately Printed, 1974, p. 18.

756. _____. The Swan and the Eagle and Other Poems. San Francisco: Privately Printed, 1974. Dedication for the Memory of Yvor Winters.

757. Stanford, Ann. The White Bird. Denver: Alan Swallow, 1949. Dedicated to Janet and Yvor Winters.

758. Stanford, Donald E., ed. The Poems of Edward Taylor. With a foreword by Louis L. Martz. New Haven: Yale University Press, 1960. Dedication for Yvor Winters, Among the first and farthest.

759. [Statement]. Stanford Today 1 (1962): n. p. Includes brief unsigned statement; reprintings of "To the Holy Spirit," "At the San Francisco Airport," and "Night of Battle"; four photographs of Winters and one of Winters and Janet Lewis (Mrs. Winters).
States that recognition for Winters has been long overdue but has finally arrived in the form of a Collected Poems in paperback, an LP of Winters reading Winters, and the Albert Guérard chair of literature at Stanford.

760. Swallow, Alan. "Series for My Friends." The War Poems of Alan Swallow. New York: Fine Editions Press, 1948, n. p.
Mentions Winters.

761. Thomas, Harry. "The Great Forger: To the Spirit of Yvor Winters." SR 11 (1975): 888.

762. Titus, Edward W. "Envoi." TQ 3 (1931): 743.
Satirical verse comment on Winters' "The Critiad." (See item 302.)

763. Trimpi, Wesley. "To Giotto: For A. Y. W." The Glass of Perseus. Denver: Alan Swallow, 1952, p. 36.

764. _____. "For the Living: To the Memory of A. Y. W." SR 7 (1971): 1040. Reprinted in SR 17 (1981): 679. Reprinted in his The Desert House. Florence, Ky.: Robert L. Barth, 1982, n. p.

765. Wescott, Glenway. The Bitterns: A Book of Twelve Poems. Evanston: Monroe Wheeler, n. d. Dedicated to Arthur Yvor Winters.

766. Yvor Winters Folio. Photographs by Harry Bowden. Bern Porter Publication. A portfolio of seven photographs: one of Winters, one of Janet Lewis (Mrs. Winters), one of the two of them together, and three interiors of the house and study.

AUTHOR INDEX

Abood, Edward, 477
Alvarez, A. , 478
Andelson, Pearl, 479
Anderson, Lee, 406
Argensola, Lupercio Leonardo
   de, 398
Arnold, Richard K. , 32
Atkinson, James, 31

Baker, Howard, 31, 33, 480,
   481
Barish, James, 482
Barth, Robert L. , 720
Barrett, William, 483
Baudelaire, Charles, 386, 389
Baxter, John, 424, 484
Bellay, Joachim du, 390
Benêt, William Rose, 485
Bilac, Olavo, 18
Blackmur, R. P. , 486, 487,
   488, 489
Bloom, Harold, 490
Bloomingdale, Judith, 491
Bogan, Louise, 492
Bowers, Edgar, 32
Brady, Frank, 425
Brooks, Cleanth, 426, 493, 494
Brooks, Van Wyck, 427
Brown, Ashley, 495
Bryant, Marjorie, 721
Bunting, Basil, 722
Burke, Kenneth, 428
Butterfield, R. W. , 429

Campbell, Gladys, 496
Campbell, Harry M. , 497
Cargill, Oscar, 498, 723
Carruth, Hayden, 499, 500
Casey, John, 501
Cassity, Turner, 502

Channing, Michael Denis, 707
Clark, David R. , 430
Comito, Terry, 503
Corbière, Tristan, 392
Cosgrave, Patrick, 431
Coxe, Louis D. , 724
Crane, Hart, 432
Crawford, Francis, 32
Crow, Charles L. , 433
Cunningham, J. V. , 31, 504,
   505

Dale, Peter, 725
Daryush, Elizabeth, 35
Davie, Donald, 30, 434, 435,
   436, 506, 507, 508, 509,
   510, 511, 512, 513
Davis, Dick, 437, 514, 515
Davis, Robert Gorham, 516,
   726
Day, A. Grove, 727
Desbordes-Valmore, Marceline,
   403
Deutsch, Babette, 517
D'Evelyn, Thomas, 518
Dickey, James, 519, 520
Dickinson-Brown, Roger, 521
Donahue, Charles, 522
Donoghue, Denis, 523, 524
Dorr, Colgate, 32
Drew, Elizabeth, 525
Drummond, Donald F. , 526,
   728, 729

Eastman, Max, 439
Elman, Richard M. , 527
England, Eugene, 528

Fields, Kenneth, 34, 529, 530,
   531, 708

175

TITLE INDEX

179

SUBJECT INDEX

"Acquainted with the Night," 10
Adams, Henry, 7, 8, 9, 10, 474, 493, 497, 498, 539, 577, 695
Adams, Leonie, 16, 65
Aeneid, The, 16, 66
Aiken, Conrad, 16, 65
American Indian Love Lyrics and Other Poems, 51
Andelson, Pearl, 16, 44
Arensberg, Walter Conrad, 15, 708
Aristotelianism, 15, 501, 515, 631, 634, 701, 710
Arnold, Matthew, 15, 77, 625

Babbitt, Irving, 474, 551, 597, 598, 599, 672, 711
Baker, Howard, 15, 505, 602
Bass, Althea, 16, 72
Baudelaire, Charles, 2, 4, 7, 9, 16, 60, 124
Being: being, consciousness, and literary technique, 1, 2, 4, 5, 7,
    9, 10; realized fullness of potential being, 4, 5, 7, 9, 10
Benito Cereno, 6
Berryman, John, 16, 107
Billy Budd, 6
Black, MacKnight, 16, 72
Blackmur, R. P., 10, 474, 571, 686
Blake, William, 7, 9, 15
Blithedale Romance, The, 84
Blue Juniata, 16, 55
Bogan, Louise, 15, 16, 54, 697
Bowers, Edgar, 15, 16, 114, 612
Bravo, The, 6
Bridge, The, 9, 16, 66, 104, 491, 626
Bridges, Robert, 4, 15, 16, 71, 77, 83, 124, 478, 663, 664
Brooks, Cleanth, 10, 474, 638, 693
Browning, Robert, 8, 15
Bryant, William Cullen, 498
Burma Shave, 664

Calvinism, 6, 9, 7, 8, 16, 103, 592, 710
Campion, Thomas, 10, 16, 54, 108
Carroll, Donald, 718
Carruth, Hayden, 109, 499
Churchill, Charles, 15, 119, 649